Hercules!

Hercules!

THE A TO Z OF

ELTON JOHN

MICK WALL

NINE
EIGHT
BOOKS

NINE
EIGHT
BOOKS

NEB 020

First published in the UK in 2023 by Nine Eight Books
An imprint of Black & White Publishing Group
A Bonnier Books UK company
4th Floor, Victoria House, Bloomsbury Square, London, WC1B 4DA
Owned by Bonnier Books, Sveavägen 56, Stockholm, Sweden

@nineeightbooks

@nineeightbooks

Hardback ISBN: 978-1-7887-0862-3
Trade Paperback ISBN: 978-1-7887-0863-0
eBook ISBN: 978-1-7887-0864-7

A CIP catalogue record for this book is available from the British Library.

Publishing director: Pete Selby
Senior editor: Melissa Bond

Cover design by Lora Findlay
Cover image © Terry O'Neill/Iconic Images Ltd
Typeset by IDSUK (Data Connection) Ltd
Printed and bound in Great Britain by Clays Ltd, Elcograf S.p.A

1 3 5 7 9 10 8 6 4 2

Every reasonable effort has been made to trace copyright-holders of material reproduced in this book. If any have been inadvertently overlooked, the publisher would be glad to hear from them.

Nine Eight Books is an imprint of Bonnier Books UK
www.bonnierbooks.co.uk

MIX
Paper from
responsible sources
FSC® C018072

Contents

FOREWORD

'The great thing about rock 'n' roll is someone like me can be a star.'

Sir Elton Hercules John, CH, CBE is the most famous living singer-songwriter in the world. A member of a select coterie of stars known only by one name – Elton, Elvis, Prince, Madonna.

By the time he'd begun his Farewell Yellow Brick Road tour, Elton John had become all things to all people. For the TikTok generation, he is chiefly known for his work with Dua Lipa, Pnau, Demi Lovato and Ed Sheeran. For others, the name Elton John is synonymous with philanthropy, charitable foundations and a tireless devotion to fundraising for HIV/AIDs research.

His rollercoaster career has been Zelig-like in bringing him into close contact with everyone: from David Beckham to Billie Jean King; Elizabeth Taylor to Eminem; Demi Lovato to George Michael; John Lennon to Ozzy Osbourne; Michael Parkinson to Graham Norton; Princess Diana to Miss Piggy; Rod Stewart to Divine; David Bowie to David Walliams; Britney Spears to Freddie Mercury; Gianni Versace to Brian Wilson; Axl Rose to Justin Timberlake . . . And on and on and on. Who doesn't know and love Elton John?

None of that would have been within reach, however, if it wasn't for his astonishing six-decade run of stone-cold classic hits. Like Queen, Elton John's various *Greatest Hits* collections would be enough to last most pop and rock connoisseurs a lifetime. For these, he has been rewarded with five Grammy Awards, five BRIT Awards, two Academy Awards, two Golden Globes, a Tony Award, a Disney Legends Award and a Kennedy Center

Honor lifetime achievement medal. He was inducted into the Songwriters Hall of Fame in 1992 and the Rock and Roll Hall of Fame in 1994 and is a fellow of the British Academy of Songwriters, Composers and Authors. Knighted by Queen Elizabeth II in 1998 for services to music and charitable services, in 2019 President Emmanuel Macron presented Elton with France's highest civilian award, the Legion d'Honneur, describing him as a 'melodic genius', highlighting his work on behalf of the LGBT+ community.

This A to Z offers a joyride through the life and times of one of the all-time greats of rock 'n' roll, a musical giant to rival the Beatles, ABBA, Queen, Bowie . . . all of whom Elton's record sales had dwarfed long before the advent of cassettes, tape-decks, CDs, streams, YouTube and TikTok. It also offers a unique perspective on Elton John himself. The pint-sized people-pleaser from Pinner named Reg Dwight, who played the piano better than he did anything else. The talented, watchful kid in glasses, who could also sing but only escaped the shadows of beckoning obscurity by transforming himself through an act of Herculean self-will into one of the most brilliant, versatile, glamorous and loved stars of all time.

I was twelve years old when 'Your Song' first became a hit for Elton John early in 1971. I was struck by the conversational, self-deprecating tone: 'Well, a few of the verses, well, they've got me quite cross . . .' It was so innocent, it tingled. 'It's a little bit funny, this feeling inside . . .' So relatable. Whenever it came on the radio it compelled you to pay closer attention. I had no idea who Elton John was: 'Your Song' was such an instant shot-through-the-heart classic, it didn't matter who it was by. Like millions of others, I was beguiled. Then forgot all about it – until the next time it came on the radio. It was the song that detained you, not the singer.

That all changed when Elton John began appearing on stage and TV in a rapidly expanding line of evermore ridiculous eyewear and stage clothes. For 'Rocket Man', lightly sequined jacket and flash maroon tie, perhaps – and big yellow glasses spelling out the word ZOOM! For 'Honky Cat', dressed as . . . a giant cat. For 'Crocodile Rock', shiny head-to-toe pink lamé. All backed up by some of the best music of the era. By the mid-'70s Elton was the biggest rock star in the world. Six straight number-one albums in America. Fourteen top-ten American singles, including five number ones. A similar story back home in Britain and everywhere else in the world that sold radios and record players.

Nobody predicted what happened next, however, over the coming decades, as his career took on the aspects of a high-speed roller coaster, hurtling from the very top of the mountain to the very bottom of the well, and then back again.

Everyone has their Elton John stories – and no one tells them better than Elton himself. In this book, we highlight the very best of them.

Mick Wall, June 2023

Ackles, David

The Troubadour's forgotten man

The most significant night of Elton John's career – the night young Reginald Kenneth Dwight's life changed for ever – occurred at the Troubadour club in Los Angeles, in August 1970. It was Elton John's first ever show in America.

The only other musician who appeared on the Troubadour stage that same night – and the subsequent nights of Elton's now-legendary eight-show run there – was someone almost never mentioned again. A mystically self-absorbed folk singer poet that nobody would remember the next day, let alone years later when the history books and biographies and documentaries and films would retell the story.

His name was David Ackles and he was one of the most extraordinary singer-songwriters on the scene at a time when LA was teeming with singing-songwriting superstars. Ackles was already thirty-three when he opened for Elton at the Troub – ancient in potential rock star terms in 1970. But he'd been a child actor, appearing in six of the eight films in the *Rusty* children's film series between 1945 and 1949. His background was church-going, but set in the land of vaudeville, where both his parents were veteran musical performers.

He got his break as a staff songwriter for Jac Holzman's innovative Elektra Records but nothing he wrote ever fitted any of Elektra's artists so he decided to record his own songs. Elton and his lyricist Bernie Taupin were awed by his music. Each night Elton would watch Ackles' set enthralled – and pissed off with the audience who coughed, talked, fidgeted and ruined the vibe.

Ackles had been through worse and actually enjoyed being there that week at the Troub. It was like one long party. At the end of the week, David bought Elton a half-bottle of whiskey and told him what a pleasure it had been working with him. Elton didn't know what to say. 'Do you know,' Elton told friends, 'that meant most of all to me.'

Bernie was so enamoured of Ackles' work he went on to produce his third album, *American Gothic*, released in 1972. Asked to describe Ackles' unique style, he said: 'There was nothing quite like it. It's been said so many times, but his stuff was sort of [like] Brecht and Weill, and theatrical. It was very different than what the other singer-songwriters of the time were doing. There was also a darkness to it, which I really, really loved, because that was the kind of material that I was drawn to.'

The only Ackles album recorded in the UK rather than America, *American Gothic* was not a commercial hit in any sense. It was regarded however as an immediate cult classic. The *Los Angeles Free Press* compared the album to the Beatles' *Sgt Pepper's Lonely Hearts Club Band*. The UK's then most influential music weekly, *Melody Maker*, crowned it 'a classic', and Derek Jewell, the eminent music critic of the *Sunday Times*, described it as 'the *Sgt Pepper* of folk'.

But even Ackles considered the 'comparison to *Sgt Pepper*' as 'overpraising'.

Such modesty didn't necessarily help boost his commercial ambitions, but the work of the forgotten man of Elton's celebrated Troubadour shows became an important influence on significant figures in the generation of songwriters that followed him.

'ARE YOU READY FOR LOVE'

Only if you wait for twenty-five years

'If you fancy living in a despondent world of unending, delusional bullshit, I really can't recommend cocaine highly enough,' reasoned Elton John in his splendid 2019 autobiography, *Me*. While Elton wasn't specifically referring to his late-'70s career lull, when his personal life overwhelmed his creativity and his music was occasionally frankly terrible, he might as well have been. After all, he never released a less enthralling record than 1979's disco disaster, *Victims of Love*, and his decision not long before that to fire his band and stop touring was nothing less than desperate. Here was a man who had sunk to his professional nadir.

Despite this, the occasional gleaming light shone like a beacon amid the slew of underachieving releases that accompanied Elton's transition from '70s superstar to '80s . . . what? Even he didn't know.

One such bright moment was *The Thom Bell Sessions*, an EP recorded in late 1977. One of its three tracks, co-composed by the songwriter and producer Thom Bell, was 'Are You Ready for Love', an emotionally moving but musically overwrought epic that clocked in eight-plus minutes. Heartfelt, very musicianly, it's a marathon to wade through for anyone who isn't obsessed with this era of Elton's career – but there's promise here, not least in the funk bass and Elton's smooth lower-register vocal melodies.

The fact that the song, like the parent EP, went largely unnoticed on its release in 1979 – two years after being recorded – is understandable. The track 'Mama Can't Buy You Love' proved popular enough on American radio to send the single version into the lower reaches of the top ten. But the original version of 'Are You Ready for Love' doesn't stand up next to any of Elton John's best-known hits from five years before and, despite Bell's best efforts, it certainly doesn't compete with disco titans like Chic or Earth, Wind & Fire.

Some people simply couldn't take Elton seriously as a contemporary soul artist, sensing correctly that he was jumping onto a passing fad. It wasn't that he was an imposter – doing glam-reggae on 'Bennie and the Jets' he was totally convincing, equally so when prog-rocking on 'Funeral for a Friend/Love Lies Bleeding' or James Taylor special-pleading on 'Your Song' or his own earlier, much superior version of Philly soul with 'Philadelphia Freedom'. Maybe the time just wasn't right for 'Are You Ready for Love'. Maybe Elton just changed his mind. He was thinking and moving fast in those days.

As neither Elton nor his American record company, MCA, seemed to know what to do with it, the song remained unknown to the world . . . until a quarter of a century later. It had reappeared twice in the interim – once as part of 1989's extended *Complete Thom Bell Sessions* reissue, comprising the original three tracks from the EP plus another three tracks they'd recorded; and as a tacked-on bonus track for 'The Last Song' CD single in 1992 – but neither release had any impact.

When the song was remixed by the famed British house producer Ashley Beedle for a TV commercial in August 2003, it somehow sounded better: more contemporary and more in touch with the mood of the day. Beedle's remix was not, as you might reasonably have expected, a Fatboy Slim or Junkie XL-style big-beat extravaganza. Instead, the new mix cut the song's running time in half, polished up the drums and brought its best feature – the chorus line – right to the front where it always should have been.

The exhilarating utterly refreshed 'Are You Ready for Love' was initially used to promote the start of the 2003/04 Premiership Football season for Sky Sports in England and found its perfect vehicle. As a relaxed, Sunday-afternoon tune that you and your kids could sing on the sofa while preparing to watch the footie, it sounded great. The song's vibes tied in neatly with the early-'00s obsession with '70s culture, from Air to ABBA and beyond.

When 'Are You Ready for Love' went to number one, on 6 September 2003, for mainstream pop fans it appeared like a bolt from the blue. But insiders nodded sagely when it became Elton's sixth British chart-topper. It also hit the top spot in Ireland and several other European countries and – in club-mix form – on the US's Dance Chart, the latest in a series of respectable chart positions that he achieved in the early years of the new century.

It helped that the accompanying video, directed by the BAFTA-winning Kate Dawkins, was so memorable. Viewed on your phone now, the video looks a little too Day-Glo and giddy perhaps, but it still works. A stylised Elton with a jawline and collar-length hair, crooning and camping his way through the song and reminding us that he too was once young.

If changing fashions helped bring Elton John's star back into focus, the success of 'Are You Ready for Love' offered more than adequate proof that quality endures, class is for ever. Not that Elton ever needed any encouragement.

ART COLLECTION

'I know what I like . . .'

If money was no object and you were a naturally needy person who required plenty of luxuries to feel good about life, you too might 'do an Elton' and build up several collections of whatever categories of luxury items caught your fancy. Over the years Elton John has bought and sold a huge number of collectables, from records to furniture, bone china, antique objects d'art, couture fashion items and beyond. Most prominent among them, however, is his art and photography collection.

While the debts of a couple of developing countries could be paid off with the money he's blown on this stuff, Elton is blissfully unrepentant, pointing out not unreasonably that he has been 'addicted to far more damaging things than buying tableware and photographs'. Besides, he has several houses across the globe to fill.

By 1988, Elton's fine art collection had reached almost comedic proportions, with crates of expensively acquired works from all over the world filling up the squash court at Woodside, his old Windsor home, with nowhere else to store their contents. His works included art by Jean-Michel Basquiat, Andy Warhol, David Hockney, Tracey Emin and others, but he grew tired of them and had them sent to Sotheby's, only holding on to a couple of sentimental treasures by Francis Bacon, Patrick Procktor and the surrealist René Magritte. The auction realised £8 million and Elton got his squash court back, but not for long as he soon switched to buying photography.

This shift in focus occurred after Elton had finally got clean and sober in 1990: before that he hadn't regarded photography as on a par with other visual art forms. At that point he'd worked alongside world-class photographers for two decades – Terry O'Neill, Annie Leibovitz, Richard Avedon, and Norman Parkinson among them – but had always considered their work to be high-end publicity pictures rather than bona fide art.

In the context of the music industry, he was right to think that way, but his horizons were expanded when a friend introduced him to the work of Herb Ritts, the American photographer best-known for his black and white portraits of celebrities, models and other cultural figures throughout the '80s and '90s, who later directed videos for Madonna, Michael Jackson and several other major artists. His photographic work was often presented in the style of classical Greek sculpture, emphasising the endless vagaries of the human shape.

Impulsive as ever, Elton bought twelve Ritts' prints in one go and the die was cast. From there he began buying the work of American avant-garde photographer and painter Man Ray, whose mid-twentieth-century body of work had helped turn photography into an accepted art form. As a young man, Elton had stuck a Man Ray reproduction on the wall at mother Sheila Dwight's house in Pinner; it must have felt like vindication when, in 1993, he paid £112,000 for a vintage print of Ray's *Glass Tears*, setting a new auction record for a photograph in doing so.

A more practical solution to the excess artworks around the house came in 2016, when an exhibition of Elton's photographic collection took place at the Tate Modern in London called *The Radical Eye*. Three years later, the Victoria and Albert Museum in South Kensington opened a photography gallery in Elton and husband David Furnish's names, containing more than 7,000 collected works.

Elton has his eye on the long term, planning a couple of ways to put his art to good use in his old age and/or posthumously: one of these is an exhibition dedicated to his life and career. More ambitiously, he has suggested the establishment of a private Elton John Museum, where his various collections can finally be displayed and stored without anyone falling over them. As a fitting way to repay a fanbase for a lifetime of support, this is a good one.

ATKINSON, ROWAN

What's in a name?

'You didn't have a solo British number one until this year,' intoned Rowan Atkinson in a priceless five-minute 'interview' with Elton John, recorded at the Hysteria 3 comedy event in 1991. 'Surely you wouldn't have had to wait so long for a number one if it hadn't been for your stupid, pointless bloody name?'

You can see the rest of this slice of comedy gold on YouTube. Essentially, Atkinson spends the whole of the conversation – jokingly billed as a serious dialogue about music – taking the piss out of his interviewee's name, insisting that it should really be John Elton. At one point he asks: 'Are you jealous of Ben Elton?' and jokes about the subject of 'Candle in the Wind' being called 'Monroe Marilyn'.

The man himself, who is visibly trying not to laugh throughout, pretends to get angry and eventually 'shoots' Atkinson with a toy pistol, remarking 'What a head dick!', and stalks off the stage accompanied by a standing ovation from the audience.

It's a genuinely great bit of comedy, but like all the best humour, there's a grain of truth inside the joke.

As we know, and indeed as Elton explains in the video clip for the benefit of the audience, he borrowed his stage name from Elton Dean and Long John Baldry, the sax player and singer in Bluesology, the band in which he and those musicians had played in 1967. In doing so, he unwittingly doomed Dean to being forever known not as a musician, but as the donor of a weird stage name. 'Elton Dean appreciated the irony that he was better known for giving Elton John half his name than for his own superlative saxophone playing,' noted *The Guardian* in Dean's obituary in 2006.

Still, did anyone know anyone called Elton – as a first name – before the former Reggie Dwight adopted it? Unlikely: Elton had always been a surname, as fans of Jane Austen's *Emma* and its dodgy character of the same name may recall.

For this reason, when Elton's debut album *Empty Sky* and the self-titled follow-up were released in 1969 and 1970, it's thought that more than a few purchasers assumed that his name had been printed in error – or at least, that it had been an ill-advised choice. Was this bloke really called 'John Elton' but had chosen to flip his name around to make it stand out? Was it a mistake? Was the record company having us all on? Hence Rowan Atkinson and his wonderfully funny sketch that stretched a single joke out for five minutes. 'Tell me, did you ever discuss changing your co-writer's name?' enquired the future Mr Bean. 'Presumably "Taupin Bernie" would have been more consistent.'

Fair play to Elton for being the butt of the joke. Mind you, if you watch his reactions closely, that infamous Elton John impatience isn't ever *too* far from the surface.

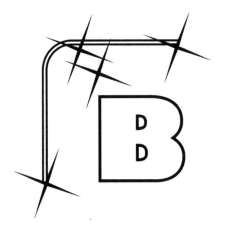

THE BEATLES
Fab gear

Most of us will never know what it's like to become friends in adulthood with our childhood idols – which is just as well, because all the evidence suggests that it's often an uneasy process that can lead to an unstable, unbalanced relationship. In the case of Elton John, who spent innumerable days as a kid poring over his collection of Beatles' singles before buddying up years later with most of the Fab Four, it's been a mixed experience, to say the least.

Like most of his generation, in his youth Elton regarded the Beatles as supermen: musicians who could do no wrong and whose songs said everything that was worth saying about the world, certainly as it was in the '60s. When he first encountered one of them in person, it was 1968 and he was a 21-year-old studio musician – and the experience left him flabbergasted. Elton often tells the story of Paul McCartney walking into the Abbey Road Studios and playing the work-in-progress 'Hey Jude' on the piano while Elton looked on, speechless.

As it turned out, McCartney never became particularly close to Elton: his influence on him has been musical rather than personal. What unites the two songwriters is a world-class talent for composing top-line melodies and there's often a heart-felt, confessional edge to Bernie Taupin's lyrics that also comes straight from the school of McCartney.

Elton bonded most with John Lennon, albeit for a fairly brief period. Although the two musos presented very differently, both came from working-class backgrounds, both overdid the drugs and both suffered agonies, thanks to their inner insecurities. Not that any insecurities impeded them throughout 1974–75, the period in which they spent most time together.

'I was intimidated when I first met John because I'd heard how he could be very abrasive, but I never found that in that friendship, ever,' he told his Facebook followers in 2019.

'I took to John Lennon straight away,' remarked Elton in his autobiography, *Me*. 'The first time I met him, he was dancing with [Apple Records manager] Tony King. Nothing unusual in that, other than the fact that they weren't in a nightclub, there was no music playing and Tony was in full drag as Queen Elizabeth II. They were at Capitol Records in Hollywood, shooting a TV advert for John's forthcoming album, *Mind Games* . . . I thought, we're going to get on like a house on fire.'

At the time, Lennon had temporarily separated from his wife Yoko Ono and was squiring his employee May Pang through an eighteen-month period of debauchery in Los Angeles – 'John's Lost Weekend', as it became known. Elton joined Lennon in what he later referred to as 'boozy madness' and frequently visited him on both coasts of the US. He also played piano on two songs from Lennon's 1974 album, *Walls and Bridges*: 'Surprise, Surprise (Sweet Bird of Paradise)' and 'Whatever Gets You Thru the Night'.

The latter session led to a career highpoint for both men. Convinced that the song would be a number-one hit, Elton placed a bet with Lennon that if he was right and 'Whatever Gets You Thru the Night' did indeed top the US charts, the former

Beatle would join him on stage. 'I just wanted to see him play live, which he'd hardly done at all since the Beatles split up; a couple of appearances at benefit gigs and that was it,' said Elton.

When Elton's prediction turned out to be correct, Lennon was as good as his word, fortunately – because his appearance on stage at New York's Madison Square Garden on 29 November 1974 has gone down as one of rock 'n' roll's most memorable moments. Mind you, Lennon was taken aback at the sight of Elton's outrageous stage wear, exclaiming: 'Fucking hell, is this what rock and roll's all about nowadays, then?' and experiencing such severe stage fright that he vomited backstage. Still, he rallied splendidly for three songs – the recent hit plus Elton's spectacular version of 'Lucy in the Sky with Diamonds', which had been recorded during the *Captain Fantastic* sessions and recently released as a stand-alone single featuring Lennon on backing vocals (credited as Dr Winston O'Boogie & His Reggae Guitars) – and also hit number one in the US. Plus a rip-roaring version of 'I Saw Her Standing There' – and an encore of 'The Bitch Is Back'.

'In my whole career, I've honestly never heard a crowd make a noise like the one they made when I introduced [Lennon],' Elton recalled. 'It just went on and on and on. But I knew how they felt. I was as giddy about it as they were . . . It was probably the highlight of our careers to that point.'

When Lennon did finally acquiesce to appear on stage with Elton, Yoko Ono, unbeknownst to them both, had acquired a ticket for the show – and brought along a date. As soon as the pair were reunited backstage, Yoko recalled to biographer Philip Norman: 'We immediately started talking, each of us totally forgetting the people we were supposed to be with. John invited me to an art show. We started dating all over again.'

They would go on to have a son, Sean, to whom Elton became godfather, and Elton would tell Sean many years later of the confidence John's friendship had given him and of the fun they had together: 'That night was so consequential in the history of his life.'

Though no one could have known it then, his performance with Elton was Lennon's final live performance, and indeed he withdrew from Elton's company on his return to Yoko, giving up the booze and focusing on fatherhood. Elton was still brushing shoulders with former Fabs, though, having become close to Ringo Starr, who he'd first met in 1973. As he noted in his daily diary, 'Got up. Tidied the house. Watched football on TV. Wrote "Candle in the Wind". Went to London. Bought Rolls-Royce. Ringo came for dinner.'

As with Lennon, Elton's relationship with Starr involved plenty of drug-influenced mayhem. The former once bought a full-scale fibreglass model of a Tyrannosaurus Rex from the latter ('at the end of a very long night,' Elton wryly noted), while Starr is said to have asked to join Elton's band during a 'mammoth drug fest'. History could have been made that night, but as Elton reasoned, 'He probably forgot he said it about ninety seconds after the words came out of his mouth.'

More productively, Elton was inspired to fork out for his Windsor mansion, Woodside, after a visit to Starr's palatial residence, Tittenhurst – formerly owned by Lennon – gave him the idea that a man in his position should really have a country mansion of his own.

In 1975, Elton found himself in the astonishing position of being more successful than the Beatles, at least in one sense, when the *Captain Fantastic* and *Rock of the Westies* albums both debuted in the US album charts at number one. 'No one had ever done that before, not Elvis, not the Beatles,' he marvelled, 'and now I'd done it twice, in the space of six months.'

This must have been a confusing experience for Elton, which may explain – along with the 24/7 coke – why he made some regrettably pointed comments in 1978. Referring to the 'Ego' single from that year's *A Single Man* album, he declared that it was 'dedicated to the Jaggers and Bowies of the world – and especially to Mr McCartney . . . [his] music has gone so far down the tubes, I can't believe it.'

On 13 September 1980, Elton and Lennon crossed paths again, this time at an after-show party on a museum ship on New York's East River. Exhausted after his show at Central Park earlier that day, Elton didn't stay long, but noted that Lennon was in great spirits and excited about his upcoming album, *Double Fantasy*. The two men promised to meet next time Elton was in New York; however, on landing in Melbourne on 8 December, a week into an Australian tour, Elton received the devastating news of his friend's murder.

'I couldn't believe it,' he later wrote. 'It wasn't just the fact of his death, it was the brutality of how it happened. Other friends of mine had died young: first Marc Bolan in 1977 and then Keith Moon in 1978. But they hadn't died the way John died. Marc had been killed in a car crash and Keith had basically died from an incurable case of being Keith Moon. They hadn't been murdered, by a complete stranger, outside their home, for no reason whatso-ever. It was inexplicable. It was inconceivable.'

Distraught, Elton sent Yoko Ono a chocolate cake instead of flowers, knowing that she had a sweet tooth, and arranged for a private ceremony to honour Lennon in Melbourne. No formal funeral was held for the most famous ex-Beatle, so perhaps Elton's own version – held at the city cathedral, hired for the occasion – was the nearest equivalent. Elton and Bernie Taupin wrote a song for their friend, 'Empty Garden', with suitably angry lyrics, but it has rarely been played since as Elton finds it too emotional to approach.

When Yoko Ono was preparing 1984's *Milk and Honey*, an album built around some half-finished recordings of Lennon songs made just prior to his death, she asked Elton to help her complete them. Although flattered by the request, he declined, wary of imposing himself on the deceased icon's music. (Yoko would later add several of her own original compositions with the aid of the production team at Geffen Records.) The meeting was uncomfortable, as he later described it, but Elton has gone on to maintain cordial relations with Yoko and her and John's son Sean, as he did with John's older son, Julian.

As for George Harrison? Elton's relationship with The Quiet One seems to have been chummy, if infrequent. A fantastic story from the late '80s involves Elton, almost psychotically coked-up, buttonholing a scruffy stranger at a garden party attended by rock 'n' roll glitterati and demanding that he change into something more glamorous. The scruff in question turned out to be Bob Dylan.

As Elton, mortified, attempted to salvage the situation, the nearby Harrison offered some sound advice. 'I heard the unmistakable sound of George's mordant, Scouse-accented voice calling out to me,' he recalled. '"Elton," he said, "I really think you need to go steady on the old marching powder."'

'One of the Beatles was publicly telling me to do something about my cocaine habit. I just laughed it off . . .'

BECKHAM, DAVID AND VICTORIA

The godfather

Elton has always been chummy with the latest pop sensations of any given era, from George Michael in the '80s to Take That in the '90s, so it's little surprise to hear that he's close friends with the ad hoc Spice Girl Victoria Beckham (née Adams) and her superstar former footballer husband, David. Elton's influence on Victoria was significant: after meeting her when he cameoed in the breathtakingly awful 1997 film *Spice World*, he inspired her to quit the girl group and go solo.

As Victoria once burbled in a public letter to herself: 'Remember years ago, watching your dear friend Elton John on stage in Las Vegas. He performed "Tiny Dancer", as if it were the first time, and you realised this was like oxygen for him. It was a life-changing moment – while singing and dancing was fun for you, it wasn't your passion. That day, you started your quest to uncover your own dreams. It was time to step away from being a Spice Girl.'

Less well known at the time was the fact that Elton had collapsed on his private jet as he flew to sing at Victoria and David's wedding in 1999. Rushed to hospital, he was diagnosed with an irregular heartbeat and had to undergo emergency surgery to have a pacemaker fitted. Leaving hospital after the operation, Elton told reporters: 'It came as a bit of a shock, but the operation was a simple procedure.'

Subsequently Elton became godfather to the Beckhams' sons Brooklyn and Romeo, inviting the family to his wedding to David Furnish in 2014 and performing at his younger godson's sixteenth birthday party four years later. Over the years the tabloids have often featured stories of Elton, Victoria and the two Davids hanging out in various glittering showbiz locales, with day-by-day updates from Instagram coming in summer 2018 when the foursome holidayed in Europe aboard Elton's Riva superyacht, named *Hercules II* (following on from his previous superyacht, a 63 Vertigo named *Hercules*). A mildly amusing moment came when David B was made over to look like his host, with the full diamond-glasses-and-Versace uniform.

Less frivolously, Elton and the Beckhams were reported back in 2005 to have bought a new holiday home in South Africa together, with a mystery third investor rumoured to be Sting. They were said to be planning to turn the nine-bedroom beachside property in South Africa's exclusive coastal village, Llandudno, into a boutique hotel.

As Elton said at the time, 'I'm addicted to buying a piece of property, doing it up and then buying another piece. My mum always wanted me to put my money in bricks and mortar instead of up my nose.'

'BENNIE AND THE JETS'

Electric boobs and mohair shoes

'Bennie and the Jets' was one of the most novel numbers on *Goodbye Yellow Brick Road*, sheer exuberant fun, catchy to its roots, with Elton indulging his Frankie Valli falsetto impression to perfection. But it was never intended to be released as a single – at least, not as far as Elton was concerned. As if to make the point, in the UK, 'Bennie and the Jets' was made the B-side of the 'Candle in the Wind' single. Both the singer and the DJM label deemed 'Candle in the Wind' classier, more polished, more serious, more classic Elton. 'Bennie . . . ' was album-filler. Now it's one for the ages.

DJM decided that 'Bennie and the Jets' would be seen as a novelty song in Britain and Europe, Elton's very own 'Yellow Submarine'. By comparison, 'Candle in the Wind' was the big statement song and again it would be hard to argue with that analysis, from DJM's point of view. 'Candle in the Wind' was cathartic, absolute. 'Bennie and the Jets' was merely comical.

In America, however, where the giant MCA (Music Company America) released Elton's records in the '70s, the strong feeling was that 'Bennie . . . ' should be the next single. There had been unexpected radio interest in the track at certain R&B stations in Detroit. It was rare to hear a white rock artist on those stations. The feeling was that even if it didn't cross over into Elton's more familiar mainstream radio audiences, 'Bennie . . .' might open up new markets for him, rather than another ballad, the safe choice, however beautifully rendered and iconic.

Elton was not happy. 'I said, "No, I want 'Candle in the Wind',"' he told the BBC. 'They fought and fought and fought, and I turned them down so many times until they told me that the record had gone to number one on the R&B station in Detroit.'

Elton's music topping the charts on black stations was an entirely unforeseen gift. Reared on vintage blues and soul, the singer-songwriter was delighted. Of course they could release as 'Bennie . . .' as the next single.

'The only reason I caved was because the song was the number-one black record in Detroit,' Elton admitted in *Rolling Stone*. 'I went, "Oh, my God." I mean, I'm a white boy from England. And I said, "Okay, you've got it".'

It became the spark that started the bushfire. Once Detroit had a 7-inch single version they could spin easily on radio, other stations – black and white – began urgently requesting their own easier-to-spin 7-inch copies.

Given full national release as a single in America in February 1974, by early April 'Bennie and the Jets' had stomped to number one on the singles' charts and sold over 2 million copies. 'It shows that, as an artist, sometimes you know nothing,' Elton graciously conceded.

Speaking to *Rolling Stone* on the fortieth anniversary of the song hitting number one, Bernie Taupin disclosed: 'I saw Bennie and the Jets as a sort of proto-sci-fi punk band, fronted by an androgynous woman, who looks like something out of a Helmut Newton photograph.'

Clad in 'electric boots, a mohair suit' and blasting out 'electric music, solid walls of sound', backed by her 'weird and wonderful' band, the Jets, the narrator tells her friends Candy and Ronnie. First heard on *Goodbye Yellow Brick Road*, it came across as a light-hearted parody of the prevailing glam scene: Bennie could have been Bowie, Freddie Mercury, Jagger or Bryan Ferry. It was all of them, though neither Elton nor Bernie ever claimed as such.

Within weeks of 'Bennie . . .' going to number one in America, a new all-white Scottish outfit called the Average White Band also hit the top of the US charts with their own funktastic single, 'Pick Up the Pieces'. The following year, David Bowie released *Young Americans*, an album he described as 'plastic soul' but from which came his first number-one single in America, 'Fame'. A year after that, the Rolling Stones had their own glam-funk faux-disco hit, 'Hot Stuff'.

But Elton and Bernie had been drawing from that well for years. When 'Bennie . . .' also got to number fifteen on the *Billboard* soul charts, Elton became the first white rock artist to be invited to perform on *Soul Train*, the weekly TV series devised by producer and presenter Don Cornelius, specifically to highlight black music in all its forms. Elton set the trend, to be followed swiftly by both the Average White Band and Bowie again in 1976.

In *The Cut: The Making of Bennie and the Jets*, the producer Gus Dudgeon recalled the moment the sauntering, shadow-dancing 'Bennie' was born: 'For some weird reason, Elton happened to have hit the opening piano chord of the song exactly one bar before the song actually started. So I was doing the mix and this chord kept coming on which you normally wouldn't expect to hear. I turned to engineer [David Hentschel] and I said, "What does that remind you of? . . . It's the sort of thing that people do on stage just before they're going to start a song.' Just to kind of get everybody, "Okay, here we go, ready?" For some reason that chord being there made me think, "Maybe we should fake-live this".'

The enterprising studio-whiz mixed in live sounds from an Elton performance at London's Royal Festival Hall in 1972, along with some raw audience crackle and thunder from Jimi Hendrix's 1970 Isle of Wight performance. A perfectionist with a featherlight touch, he also included a series of whistles from another concert in Vancouver, with added-on handclaps and generic audience excitement.

'Bennie' may have sat comfortably as a hip glam 'parody', last track side one of *Goodbye Yellow Brick Road*, but as a standalone single, out from under the weight of the mothership, this prefigured Bowie's plastic soul period by at least two albums and quickly reached the stratosphere as one of Elton John's best-loved and most instantly recognisable hits.

It was no more plastic than Elton trying to be badder than Jagger on 'Saturday Night's Alright for Fighting', or more plangent than Dylan on 'Goodbye Yellow Brick Road'. Elton wasn't posing, not when it came to music. Call it plastic funk if you wish, but this was simply a great band with its own sound now and who felt they could do anything. Its main calling card was that 'Bennie and the Jets' was simply fun and quirky. A scarcity for most of Elton's early albums, now becoming more of a feature, starting with 'Honky Cat', jive-jumpin' ahead with 'Crocodile Rock' and the carefully choreographed aggro of 'Saturday Night's Alright for Fighting'.

That 'Bennie . . .' started with the convincingly faked sound of a live concert where the crowd are in full swing – the track was recorded entirely in the studio – paradoxically made the moment more real. You suspend belief because this is 1973 and no one in rock does belief any more. This is better. More make-up, higher heels . . . Just for you alone in the crowd. It's subsequently been covered dozens of times by artists from an array of different genres, the hallmark of a true classic. Samples at random: the bibulously camp Beastie Boys and Biz Markie version in 1999; the seductive sample to Frank Ocean's slinky 'Super Rich Kids'; the mournful slightly crazed neo-classical version in 2020 by the defiantly obscure Midnite String Quartet; or how about '80s pop crooner Paul Young's bizarrely fetching swing version of 2006?

'Bennie . . .' has also been used in various TV shows and movies, from the wincingly funny Andy Bernard character in the US version of *The Office* spontaneously bursting into song in one episode, to the famous bar scene in the 2008 Hollywood rom-com *27 Dresses*, where the Katherine Heigl and James Marsden characters begin belting it out while making up their own lyrics: 'She's got electric boobs and mohair shoes,' sings Heigl. 'You're gonna hear a handsome music so the walrus sooouuund!' And, in her much-heralded Netflix docuseries, Meghan Markle revealed that her son Archie's favourite song is 'Bennie and the Jets'.

There have also been some truly breath-taking versions of 'Bennie and the Jets' over the years. Billy Joel delivering it convincingly at the 2004 Kennedy Center Honors show, old school style, fully leaded, Elton beaming down at him from his perch next to President George and Barbara Bush. Taron Egerton giving it all he's got, starring as '70s Elton in the 2019 biopic, *Rocketman*. A showstopping live performance by H.E.R. at the 2021 iHeartRadio Music Awards, during an Elton Tribute that also featured Demi Lovato and Brandi Carlile.

Earlier the same year, Elton had duetted on the song with Dua Lipa during his 2021 Oscars afterparty. The year before, Elton and Bernie Taupin had won the Oscar for Best Original Song for '(I'm Gonna) Love Me Again' from *Rocketman*. Whenever he isn't at the ceremony though, Elton hosts a glitzy Oscar-night watch party. In 2021, with the world still observing Covid restrictions, he turned it into a virtual event, with a livestreamed pre-show and a series of special performances tied to the commercial breaks of the actual Oscars.

The event, a fundraiser for the Elton John AIDS Foundation, was hosted by comedy-drama star Neil Patrick Harris, a past Oscars' host, and featured appearances from Lady Gaga, Cynthia Erivo and the cast of the Russell T. Davies' TV hit, *It's a Sin*. A gorgeously glammed-out Dua Lipa joined Elton for a brilliant performance of 'Bennie . . .' that seemed to find her channelling Bennie's weird and wonderful sound.

This author's personal favourite version of 'Bennie and the Jets', however, is still the unsurpassable performance by Elton on a 1978 episode of *The Muppet Show* accompanied by Kermit the Frog and half a dozen of his colourful friends.

Ironically, given how loved the song has become, Elton in concert has rarely matched the intensity that his famous admirers bring to it. He never quite plays the intro the way it was conceived for the album; he tends to over-elaborate on the extended piano section in the middle and likes to draw out the ending or simply bring the song to an early conclusion. In the past, he has included music phrases from Glenn Miller's 'In the Mood' and closed with the hypnotic five-note heavenly call from the famous John Williams' score for *Close Encounters of the Third Kind*. Occasionally, he swerves back towards the studio version, but tends to swing quickly back towards improvised extended versions. Nevertheless, its pride of place in the Elton canon was confirmed nightly on the Farewell Yellow Brick Road tour, where it opened the show.

Interesting endnote: in most countries outside the US where the track was the B-side to 'Candle in the Wind', it was spelled 'Benny'. But in the US and Canada, where it was the A-side, it was spelled 'Bennie'. Meanwhile, on the back-cover artwork of *Goodbye Yellow Brick Road* and the original centre-panel design, the track listing has the name spelt as 'Bennie'. However, to make things even less clear, various vinyl versions of the original album list the song as 'Bennie' or 'Benny', depending on the territory. And if you must know, when it was belatedly released as an A-side single in the UK in 1976, it bore the title 'Benny and the Jets'. Now a signature Elton John classic to rank with 'Your Song' and 'Rocket Man', 'Bennie and the Jets' was more fun than the Faces, more daring than Bowie and sillier than Sweet.

BILLY ELLIOT: THE MUSICAL
Tiny dancer

Everyone will no doubt recall *Billy Elliot* (2000), the deeper-than-it-looked film about a kid from a tough County Durham town who defied his family and community conventions by becoming a ballet dancer. Simultaneously a well-delivered treatise on gender politics and a tragicomic family drama, as well as commenting starkly on its setting at the time of the 1984 miners' strike, the film was adapted for the stage in 2005 by its screenwriter, Lee Hall. Elton John provided the music.

The show was a smash hit: it premiered in London's West End at the Victoria Palace Theatre on 11 May 2005 and ran for 4,600 performances over eleven years, closing on 9 April 2016. It won four Laurence Olivier Awards in its first year, with critics delivering enthusiastic notices, as did their American and Australian counterparts over its four- and one-year run on Broadway and in Sydney, respectively. In the US, even though reviewers were presumably less familiar with British working-class mores under Thatcherism, the musical scooped an astonishing ten Tony Awards and a further ten Drama Desk Awards in a single year, 2008.

David Furnish, one of the show's producers, explained that the idea of his husband supplying the music for the stage adaptation came about the moment they saw the original film, saying: 'I sat there as the movie unfolded and I thought, "Oh my God, this is Elton's life," and I didn't know how he'd react. I finally looked over and saw how profoundly moved he was.'

Elton was emotionally invested in the project for obvious reasons, telling the *Toronto Star*: 'My father never came to see me sing. Never . . . The scene at the end where Billy's father comes to see him dance and finally gives him the seal of approval did me in. [My father] has been dead for so many years, but I'm still trying to impress him. That's what gave me my drive. Look at me, Dad, I've succeeded.'

Billy Elliot: The Musical was, as Elton noted in his memoir, *Me*, one of a small number of projects that impressed his never-happy mother, Sheila. 'It was apparently one of the few things I'd done in the last ten years that was any good,' he sighed. 'Mum went to see it dozens of times.'

When the next stage musical Elton provided the score for – *Lestat: The Musical*, based on Anne Rice's 1985 novel, the gothic masterpiece *The Vampire Lestat* – was cancelled after just thirty-nine performances in New York in 2005, according to Elton, it provided his mother 'with the opportunity to tell me that she knew it would be a flop.'

BLAUEL, RENATE
My funny valentine

'Many years ago, I chose Australia for my wedding to a wonderful woman for whom I have so much love and admiration,' tweeted

Elton in 2017. 'I wanted more than anything to be a good husband, but I denied who I really was, which caused my wife sadness, and caused me huge guilt and regret.'

Well, it was an unexpected move, everyone had to admit. Elton was as openly gay as anyone could feasibly be in the homophobic early '80s, and the idea of him being a husband to a wife was a truly difficult concept to grasp. The question on everyone's lips, including some of his closest friends, was: why? What did Elton think he stood to gain from this? Over the years, however, his four-year marriage to the Berlin-born studio engineer Renate Blauel has started to make a strange kind of sense, particularly once you understand the context.

Renate, a former air stewardess born in 1953, relocated from West Germany to London in 1975. In 1982, she met Elton when he was recording *Too Low for Zero* at George Martin's studio in Montserrat. Now working as a sound engineer, Renate struck Elton as 'quiet but tough and self-possessed'. As he explained, 'Recording studios in those days were a real boys' club, you really didn't find many women working in them, but she was making a career for herself just by being incredibly good at what she did.'

The singer-songwriter soon found himself spending as much time as he could with Renate. It was the companionship that was key. Elton had many lovers, but no real love in his life. He was still turning every night into a party and every party into an orgy of sex and drugs.

Renate was different, Renate was real. Had Elton only been attracted to men thus far because the right woman had never come along? Was it an idea implanted into him from an early age, at a time when England lived behind net curtains and young gay men could be 'turned normal' by simply meeting the right woman?

With typical impulsiveness and no little theatricality, while touring Australia in February 1984, Elton took Renate to dinner and popped the question. One wonders if Renate assumed Elton was joking, but she duly accepted the offer of becoming Mrs John.

It's hard not to feel for a woman walking straight into such an emotional boobytrap. At the time, though, there were many fans and media more likely to see Renate's arrival into Elton's life as entirely suspect. She was either a gold digger or merely in it for the fame. It didn't seem to occur to them that maybe – just maybe – Elton and Renate might have had a good thing going?

Nobody in the touring party knew what to say when Elton broke the news, not least his current squeeze Gary, but they didn't have to wait long: just four days later, the couple tied the knot on Valentine's Day. When anyone pointed out that Elton marrying a woman was a terrible idea, he responded violently. 'People got screamed at and inanimate objects got thrown and smashed,' he recalled ruefully.

Those regrets came home to roost sooner rather than later. Although neither husband nor wife have ever revealed what happened between them, they officially called it a day in 1988. The doomed marriage is said to have inspired a couple of wistful songs – 'Blue Avenue' from *Sleeping with the Past* (1989) and 'Original Sin' from *Songs from the West Coast* (2001).

'It was the right thing to do, but it was a horrible feeling,' Elton wrote in his autobiography, *Me*. 'I'd broken the heart of someone I loved and who loved me unconditionally, someone I couldn't fault in any way. She could have taken me to the cleaners, and I wouldn't have blamed her.'

A state of post-marital harmony lasted a further thirty-two years until Renate slapped a hefty legal case on Elton. As *The Guardian* reported in October 2020, she filed proceedings at the High Court in London after the publication of *Me* and the release of *Rocketman*. Having spent some years under a new name and living happily away from the limelight, she had – the lawsuit claimed – been upset by the depiction of her marriage in the book and film.

According to Renate's legal representative, the divorce settlement had included a clause banning either side from discussing 'the marriage or the reasons for the separation' except with immediate family members or legal advisers. Renate's lawyers also claimed that her mental health had been fragile following the divorce and even that she had required electroshock therapy. Consequently, *Rocketman* had caused a 'devastating mental relapse' with 'recurring nightmares, agoraphobia, anxiety, depression, fear . . . [she] has had to relive her past constantly'.

Little wonder that the case was settled, privately and fast. An official joint statement read: 'The parties are happy to announce that they have resolved this case, in a way that acknowledges Renate's need for privacy. For her part, Renate acknowledges that Elton has acted in a dignified and respectful way towards her in the past thirty years and has always been happy to help her. They will not be discussing each other, or their marriage, in future and will be making no further comment about the case.'

Speaking in 2007, Elton said: 'A drug addict thinks like this: "I've had enough boyfriends, and that's not made me happy, so I'll have a wife – that will change everything." And I loved Renate. She's a great girl. I really, really loved her. But, you know, it is one of the things I regret most in my life, hurting her.'

BLUE MOVES

'Not exactly the work of two people cartwheeling down the street'

Because Elton John is so well known for his stirring, melodious rock songs and piano ballads, we sometimes forget that the man is in fact a consummate musician. But his fans don't necessarily want to hear 'difficult' music from him, either, as the lukewarm reception to his 1976 album *Blue Moves* clearly proved.

'I'm very proud of it,' he later claimed, 'but the music was complex and hard to play, quite experimental and jazz-influenced. And its mood was very sombre and reflective: Bernie pouring his heart out about his divorce from [first wife] Maxine and me writing music to match . . . It's a great album, but it's not exactly the work of two people who are cartwheeling down the street, overflowing with the joys of life.'

Is it really that great an album though? Like most double albums, it's a bit of a marathon to get through. Recorded in March 1976, at Eastern Sound in still wintery Toronto, it made for a very different atmosphere to the sessions produced at Caribou or the Château. Less full-spectrum, more introspective and dreamlike.

When *Blue Moves* hits its stride, though, it's genuinely great. The first of his albums to be released on his own label, Rocket, Elton wisely elected to release the best song on there as its first single. 'Sorry Seems to be the Hardest Word' is the album's most fully dimensioned song, an almost hymnal ballad with a topline melody that remained firmly in the listener's ear. Lyrically, it was almost gothically gloomy, with Elton writing some of the lyrics for a change, inspired by yet another failed real-life romance.

In case anyone was in any doubt about the song's theme, Bernie Taupin explained: 'It's a pretty simple idea but one that I think everyone can relate to at one point or another in their life. That whole idealistic feeling people get when they want to save something from dying when they basically know deep down inside that it's already dead . . . that heartbreaking, sickening part of love that you wouldn't wish on anyone.'

It seems that the thrill was gone for Elton in 1976, at least judging by this slightly misguided collection of songs. A point rammed home when he shocked his fans and band alike by announcing at a show at the Empire Pool Wembley (now Wembley Arena) on

3 November 1977 that he would be retiring from live perfor-
mances. You can see him utter the historic words on YouTube:
'I've made a decision tonight – this is going to be the last show . . .
There's a lot more to me than playing on the road.'

What's equally remarkable about this video clip is the way
Elton dresses for the show, which also featured Kiki Dee, with
whom he'd enjoyed his first number-one single in the UK with
'Don't Go Breaking My Heart', which Bernie loathed but Elton
and Kiki clearly had a ball charming the nation with. There was
also a show-stopping appearance by Stevie Wonder.

Nevertheless, Elton's old flamboyance had vanished. Certainly
when it came to his stagewear. No crazy glasses, no shazam costumes,
zero pizzaz. Instead, he opted for a beret, a figure-hugging leather
jacket and sombre colours. Wherever the Elton John of the *Captain
Fantastic* days had gone, he was nowhere near Wembley that night –
and *Blue Moves* is the soundtrack to his departure.

BLUESOLOGY

Long Johns and short memories

Most teenage musical prodigies don't form a band, tour the
world with a list of renowned artists and release original material,
then do that for six years before finally taking the step up to individual fame. Then again, most of those kids aren't little Reggie
Dwight, who was just fifteen when he put together a band called
Bluesology.

No one apart from a relatively small number of British blues
devotees has ever heard of this long-lost group, but many millions

of Elton John fans have Bluesology to thank for his five decades of hits, to date. That's how important they were to Elton's artistic development. While young Reggie was a member of that band, he evolved his stage performance, learned how to arrange, record and even – to an extent – write songs. Crucially, the group also gave him his stage name.

After Reggie's school band the Corvettes split in 1961, he and his neighbour, singer and guitarist Stewart Brown, along with drummer Mick Inkpen, asked bassist Rex Bishop to join them in a new band, Bluesology. The name was adapted from the 1949 Django Reinhardt album *Djangology* and in 1962 helped them secure London pub gigs, especially when horns were added to the sound.

Bluesology's sound was their key selling point. Reggie was a fan of Little Richard and Jerry Lee Lewis, and he could easily have pushed Bluesology in a similar rock 'n' roll direction. Instead, his group adhered to focused, horns-driven R&B, an elite sound that purists of the day preferred to the raucous new pop of the Beatles and their many overnight imitators.

In the spring of 1964, Reggie dropped out of Pinner Grammar School, a couple of weeks before he was due to take his A-levels. Fortunately for him, by then Bluesology had a weekly residency at Peter Cook's much-lauded Establishment Club in Soho, with their profile increasing thanks to taut covers of songs by artists such as Memphis Slim, Muddy Waters and Jimmy Witherspoon among others. The last of these was particularly popular with Bluesology, as Elton noted many years later.

'We played Jimmy Witherspoon numbers like "The Times are Getting Tougher than Tough" and "When the Lights Go Out",' he recalled. 'Our lead singer Stewart "Stu" Brown was Jimmy Witherspoon crazy, so that's what we used to play . . . all I really wanted to do was play like Jerry Lee Lewis or Little Richard.'

That could well have been as far as Bluesology ever got, as a respected but ephemeral footnote in British music history. However, a watershed moment came when they caught the attention of the Roy Tempest Agency, which signed them up as professional musicians. This entailed being hired out as backing performers for a host of visiting American entertainers, mostly of a decent B-league status, who were playing British dates.

'Touring was just great fun. We couldn't believe our luck,' enthused Elton in a *Billboard* interview in 1997. 'We were backing people whose records we used to buy . . . I did two tours with Patti LaBelle, and I remember that "A Groovy Kind of Love" was the B-side of one of her singles, and when Wayne Fontana & the Mindbenders had a hit with it [in 1966], she went through the roof. And she still goes through the roof, because Phil Collins had another hit [in 1988] with it!'

Other musicians who benefited from the unmistakable Dwight touch on the piano – or sometimes an electric organ for that authentic swelling R&B sound, although our man preferred the original ivories – included the Isley Brothers, Doris Troy and Billy Stewart.

'The people were well-known in England, but not too well-known in America, sometimes,' he remembered. 'Billy Stewart was another one I backed who was fantastic. He did "Sitting in the Park", which Georgie Fame & the Blue Flames covered in England, and "I Do Love You" . . . we were getting to play with people who were our idols. Even though we weren't getting paid very much – in fact, hardly getting paid at all – and doing three or four shows a night, it was a great way to start off one's professional career. I mean, it couldn't get any better for me.'

Read between the lines: thirty years after the fact, Elton was revelling in those memories. Who wouldn't? Life must have been immeasurably simpler for him back then. Still, the young backing pianist had ambition and wasn't planning on staying in the background for much longer.

A deal for original music was signed with Fontana Records, who preferred Reggie's voice to that of Stewart Brown, so the piano player got his wish. It's a shame that Bluesology's July 1965 single, 'Come Back Baby', wasn't better, though.

'That was our first record and we were real proud of it, but when you look back on it, it was a moronic song,' said Elton with the benefit of hindsight. 'Beyond dreadful! Yes, I wrote it, but it was an absolute nightmare. I mean, I was not the singer in Bluesology, but when we went to audition at Philips/Fontana Records, under a guy called Jack Baverstock, he didn't like the singer Stuart Brown's voice, he liked my voice . . . it's one of those real cheesy records that has to be heard.'

A second, equally unspectacular single, 'Mr Frantic', again written and sung by Reggie, went nowhere. A third and final effort, 'Since I Found You Baby', was the final nail in the coffin of Bluesology as an originals act, even though it came out on the rather bigger Polydor label and was produced by the singer Kenny Lynch, who had enjoyed a couple of hits.

After dates in Germany, Reggie and singer Stu refined the line-up to include Pat Higgs (trumpet), Dave Murphy (saxophone), Fred Gandy (bass) and Paul Gale (drums) for a stint backing the American R&B singer Major Lance, but yet another sea change awaited them – one that would lead to Bluesology's demise.

This came in September 1966, when the singer Long John Baldry invited Bluesology to become his backing group. Fresh from a stint with then unknown fellow vocalists Rod Stewart and Julie Driscoll in the group Steampacket, Baldry was hot property.

With few other options available to them, Reggie and Stu signed up, shedding everyone else except bassist Gandy and adding a new set of musicians. These included Pete Gavin (drums), Neil Hubbard (guitar), Marc Charig (cornet and flugelhorn) and Alan Walker (vocals). Notably, the singer Marsha Hunt – known for her musical career in the play *Hair* and elsewhere, as well as relationships with Mick Jagger and Marc Bolan – was a member for a while, as was the saxophonist Elton Dean, later of Soft Machine but best known now for quite another reason.

Despite a Baldry-free support slot with none other than Little Richard at London's Saville Theatre on 11 December – arguably the highlight of Bluesology's career – the writing was on the wall for Reggie, who now decided he wanted out. In early 1967, Baldry moved the group to the more lucrative cabaret circuit, the last straw for the piano player, who began actively looking for solo work then looked on askance as Baldry hit number one later that year with the song, 'Let the Heartaches Begin'.

Reggie answered an advert in the *New Musical Express* in June 1967, placed by Ray Williams, who was soliciting talent for Liberty Records. It so happened that a certain Bernie Taupin replied to the same ad and the die was cast.

The newly named Elton and Stewart Brown quit Bluesology in late 1967 and while that band attempted to continue with Caleb 'Older half-brother of Finlay' Quaye on vocals, they called it a day the following year.

Brown subsequently performed in a country rock band called Cochise, drummer Gavin played in Heads Hands & Feet alongside bassist and future Chas & Dave star Chas Hodges and Vinegar Joe, featuring young, pre-fame singers Elkie Brooks and a young Robert Palmer; other Bluesology alumni enjoyed moderate success as session musicians. The band's true legacy however is that they were the jumping-off point for Elton John – and for that alone, they deserve our respect.

BOLAN, MARC

Birds of a feather

If Elton John was the ugly duckling who grew into something more beautiful, Marc Bolan was already a white swan – a natural-born pop star whose effortless charisma and taste for glamour were a huge influence on Elton. The two men, only six months apart in age, emerged into the limelight at more or less the same time, having spent the tail-end of the '60s as a hippy folky (Bolan) and a jack-of-all-trades session pianist (Reggie) before rebranding themselves as kings of glitter in the early '70s.

This was a magical time, recalled Elton in his autobiography, *Me*, with like-minded musicians pushing boundaries out more every day. 'There was a new wave of artists that were all starting to make it at the same time: me, Rod Stewart, Marc Bolan, David Bowie,' he recalled. 'Musically we were all very different, but in some ways, we were birds of a feather . . . And we all knew each other.'

While the friendship between Elton and Bolan was necessarily a relatively short one, the latter losing his life in a car accident in 1977, the two men enjoyed some good times together. As Elton expresses it these days, Bolan showed him the ropes of pop stardom, simply by virtue of his extravagant, otherworldly presence.

With his Clara Bow eyes and naughty pixie smile, 'Marc seemed like he had come from another planet, just passing through Earth on his way somewhere else,' Elton told *The Guardian* in 2020. 'At a time when I was still becoming Elton John, he was a great mentor, and it was a privilege to play "Get It On" with T. Rex on *Top of the Pops* in 1971.'

A piano part isn't immediately obvious on 'Get It On' – although one is credited to the keyboard master of the period, Rick Wakeman – but that doesn't stop Elton hammering out chords and a melody throughout the song. He's mostly only visible from in front of the piano: in other words, you can only see his face and he doesn't get the chance to show off – but again, that's fine, because Bolan is quite rightly the centre of attention.

This clip serves as proof that, as Elton said, Bolan was the master and he was the student, tinkling away while the main talent twirls his Gibson Flying V and overdoes the Jimmy Page-style pout. Notice, though, how the relationship had changed by 1972: in that year, Bolan starred in the Ringo Starr-directed movie, *Born to Boogie*.

You'll notice straight away that the once-timid piano player has evolved into quite the extrovert. The scenes, which take place fourteen minutes into the film, find Elton flailing away on the piano, delivering a Little Richard-via-Pinner impersonation that could only come from a fully leaded rock star. Immediately afterwards, we cut to the sight of Bolan's head sticking up through Elton's piano as they jam on 'Children of the Revolution'. While Elton seems debonair and confident throughout, the man himself disliked his appearance in the film, describing himself as 'ugly . . . like a gorilla'.

Marc and Elton would go to gay clubs together, sometimes accompanied by David Bowie. But then gay clubs, as now, were frequented by all sorts of showbiz crowds and tended to stay open a lot later than the 'straight' nightspots. Asked about his sexuality by journalist Jan Iles in 1975, Bolan said: 'Bisexual, but I believe I'm more heterosexual 'cos I definitely like boobs. I always wished that I was 100 per cent gay, it's much easier . . . I think if you're gay or whatever, you have just so much fun.'

Bolan and Elton had fun all right. As a cheeky gag, Elton sent his chum a life-size photo of himself as a birthday present in September 1971. The following March, Bolan returned the favour for Elton's twenty-fifth – by delivering a 30-foot-tall print of his own image, as well as a silver disc for the 'Jeepster' single. The Bolan picture was so huge that Elton simply left it in the garden of his Wentworth bungalow.

'He was the perfect pop star,' recalled Elton many years later. 'His songs were great, his records rocked, he had attitude, he had performing skills, he looked fabulous, he dressed the part. I thought: "This guy doesn't give a fuck, he's just being who he is and he's loving every single minute of it." And that had a great effect on me.'

Elton's appreciation of his friend lasted a lifetime: he went on to perform 'Children of the Revolution' with Pete Doherty of the Libertines at Live 8 in 2005 and recorded a guest piano part for U2's cover of 'Get It On' for a 2020 Bolan tribute album, *Angel-Headed Hipster: The Songs of Marc Bolan and T. Rex.*

Not that this genuine respect prevented Elton from mocking Bolan's tendency to exaggerate his own success. 'He somehow managed to be simultaneously completely charming and absolutely, brazenly full of shit,' he chuckled. 'He'd say the most outrageous things with a straight face: "Darling, I sold a million records this morning." I'd think: 'Marc, no one in the history of music has ever sold a million records in a morning, let alone you."

'But something about him was so beguiling and endearing, you would never actually say that out loud. Instead, you'd find yourself agreeing with him: "A million, Marc? Congratulations! How fabulous!"'

Bowie, David
Rocket Man vs Star Man

On paper, Elton John and David Bowie should have been the best of pals, or at least artists from the same era sharing a well-won mutual respect.

They were the same age, both born in 1947 just two months apart. Both London boys from opposite sides of the river: David Jones, as he was then, from Brixton in the south, Reg Dwight in the north. Both were singers and musicians. Both toiled throughout the '60s in numerous alter-ego bands and one-offs, trying everything they could to make it. Both finally made it with huge hit singles – 'Your Song' for Elton, 'Space Oddity' for Bowie – at the dawn of the '70s, both tracks were produced by Gus Dudgeon – and both artists failed to follow up that success immediately.

When both Elton and Bowie finally found the charts again with a single that proved they weren't one-hit-wonders – 'Rocket Man' in Elton's case and 'Starman' in Bowie's – they were actually released within ten days of each other in April 1972. Moreover, both seemed to be drawing from the same well of inspiration: science fiction given extra ballast by the fact that NASA was now routinely sending manned space missions to the Moon.

Both men were also bisexual – openly in Bowie's case, who had 'come out' in a famous interview with the *Melody Maker* earlier that year – enjoying gay relationships while having numerous girlfriends, even a wife in Bowie's case and almost a wife in Elton's (before he bailed out at the last minute from his wedding to Linda Woodrow).

Most obviously, both newmade stars arrived in increasingly flamboyant style just as the pop world was being transformed by a new phenomenon called glam rock. But while Elton could so easily have been mistaken for the kind of ordinary-bloke-in-shiny-silks-and make-up that Slade embodied, Bowie became the ultra-fashionable new face of rock in 1972: tall and thin and radiantly androgynous while Elton was short and bespectacled and more obviously putting on a show in his 'crazy' glasses and à la mode glam-rags.

Suddenly both Bowie and Elton were something new and fun, yet at the same time now quite different. David had the screaming girls as well as the music-divining guys. Elton had all that plus mums and dads, and the more resolute members of the singer-songwriter fraternity still mostly clad in straggly beards to give the guy at the piano their consideration. The ones Bowie would never appeal to. Bowie could write amazing lyrics and Elton couldn't. David always looked fabulous and in the height of fashion, while Elton always looked cuddly and comically over-dressed. Bowie had the most fabulous hair since Elvis in his prime, Elton was all tasteful combovers and funny hats.

None of which should have altered the fondness of their personal relationship. Except it did when Bowie somewhat sneeringly described Elton as 'rock 'n' roll's token queen' in an interview with *Rolling Stone* in 1975. He had never forgiven Elton for what he saw as stealing his thunder in America, where 'Rocket Man' was a huge top-ten hit and 'Space Oddity' only got to number fifteen. 'Space Oddity' had originally been released before 'Rocket Man' and had been a huge hit everywhere except America. Indeed, he suspected that Bernie Taupin's lyric may have been 'influenced' by his own words. By the time Bowie's US label re-released 'Space Oddity' in 1973, however, it followed 'Rocket Man' onto American radio and many assumed it was Bowie who had 'borrowed' the idea from Elton.

His wife Angie tried to tell him: 'Other people can sing about space travel too, David.' But Bowie had held a grudge about it ever since. Not that Elton was aware of any of this at the time.

So that when he read Bowie's spiteful quotes in *Rolling Stone*, it hurt Elton, even knowing that David was strung-out and wouldn't even remember what he'd said ten seconds later. How dare he reduce his talent to a taunt, it was unforgivable. Rod might have got away with it; Elton might have said something even worse about Stewart. But that would have been two mates having a laugh and a joke. What Bowie said stayed with Elton even after Bowie's death in 2016.

'David and I were not the best of friends towards the end,' Elton confessed in *The Independent* a few weeks after Bowie's death from cancer. 'We started out being really good friends. We used to hang out together with Marc Bolan, going to gay clubs, but I think we just drifted apart.'

Then he got to it: 'He once called me "rock 'n' roll's token queen" in an interview with *Rolling Stone*, which I thought was a bit snooty. He wasn't my cup of tea [and] I wasn't his cup of tea.'

He did allow though that his old rival had found a uniquely wonderous way to deal with his death.

'But the dignified way he handled his death.' He shook his head. 'I mean, thank God. I knew he'd had a heart attack on stage in Berlin years ago, but not about the cancer. Everyone else take note of this: Bowie couldn't have staged a better death. It was classy.'

Elton had been at home in Los Angeles, asleep, when his phone woke him. It was 3 a.m. 'I immediately panicked, as when you get a phone call at three o'clock in the morning you think something is wrong. I thought of the kids, something has happened to the kids.'

It was his husband David Furnish on the line. 'David said, "I thought I better let you know, David Bowie has died." And I was shocked . . . I couldn't go back to sleep.'

Just three days after Bowie's death was announced, Elton sat alone at his piano on stage at The Wiltern theatre in Los Angeles, where he was videoing and recording a special two-hour concert to launch his new album, *Wonderful Crazy Night*. In an impromptu tribute, Elton played an extended instrumental version of 'Space Oddity', which led delicately into 'Rocket Man', with his full five-man band coming in on the chorus.

When it was over, Elton dedicated the moment to 'the Starman', then told the story of how he'd come to meet Gus Dudgeon, who had produced all his classic records from the '70s, after he 'heard a record which blew me away. It's called "Space Oddity".' Speaking to *Rolling Stone*'s David Fricke, Elton said of Bowie: 'He was innovative, he was boundary-changing, and he danced to his own tune – which in any artist is really rare.'

And Elton would know.

BUCKMASTER, PAUL
Strings attached

Many of the world's most talented people have no formal training in their chosen fields but still excel at their jobs, simply through instinct and application. The late arranger and orchestrator Paul Buckmaster was precisely such a person. The spiralling, textural strings that he applied to a long list of classic songs, many of them recorded by Elton John, gave those compositions both emotional depth and commercial appeal – and yet Buckmaster began his career with little idea how that was done, technically speaking.

'Paul seemed a bit eccentric, which, as it turned out, was a false first impression,' wrote Elton. 'Paul wasn't a bit eccentric. He was so eccentric as to suggest he might be genuinely nuts. He would stand in front of the orchestra and make noises with his mouth to indicate what he wanted them to do: "I don't know how to describe what I want, but I want you to make a sound like this." They got it exactly right. He was a genius.'

Elton wasn't overstating Buckmaster's talent: the half-British, half-Italian string arranger had impressed him deeply with his work on David Bowie's 1969 hit single 'Space Oddity', adding the layers of strings that helped to give the song its unearthly sound. Keen to give his own songs the same sophisticated atmosphere, Elton invited Buckmaster to work on his self-titled second LP in 1970. Its first cut, 'Your Song', was uplifted hugely by the resulting string arrangement – and made Buckmaster permanently in demand by songwriters and producers from then on.

Elton was Buckmaster's most regular employer in the '70s and indeed the two musicians collaborated for a further seven albums, all the way through to 2002's *Songs from the West Coast*. There were upsets along the way, as is par for the course in Elton's world, one of which came close to derailing the partnership permanently.

As Elton later recalled: 'We recorded *Madman Across the Water* in four days [in 1971]. It was supposed to be five, but we lost a day because of Paul Buckmaster. He stayed up the night before the sessions began to finish the arrangements – I suspect with a certain amount of chemical assistance – then managed to knock a bottle of ink all over the only score, ruining it.'

Although enraged by the extra studio costs incurred by Buckmaster's zonked clumsiness, Elton confessed to being impressed by the errant orchestrator's reconstruction of the entire score in a single day: 'Even when Paul screwed up, he screwed up in a way that reminded you he was a genius,' he reflected.

Despite his lack of training as an orchestral arranger, Buckmaster had had a solid education as a musician – hence his ability to rewrite Elton's *Madman* score. Born in London in 1946, he enrolled at the London Violoncello School at the age of only four, going on to become a masterful cello player. Further studies at a conservatoire in Naples, Italy, and a diploma from the Royal Academy of Music in 1967 led to a job in an ensemble backing a variety of then top-of-the-bill artists such as former Manfred Mann singer Paul Jones, the Scaffold, the Hollies and the Bee Gees, the last of these on tour in Germany in 1968.

Returning to London, Buckmaster met the producers Tony Visconti and Gus Dudgeon at a recording session. The latter, impressed with Buckmaster's cello skills, asked him to have a go at arranging some strings for 'Space Oddity' – and, after quickly studying Beethoven and Haydn scores borrowed from his local library, he did just that.

After the *Elton John* album, Buckmaster worked wonders on *Tumbleweed Connection* in 1970 and – not entirely smoothly, as we have seen – on *Madman Across the Water* the following year. His progress from the early '70s was both rapid and impressive, leading to collaborations with a number of prominent musicians.

Buckmaster's versatility was his strength: Harry Nilsson's huge number-one hit, 'Without You' (1971) possesses a 'Your Song'-a-like orchestral sheen. Recall Carly Simon's masterful 'You're So Vain' (1972) for a much more upbeat, whimsical strings accompaniment. He continued to expand his palette on Leonard Cohen's *Songs of Love and Hate* and the Rolling Stones' *Sticky Fingers* (both 1971) and with Miles Davis' game-changing jazz-fusion albums, *On the Corner* (1972) and *Big Fun* (1974).

He also played cello with David Bowie and his band in the recordings for the original soundtrack to the British movie-maker Nicolas Roeg's dystopian masterpiece *The Man Who Fell to Earth* in 1976. Based on Walter Tevis' 1963 sci-fi novel of the same name, Bowie starred as the alien Thomas Jerome Newton. Unfortunately, Roeg changed his mind about having an original soundtrack and the recordings have never seen the light of day.

Unlike many musicians of his era, Buckmaster never lost momentum, creatively speaking. Through the '80s and '90s, you could hear his impeccable work on songs by Mick Jagger, Lionel Richie, Celine Dion, Counting Crows and others. He continued into the '00s with Tears for Fears, the Darkness, Guns N' Roses, even Taylor Swift. Along the way he found the time to contribute to several movie and TV soundtracks, including *Son of Dracula* (1974), *The Spy Who Loved Me* (1977), *Midnight Crossing* (1988) and *12 Monkeys* (1995).

Paul Buckmaster finally won a Grammy in 2001 for Best Instrumental Arrangement for the song 'Drops of Jupiter' by the American rock band Train. He died peacefully at home in Los Angeles in 2017. Long before you could do everything with a laptop, Buckmaster expanded the limits of what rock and pop were supposed to be capable of. Never more memorably though than with Elton John.

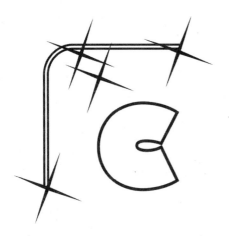

'CANDLE IN THE WIND'

Elton blows minds

If Diana, Princess of Wales – as she was formally known after her 1996 divorce from the then Prince Charles – had not perished in a car crash in Paris on 31 August 1997, Elton John's best-known song might well have been 'Your Song', 'Rocket Man', 'I'm Still Standing' or possibly 'Don't Go Breaking My Heart' with Kiki Dee. Instead, the song that most people think of now when they think of Elton John, and forever will be, is 'Candle in the Wind'.

A cathedral-like ballad with a beautifully simple but impossible to resist guitar motif, the original song was first heard in 1973 on the *Goodbye Yellow Brick Road* album and was released as a single in February the following year. It's an affecting composition, written ostensibly as a tribute to the legendary Hollywood star Marilyn Monroe, who had died eleven years before, still in her thirties, adjudged to have taken a deliberate overdose of sleeping tablets and referred to by her real name of 'Norma Jean' in the song. However, as its lyricist Bernie Taupin often tried to point out, the song is more universal than that. For Bernie, 'Candle in the Wind' was in fact a threnody for the premature passing of youth. The title was a phrase that Taupin had heard in conversation with Columbia Records' then-president and industry magus Clive Davis, in reference to the late American vocalist Janis Joplin.

Taupin clarified this some years later when he told the BBC: 'It's not that I didn't have respect for [Marilyn]. It's just that the song could just as easily have been about James Dean or Jim Morrison, Sylvia Plath, Virginia Woolf . . . any writer, actor, actress or musician who died young and became this iconic picture of Dorian Gray, that thing where they simply stopped ageing. It's a beauty frozen in time.'

Or indeed a tragic princess.

The single did just fine on its original release in the UK, where it reached number eleven, but it wasn't released in North America for reasons that defeated Elton at the time. 'I remember the record company phoning up and saying, "Bennie and the Jets" should be the single in America.' A decision, puzzling at the time from a UK perspective, that was vindicated when 'Bennie and the Jets' became Elton's second American number-one single.

'Candle in the Wind' remained popular in subsequent years, as evidenced by the success of a live version recorded on tour in Australia in December 1986. Released the following year, it unexpectedly went platinum in the US and hung around the charts all the way into 1988 when it reached number five in the UK and scored a Grammy nomination that year for Best Male Pop Vocal Performance. While Elton would no doubt have been pleased at the warm reception afforded the fifteen-year-old song, he must also have recognised the clear message this sent from his public, who had largely ignored his latest album, 1986's *Leather Jackets*.

That was it for another nine years, until the appalling death of Diana, Princess of Wales, and mourners started writing excerpts from 'Candle in the Wind' in books of condolence at St James's Palace. Elton had been friends with Diana for some years, although the relationship had occasionally been strained by her miserable, conflicted position, in and out of the Royal Family.

He was alerted to the 'Candle in the Wind' phenomenon by the Virgin founder, Richard Branson. The song was also enjoying a lot of radio airplay as the British population – many of whom were still reeling from genuine shock and sadness at the princess's death – turned to more sombre music for comfort and consolation.

It turned out that Diana's family, the Spencers, had asked Branson to convey a request to Elton: they wanted him to rewrite the lyrics of 'Candle in the Wind' and perform the song at Diana's funeral on 6 September. The Dean of Westminster Abbey, where the funeral took place, Wesley Carr, had personally appealed to senior aides at the palace to ensure Elton's performance at the funeral, insisting on the 'inclusion of something of the modern world that the princess represented'. A solo performance by a saxophonist had been considered as a second option. Although he was taken aback by the request and concerned that Bernie Taupin wouldn't be able to rewrite the lyrics at such short notice, Elton immediately agreed to the request. How could he refuse?

Taupin duly complied, changing the opening line from 'Goodbye, Norma Jean' to 'Goodbye, England's rose' and coming up with four completely new stanzas, quickly approved by the Spencers via Branson. The original Marilyn version's line, 'The press still hounded you', would have been appropriate for the new version, given that Diana had died while being chased by paparazzi, but perhaps this would have been a step too far.

Elton was given a chance to rehearse the song at Westminster Abbey on 5 September and was struck by the positive attitude of the various participants, from the Archbishop of Canterbury down. He chose to use a teleprompter both then and at the actual event, reasoning that one was appropriate given the importance of the occasion, although he was normally against their use.

Elton performed the retitled 'Candle in the Wind 1997' to a TV audience estimated to be around 2.5 billion people. Studying the footage, he does his job perfectly, although one of his eyebrows flicks up and down throughout: he was asked about this afterwards and admitted that it was a symptom of the nerves he was feeling. He later wrote that he was worried about singing the wrong version of the song, understandably enough. But of course he didn't. The consummate pro, the veritable man for the very biggest occasion, Elton's performance was pure silk.

The biggest gig of his life over with, Elton was transported immediately after the funeral to Townhouse Studios in Shepherd's Bush. The former Beatles' producer George Martin recorded two takes of his vocals and added a string section for a planned charity single, which was then rushed into production in time for a 13 September release.

Once back at Woodside in Windsor, Elton and David Furnish watched the aftermath of the funeral on TV. At this point, Elton's emotions finally got the better of him and he broke down with grief, having had to stay calm until both the funeral and the studio session were successfully completed.

On its release, 'Candle in the Wind 1997' – accompanied on the CD single by Elton's then-current song, 'Something About the Way You Look Tonight' – immediately broke records, set them and broke them again. People bought multiple copies, swept up by the national wave of grief over Diana and the plight of her young sons, William and Harry, buoyed by the single's charitable status.

The new song instantly went to number one, selling 658,000 copies on the first day of release in record stores and over 1.5 million copies in its first week. It stayed at the top of the charts for five weeks and became the best-selling charity song ever released in the UK, outselling Band Aid's 'Do They Know It's Christmas?'. Soon it became the best-selling single of all time in the UK, charity or not.

The Americans loved the single, too, buying 3.5 million copies and keeping it at number one for fourteen weeks. It stuck around on the US charts for the best part of another year. In Canada, it went platinum nineteen times, taking up residence in various charts there for several months, and is still today the biggest-selling single in Canadian history. In fact, the single sold massively all around the planet, ultimately shifting over 33 million copies and becoming officially the biggest seller of all time. Only Bing Crosby's 50-million-selling 'White Christmas' has come close.

Elton himself has mixed feelings about 'Candle in the Wind 1997'. He sang it only three times, once at Princess Diana's funeral and twice at the studio, and claims never to have listened to it after he approved the mix. He didn't even perform the song at the Concert for Diana at Wembley Stadium in 2007 and has always refused its inclusion on any singles compilation, even for charity.

As you might agree if you had heard the song blaring from the radio for what felt like every single day from the summer of 1997 into 1998, enough is enough.

Elton certainly seems to have thought so.

THE CAPTAIN & THE KID

You the Brown Dirt Cowboy and me a Rocket Man

At the suggestion of management, in 2005 Elton John and Bernie Taupin began work on a sequel to 1975's *Captain Fantastic and the Brown Dirt Cowboy*, the idea being to chronicle the two men's lives over the intervening three decades. The urge to dismiss the new album, to be titled *The Captain & the Kid*, as a mere marketing stunt was, and remains, strong, but an open-minded listen to the songs they came up with revealed a truer spirit and musical logic behind the concept.

There's certainly plenty of emotional food for thought here. Elton, via Bernie, reflects on the duo's absurd overconfidence in 'Wouldn't Have You Any Other Way (NYC)' then peers inward at their enduring relationship in 'Tinderbox'. Inevitably at this stage, there is sadness, with 'Blues Never Fade Away' a heartfelt farewell to departed friends, the list of which was growing, and 'The Bridge' asking out loud how long the fun can last.

In case that sounds too down, 'Just Like Noah's Ark' is a gleeful barrelhouse rocker that celebrates the crazy times, as Taupin looks back with amusement at their antics in 'I Must Have Lost It on the Wind': 'You couldn't tell me I was wrong / You couldn't tell me anything,' chirps Elton. The album closes with its defiantly nostalgic title cut, Elton solemnly intoning: 'We stuck around for the battle, waiting for a plan to turn you into the Brown Dirt Cowboy and me into a Rocket Man.' If you were one of the lucky ones to have been teenagers when Elton was at his absolute peak in the first half of the '70s, that line will always clutch at your heart.

The critics mostly liked *The Captain & the Kid*, although they were in a strange place in 2006 when it came to their own perception of Elton John. A huge wave of hype had accompanied Elton's 2001 album, *Songs from the West Coast*, but he had failed to sustain that momentum with *Peachtree Road* three years later, leaving reviewers feeling disappointed. They were understandably cautious when it came to the new *Captain* album, especially as it came with obvious gimmick potential. The tail wagging the dog.

'It's a confident return to vintage form,' acknowledged *The Guardian*, 'but almost every tune here sounds hammered and wrought out of the songsmith's forge rather than from a moment's white-hot inspiration.' In America, *Billboard* were more upbeat, stating: 'Thanks to organic, piano-driven production, stellar storytelling and Sir's rededication to his vocal craft, this is a triumph.' *Entertainment Weekly* trumpeted: 'It's not crying wolf to warn you that *The Captain & the Kid* is EJ's best since the Carter years,' while *Rolling Stone* decreed it, 'the third album in a career-resurrecting run that began in 2001, when Elton John took the novel approach of sitting down at a piano and writing songs that sound a lot like Elton John.'

The 'closing the cycle' idea – referred to by Elton in the album's liner notes, alongside a wad of nostalgic images of him and Bernie – went down well with his fans. It reached number six in the UK and number eighteen in America. Good, not great but an upward tick. However, *The Captain & the Kid*, despite its royal ancestry, vanished quickly from view in the modern zero-attention-span age.

Elton wasn't used to the speed of the news cycle, the sudden importance of the internet, or the fact that he was nearly sixty. Most of all, he was extremely piqued by what he saw as a lack of promotion by his label, Interscope. As a result, a new Elton John album would not appear for another seven years.

CAPTAIN FANTASTIC AND THE BROWN DIRT COWBOY
Songs about trying to write songs

Nostalgia is a fundamentally untrustworthy emotion because it can trick you into thinking that your life used to be better, when often that's not the case. Most songs written about the good old days are superficial for that very reason and only a tiny number of musicians ever pull off the combined trick of looking back into the past – telling the actual truth of those times, the funny and the sad, the cringeworthy – and making a huge success out of it.

Elton John and Bernie Taupin joined that gilded elite when they wrote and recorded their ninth studio album, *Captain Fantastic and the Brown Dirt Cowboy*. Composed and recorded in 1974 and released in May the following year, it came at exactly the right time for Elton. He was at the very height of his career, able to do no wrong it seemed, yet it was now he and Taupin decided to focus on the sometimes painfully autobiographical subject of their own relationship and their shared journey from nothing to something to everything.

There was also the feeling, aired here and there, and not unfairly, that his previous album, *Caribou*, had been good enough without coming close to the grandeur of its predecessor, *Goodbye Yellow Brick Road*. But in 1974 Elton John was still at a point where people cared enough about him to invest in whatever he did next. He hadn't been around long enough for his fans to become jaded.

In order to understand the real significance of *Captain Fantastic*, we need to consider where Elton was at commercially in 1974: *Caribou* had been one of the big summer-long million-sellers. It might not have had the artistic heft of his other recent work but it had 'The Bitch Is Back' on it and 'Don't Let the Sun Go Down on Me'. Wherever you roamed in the world, Elton was on the radio. There seemed to be no off switch. He was already working on the album's successor when the news came through that *Caribou* had gone platinum in America.

Then in November came *Elton John's Greatest Hits*. Ten singles cherrypicked from the four astronomical years since *Elton John*, nine of them million-selling hits, it became one of his biggest selling albums, spending ten weeks at number one in America and going on to certify seventeen times platinum across the next thirty years. At home in Britain, it went straight to number one and earned Elton his second platinum UK album.

The spark that lit the bonfire was an absolutely inspired choice stand-alone single released to coincide: Elton's cover of the Beatles' 'Lucy in the Sky with Diamonds', featuring John Lennon.

Elton-mania continued into 1975, with a reissue of *Empty Sky* doing decent business and another non-album number-one single in April with 'Philadelphia Freedom'. Shrewdly, Elton had employed the services of American composer and arranger Gene Page to come up with a string arrangement that closely resembled the Philadelphia soul style of producers Kenny Gamble and Leon Huff, then enjoying huge success with acts like the O'Jays, Harold Melvin & the Blue Notes and the Three Degrees, bringing flutes and horns to the Elton sound.

The fourth of the six number-one singles Elton would enjoy in America, the song took inspiration for its name from Elton's newest best friend, Billie Jean King – the American women's tennis legend and social pioneer, who had beaten Bobby Riggs in the famous Battle of the Sexes tennis match the previous year. King was now part of the Philadelphia Freedoms, a newly formed professional tennis team. The B-side was a frenzied live recording from Madison Square Garden of Elton and Lennon belting out 'I Saw Her Standing There', a McCartney Beatles-era classic, with Elton taking Paul's lead vocal part.

Elton was rock's mid-'70s Midas. Expectations were high for his next album, the already hyped to the heavens before it was even released, *Captain Fantastic and the Brown Dirt Cowboy*. We couldn't wait.

Released in June 1975, *Captain Fantastic* landed at the giddy peak of Elton fever. Sure, rubbing shoulders with Lennon reflected well on him, but now he wanted you to know he didn't just hang out with the biggest rock stars in the world – he *was* the biggest rock star in the world.

Concept albums were all the rage, everyone had done one: Bowie, Floyd, the Beatles, the Who, Genesis, Dylan. Elton's new album was based on a simple concept: Elton's shared history (Captain Fantastic, who else?) with Bernie (the Brown Dirt Cowboy). Its ten songs – written in the order that they appear on the album, according to Taupin, adding to the sense of import – tell the seven-year story of their early lives and work together, their slog towards recognition and the blossoming of their success. Crucially, none of this comes over as an exercise in self-indulgence. Bernie's lyrics are honest and open, despite his trademark cluttering of metaphors and images, expressing with clarity where the two men had come from and how their shared trajectory unfolded.

As Elton later put it, *Captain Fantastic* was 'songs about trying to write songs. Songs about no one wanting our songs. A song about my stupid failed suicide attempt in Furlong Road and a song about the weird relationship we had developed.'

The bare bones of the songs were put together in 1974 while Elton was aboard an ocean liner, the SS *France*, travelling from Southampton to New York with Cynthia Lennon and her son, Julian. John had asked him to escort his estranged wife and child over to visit him. Still unable to sit quietly, Elton found himself borrowing the ship's music room for a couple of hours of song-writing every lunchtime.

The resident pianist, he later recalled, resented this intrusion and made a point of playing on the deck above him, drowning him out often with the help of an opera singer. It was in this claustrophobic atmosphere that Elton composed his new songs. They came easily, fortunately, although he was obliged to commit them to memory as he didn't have a tape recorder with him. Once back in Caribou Studios in Colorado, however, Elton assembled the band, flew Gus Dudgeon in and the songs were committed smoothly to tape.

Then there was the small matter of the album artwork, created by the psychedelic artist and illustrator Alan Aldridge, whose work designing album covers and books for the Who (*A Quick One*) and the Beatles (their 1969 illustrated book of lyrics) had brought Aldridge to Elton's attention. Album artwork was another big thing in those 12-inch vinyl years. Before the listener even pulled out the record – a limited chocolate-brown edition, if they were lucky – and put it on the turntable, their attention would have been gripped, their mind suitably blown, by the astounding landscape that occupied the gatefold sleeve.

Aldridge's work for the *Captain Fantastic* cover has often been described as being based on Hieronymus Bosch's unnerving medieval triptych *The Garden of Earthly Delights* and there is something to that comparison – namely that both artists appear to have been 'tripping balls', as they say, when they put paintbrush to canvas.

Take a closer look. Elton appears, leaping from a piano, front and centre, while Bernie is tucked safely away inside a glass globe. A bevy of monstrous creatures surround the two men, part human, part animal: they caper, dancing and grinning, through an elaborately bizarre collage of broad and minuscule details.

Fans of Aldridge's books, *The Beatles Illustrated Lyrics* (1969 and 1971), and the Deep Purple side project, *The Butterfly Ball and The Grasshopper's Feast* (1973), will recognise the characters' trademark twisted grins and creepy, elongated fingers, while many a youngster was captivated by the two naked women, crocodile- and bird-headed, respectively – as well as a strange ceramic jug figure who appears to be excreting sunflower seeds.

The artwork was the perfect entrée to the music, which begins with the title track. It appears at first a gentle song, based on acoustic guitar and Elton's cod-American drawl: he considers his 'raised and regimented' upbringing, while Bernie wonders, 'Shall I make my way out of my home in the woods?' When the rhythm section wanders in, Dudgeon gives them a wonderfully warm, uncompressed sound – the essence of the mid-'70s, in effect.

'Tower of Babel' is equally restrained at first, although its terse chorusing of 'Sodom meet Gomorrah, Cain meet Abel' and Johnstone's layers of lead guitars soon add intensity. The album really amps up with 'Bitter Fingers', a musically joyous but lyrically downbeat tale of the Dick James's years. 'It's hard to write a song with bitter fingers,' intones Elton, although he sounds ebullient rather than depressed.

Strings waft through, 'Tell Me When the Whistle Blows', courtesy of the arranger Gene Page, who gives a sophisticated sheen to this opaque tale of youthful uncertainty. 'Long lost and lonely boy / You're just a black sheep going home,' writes Bernie, recalling long train rides back to rural Lincolnshire after early songwriting sessions in London with his new best friend.

This leads into the album's best-known song and only single, 'Someone Saved My Life Tonight'. At this point in his career, Elton's high vocals could be emotional beyond words and as he sings, 'You almost had your hooks in me, didn't you dear' to his ex-girlfriend Linda Woodrow, we're taken back to the miserable moment in 1968 when he made a feeble attempt at suicide. The 'Someone' was Long John Baldry, who had been the one who talked him into breaking off the engagement to Woodrow rather than destroying his budding career in a loveless marriage.

In a 2006 interview with the film director and former *Rolling Stone* writer, Cameron Crowe, Elton said, 'I've always thought that *Captain Fantastic* was probably my finest album because it wasn't commercial in any way. We did have songs such as "Someone Saved My Life Tonight", which is one of the best songs that Bernie and I have ever written together, but whether a song like that could be a single these days, since it's [over] six minutes long, is questionable. *Captain Fantastic* was written from start to finish in running order, as a kind of story about coming to terms with failure – or trying desperately not to be one. We lived that story.'

Flip the vinyl over and we're into rather more rock-indebted territory with '(Gotta Get a) Meal Ticket', an up-tempo paean to money and the pain of being without it. Keep an ear open for Murray's fabulous bass part, a disco line years before the genre was invented. For 'Better Off Dead', Bernie is in full storyteller mode: 'Through the grease-streaked window of an all-night cafe / We watched the arrested get taken away'.

'Writing' may be a deep cut here but it's another emotionally incisive moment, telling the tale of the burden of a lifetime of composition. 'I know you and you know me / It's always half and half,' sings Elton to Bernie, foretelling decades of collaboration and wondering if it will be any good.

'We All Fall in Love Sometimes' is *Captain Fantastic*'s big ballad and a beautiful song it is too, beginning with Elton's soulful piano and vocal. It builds in the patented manner, but never loses the listener along the way, with a fully leaded finale leading into the album's closer, 'Curtains'. Here, we say a slow goodbye to the Captain and the Cowboy over six minutes of thoughtful musings on the first recordings that the two ever made, seven years and two whole careers beforehand.

To say that Elton's fans took to the new songs is something of an understatement: *Captain Fantastic* became the first album in history to enter the American chart at number one. It remained at the top for seven weeks, turning gold overnight for over half a million sales, and although more than a few critics deemed it too indulgent, too whimsical, the public didn't care. It reached number two in Britain and number one almost everywhere else.

As Elton told the *Melody Maker*: 'I can't understand the critics who say that Bernie and I must be egomaniacs. The album wasn't meant to say, "Here we are, we're wonderful!" . . . for me it's a completely honest album. I've laid myself on the line. It's the truth, and I don't see why people should criticise me for being autobiographical.' He added: 'I identify with this album so much more than anything else I've done. For me it will always be my favourite album.'

Perhaps more than any other of Elton's albums, *Captain Fantastic* is the full package in today's multimedia sense. Like the Beatles' *Sgt Pepper's Lonely Hearts Club Band*, eight years old when this album was released, it came with extra materials – in this case a book of printed lyrics and another of memorabilia. The extra expense caused DJM to price the album in the UK as a double LP, causing Elton to comment: 'It's their decision, not mine . . . There's only one album left to do in the DJM contract. After that, I'm free.'

Of course, there were upsets around the album's release, as there have been at every stage of Elton's career. One came when he fired two members of his band on the eve of *Captain Fantastic*'s release.

Nigel Olsson told the press in January 1975: 'The next LP is perfect. It really is the one . . . It's a concept album and tells how Bernie and Elton started writing songs. For me – it's my favourite album to date', but the drummer might have been less fulsome in his praise had he known that he was about to be fired – over the phone.

Dee Murray received the same treatment while on holiday in the West Indies. Picking up a call from London, he heard Elton say, 'I've decided to change the band. I think you, Nigel and I have gone as far as we can together.'

Elton revealed that he'd been considering the change since the gigantic 1974 US tour: 'When I got back home afterwards, I was depressed for about two weeks,' he said. 'At first, I didn't know why – I thought I was just unhappy. Then I realised: I had to change the band.'

Another colourful episode occurred at the Los Angeles press reception for *Captain Fantastic*. An equivalent New York event had gone smoothly, but at the LA venue the sound was adjusted wrongly. As Dick James's son Stephen later confided to the biographer Philip Norman, 'When the first side ended, the house lights went up. Manager John Reid got out of his seat and stormed down to the engineer who was in charge of the hi-fi monitors. John screamed at this guy, something like "The sound's a fucking shambles!" . . . and he swung at this guy and hit him straight in the mouth.'

Finally, Elton himself proved that he was still capable of making errors of judgement when it came to the live debut of the new album, presented as a grand opening, a musical state occasion. Assisted in this foolhardiness perhaps by a chemically heightened state, he decided to play the album in its entirety at Wembley Stadium. It was Saturday 21 June 1975 and the album had only been on sale for a few weeks. Most people didn't know the songs yet.

After sets from Stackridge, Rufus with Chaka Khan, Joe Walsh, the Eagles and the Beach Boys – the last of whom played a full complement of non-stop hits – Elton's headlining set was met largely with restless indifference from the audience, tired after a long day and night of grooving around and having fun. They loved Elton but this new stuff they didn't know yet, it was kind of a downer: time to split.

'People started to leave. I was terrified,' Elton recalled. 'It was years since I'd lost an audience . . . I couldn't just suddenly strike up with "Crocodile Rock" halfway through. We eventually got round to the hits, but it was too little, too late, as the reviews quite rightly pointed out.'

Still, these were mere speed bumps on Elton John's path to supremacy. The *Captain Fantastic* album was and remains a spectacular achievement, critically, commercially, artistically. What *Captain Fantastic* reflects is the peak of Elton's ambition, certainly at this stage in his career. What do you give the rock star who's got everything? Credibility. Deep respect. Legendary status. *Captain Fantastic* is the closest Elton ever came to a *Sgt Pepper* of his own, from its gritty core concept to that world-class artwork. Importantly, it demonstrated again that Elton John had no limits when it came to creativity. It would be many years before he made another album of such scope and ambition.

CARIBOU

The sun going down

When the man who produced one of your best-known albums later describes it as 'a piece of crap' and complains, 'The sound is the worst, the songs are nowhere, the sleeve came out wrong, the lyrics weren't that good, the singing wasn't all there, the playing wasn't great and the production is just plain lousy,' then you know you've failed to hit the mark.

That man was Gus Dudgeon, who knew a substandard Elton John album when he heard one, having produced six of his previous albums at the time of *Caribou*, in 1974. It was Elton's eighth album in five years, ninth if you consider the double *Goodbye Yellow Brick Road* as two albums. Inevitably, he would find inspiration harder to come by. He needed a long break, but nobody had long breaks in the frenzied here-today-gone-later-today music biz of the mid-'70s.

Oddly in that context then, the *Caribou* album yielded two of Elton John's most memorable hits in the thunderous Stonesy 'The Bitch Is Back' and an Elton ballad for the ages, 'Don't Let the Sun Go Down on Me'. Both only got as far as the top twenty in the UK, but in America they both went Gold for over half a million sales, as they arrowed into the top five.

The album was another instant UK and US number one and showed up in the top-twenty charts all over the world; selling over 2 million copies in the US alone. And yet . . . and yet . . .

Tom Nolan described the album in *Rolling Stone* as 'dispiriting', declaring: 'Nearly every song on *Caribou* suffers from a blithe lack of focus, an almost arrogant disregard of the need to establish context or purpose . . . Shifting from sentimental, to heavy, to mocking, [John and Taupin] not only fail to touch all bases but undercut what credence they might possibly have achieved.' Criticising the album's production and the superficiality of the songs, he concluded that *Caribou* is 'a startlingly empty experience'. That doesn't seem entirely fair, given the two classic Elton tracks *Caribou* contained. In truth, however, the critics were correct: the material was thin. The singing and playing were still great but there was something off about it. It felt rushed. It *was* rushed. Coming after the extravagant critical acclaim he'd rightly basked in, in 1973, *Caribou* felt a little too off-the-peg.

The fact it fell between two epoch-shaping Elton albums, in *Goodbye Yellow Brick Road* (1973) and *Captain Fantastic and the Brown Dirt Cowboy* (1975), means its legacy is of an undercooked folly. Even the cover art felt rote, as bad as Dudgeon had described it: a zero-effort portrait of Elton looking faintly ridiculous in his latest fun specs and long black baggy trousers disguising boots so high they could be stilts. Set against the cheesiest, cheapest-looking blown-up print of some mountains, Elton chuckled fatuously into the camera.

The reviews all said much the same thing as *Rolling Stone*. Elton and Bernie Taupin seemed to be taking it easy, indulging in tomfoolery ('Solar Prestige a Gammon') or just treading water. It's not that 'You're So Static' (a twee soul workout), 'Grimsby' (a half-hearted rocker with, let's face it, a terribly boring title) or 'Ticking' (a lukewarm murder ballad) were frankly not up to standard: at best, they were simply mundane. At worst, eminently skippable.

The real issue was that Elton and Bernie were doing too much, having allotted only ten days to the recording sessions even though they barely had any songs ready. The sessions, at the Caribou studio ranch in the Colorado Mountains, started badly when the crew required two days to learn the monitoring system and a further day was lost when Elton flounced off in a huff.

He also despised 'Don't Let the Sun Go Down on Me', screaming or mumbling the vocal takes just to annoy Gus

Dudgeon, and famously sneering at session's end, 'That's a load of fucking crap! You can send it to Engelbert Humperdinck and if he doesn't like it, you can give it to Lulu as a demo.'

In the end, Dudgeon saved the day by creating most of the album from the various pieces Elton and the band had laid down, partially or together, after the singer had gone on tour, adding extra vocal tracks by Dusty Springfield, Beach Boys' Carl Wilson and Bruce Johnston, and Toni Tennille (later of Captain & Tennille) as well as brass parts from the amazing funk band, Tower of Power.

The fact that *Caribou* actually turned out as well as it did, let alone gave Elton a couple more enduring hits, is damn near miraculous. All these years later, we should probably regard the album a little more charitably. The other thing to remember is that when you have a back catalogue to live up to like Elton John's, any old song won't do. Good is not enough, you need great. You need solid-gold hits churned out one after another – and who of the great songwriting canon ever managed to do that for two albums a year, five years in a row?

Makes you tired just thinking about it.

CHÂTEAU D'HÉROUVILLE

A ghost in the house

In the history of popular music, there are certain recording studios that have assumed legendary status, either for the extraordinary artists that recorded there, the astonishing records they made there, or sometimes just the place itself.

HERCULES!

EMI Recording Studios in north London is the most iconic in Britain, particularly its Studio Two room, because it's where the Beatles recorded all their albums – to the extent that in 1976 EMI renamed it Abbey Road Studios in honour of the very last album the Beatles made there. Sun Studio in Memphis, Tennessee, is another such venue, due to the fact it's where Elvis Presley recorded no less than sixteen American number-one hits in the '50s and '60s, including such all-time classics as 'Heartbreak Hotel', 'Hound Dog', 'Love Me Tender' and 'Jailhouse Rock'.

Hansa Studios in Berlin, located next door to the Berlin Wall, is one of those places that seemed to imbue every artist that recorded there with a certain dark glamour to the extent that it attracted a particular kind of artist, from David Bowie and Iggy Pop to Depeche Mode, Killing Joke and U2, to name just a few. Motown's Hitsville USA in Detroit, Michigan, achieved seventy-nine American top-ten hits between 1960 and 1969.

Added to this select category in the '70s was the Château d'Hérouville, first made famous by Elton John and which subsequently became the hip recording spot for Pink Floyd, David Bowie, T. Rex, Cat Stevens, Bad Company and many others. Located in the village of Hérouville, in the Val-d'Oise département of France, 40 miles north of Paris, the original had been built in the eighteenth century by Gaudot, an architect of the school of Rome, from the remains of an earlier sixteenth-century château. In the nineteenth century, it was used as a courier relay station and stabled hundreds of horses. An octagonal stone drinking trough in the courtyard is now a protected historical monument.

Its reputation for arty indulgence began when the composer Frédéric Chopin was said to have lived there while having an illicit affair with George Sands – penname for the nineteenth-century French novelist Amantine Lucile Aurore Dupin de Francueil. The château gained further fame when it became the subject of a painting by Vincent van Gogh, who was buried in a nearby graveyard.

The French film and experimental composer Michel Magne bought the château in 1962. It was he who converted the building into a sixteen-track residential recording facility after a fire devastated the left wing in 1969.

The studio has been listed under several names in various album credits over the years, including Studio Hérouville, Château d'Hérouville, Michel Magne Studios, Strawberry Studios and by the nickname Honky Château. It wasn't Elton John who gave it that name though, but Rex Foster, whose *Roads of Tomorrow* was the first album recorded at Château in 1969–70. On Foster's website it claims it was he who gave it the nickname 'the Honky Château'.

But it was Elton who led the way for the château to host several big-name artists. When word spread of two wings, thirty rooms, plus several outbuildings, a swimming pool and a tennis court, set in more than 6 acres of scenic French woodland, it became the must-have venue for a generation of '70s rock stars to call home.

Not everyone found the Honky Château quite so agreeable, however. When David Bowie recorded his 1973 *Pin Ups* album there, he claimed to have felt a supernatural presence. Apparently, he took one look at the master bedroom and declared, 'I'm not sleeping in there!' He said there was a darkness and coldness in the master bedroom. Bowie took the smaller bedroom next door.

In 1977, when the rock band Rainbow recorded there, their singer Ronnie James Dio nicknamed it the Château Horrorsville. Rainbow guitarist Ritchie Blackmore was fond of getting out the Ouija board and holding nightly séances throughout the band's stay. Blackmore, who did stay in the spooky master bedroom, claimed that when he looked in the mirror once, he saw Mozart staring back at him.

According to Dio, during one of Ritchie's nightly séances they conjured up Thor, the God of Thunder – and asked for a sign. 'Huge storms immediately cracked open the sky,' Ronnie recalled, 'which began to pour with rain, thunder and lightning.' When they went into the studio the next day to record, the tape had been wiped clean. According to Dio, it was a regular occurrence. 'The 24-track machine would actually turn itself on and off.'

The next morning, ashen-faced drummer Cozy Powell told them someone had locked him in his room and all the books had flown off the shelf.

Blissfully unaware of any of this, when Elton and the band, along with Bernie Taupin and producer Gus Dudgeon, arrived for their first visit in January 1972, they found the elegantly half-ruined château breathtakingly beautiful. Living together meant that while Bernie was upstairs feverishly wording his latest lyric, Elton was downstairs at the piano in the large dining hall, putting music to whatever Bernie had come with earlier. Songs like 'Rocket Man' were thus begun and often completed in less than twenty minutes. Recording would commence immediately by strolling across the courtyard to the purpose-built studio. It would take fewer than three weeks to write and record all ten tracks.

The château also boasted exquisite cuisine and possessed its own vineyard. Elton soon became friends with the studio manager, Catherine Philippe-Gérard. They grew devoted to each other, to the extent that Elton brought Catherine into his inner circle, along with Bernie, Gus and John Reid. Elton was so happy he announced that the album would be dedicated to her.

CHEN, NATHAN
Skating for gold

When the 22-year-old American figure skater Nathan Chen set a new world record on his way to winning the gold medal at the 2022 Bejing Winter Olympics, with a free skate programme sound-tracked by a medley of Elton John's music, he became only the second American male to win the figure skating men's singles gold in thirty years.

Chen – a three-time (2018, 2019 and 2021) world champion figure skater – delivered a near-faultless four-minute skate routine that featured reworked versions of 'Goodbye Yellow Brick Road', 'Rocket Man' and 'Bennie and the Jets' with the majority of Chen's gold-worthy jumps and axels fittingly taking place during the 'Rocket Man' portion of the programme.

After Chen won the gold, Elton, who was watching from his hotel suite while on tour, was moved to tweet: 'Congratulations @nathanwchen for winning Gold skating to "Rocket Man" in the free skate finals in Beijing.'

Chen's Elton John-themed routine scored 332.60 points with the judges, well ahead of the 310.05 points from the silver medalist Yuma Kagiyama of Japan. The gold medal was also a redemption of sorts for Chen, who – despite being considered the best figure skater in the world by 2022 – only finished fifth and off the medal podium at the 2018 Winter Olympics in South Korea.

'I never thought I would actually be able to make this happen,' Chen told the *New York Times*. 'It's hard. It's always been a dream, of course. It's a pretty daunting mountain.'

Famous for his varied and unusual musical choices to accompany his exhilarating free skate style, Chen had previously utilised musical extracts from the ballet *Le Corsaire* to atmospheric contemporary works by Philip Glass and Stravinsky.

Chen previously starred in three episodes of the TV show, *From the Top: Olympians and Rockstars*, alongside singer-songwriter Hayley Kiyoko, which Elton executive produced for the official Olympic Channel in 2021. A show that paired Olympic athletes with music stars, as Elton explained: 'There has long been an inextricable connection between music and sport, two worlds that often come together for cultural moments around the world.'

When Elton joined forces with Britney Spears on his *Lockdown Sessions* album for an acoustic version of his song 'Hold Me Closer', he released it as single in 2022 accompanied by a stunning video starring Chen skating in Yale's Ingalls Rink, commonly referred to as 'The Whale' due to its distinctive shape and architecture.

COMING OUT

Can we get personal?

Elton John first revealed his sexuality to the public in 1976, but not because he was crusading for gay rights or determined to live his life as out and proud. No, he did it because he was bored.

Sequestered in his tenth-floor suite at the famously plush Sherry-Netherland hotel on New York's Upper East Side while executing a seven-night run of shows at Madison Square Garden, Elton agreed to an interview with the writer Cliff Jahr of *Rolling Stone* simply to pass the time. Jahr, who sadly succumbed to AIDS in 1991 at the age of fifty-four, was an out-and-proud gay man who was determined to ask Elton the big question, to the extent that he and the accompanying photographer had arranged for the latter to leave the room so he and Elton could be alone at the time.

In the end, there was no need for this subterfuge because Elton raised the subject himself. When Jahr asked, to his credit, 'Can we get personal? Should we turn off the tape?' and Elton replied, 'Keep going,' the journalist inquired, 'What about Elton when he comes home at night? Does he have love and affection?'

Elton then said, 'I'd rather fall in love with a woman eventually, because I think a woman probably lasts much longer than a man. But I really don't know. I've never talked about this before . . . I'm not going to turn off the tape. I haven't met anybody that I would like to settle down with – of either sex.'

Jahr then asked straight out if Elton was bisexual and while the singer didn't say yes or no, he did explain: 'There's nothing wrong with going to bed with somebody of your own sex. I think everybody's bisexual to a certain degree. I don't think it's just me. It's not a bad thing to be. I think you're bisexual. I think everybody is.'

Although he stopped short of admitting his affair with John Reid, not wishing to publicly out his manager, Elton was clear that he and Bernie Taupin had never been an item ('We're more like brothers than anything else') and joked that Watford FC were going to find his admission difficult to accept.

'But I mean, who cares! I just think people should be very free with sex – they should draw the line at goats,' he chuckled and indeed he was right to be relaxed about all this. Hardly anyone batted an eyelid about Elton coming out, apart from a couple of religious freaks, who wrote letters complaining to *Rolling Stone*, and some conservative radio stations that withdrew their airplay.

Quite correctly, Elton didn't give a damn and in fact he made his position even clearer in 1992, telling *Rolling Stone* in another frank interview: 'It's wonderful to be gay. I love being gay. I really do. I think I wouldn't have had the life I've had if I hadn't been gay. And I'm very proud of that. I'm very proud that I can appreciate that . . . Be proud of who you are. There are so many wonderfully diverse people in the world. Straight people, gay people, transgender people. We're all God's kids.'

COOPER, RAY
Hit it!

Drummers often become bona fide rock stars, but percussionists – their subtler colleagues in the hitting-things-hard industry – tend to remain out of the limelight, no matter how many claves or triangles they wield. Take Ray Cooper, for example, who has brandished a mallet with Pink Floyd, Carly Simon, Billy Joel, Mark Knopfler, the Rolling Stones and sundry former Beatles – and yet hardly anyone knows who he is.

Cooper's importance to Elton John's career cannot be under-estimated, though. Born in 1947, he made his bones in the pop group Blue Mink – a Dick James's act famous for their huge 1969 hit, 'Melting Pot', whose members had appeared on the *Elton John* album – before playing on *Madman Across the Water* in 1971. Since which time, Cooper has appeared on eleven more Elton John albums, surviving the great band cull that followed *Captain Fantastic* . . . four years later and eventually occupying an indispensable role.

Cooper has now played more than 800 shows with Elton and not only as part of a full band: tellingly, when Elton played a stripped-down tour in Russia in 1979, Ray was the only other musician on the stage. For the percussionist, those dates – 21–24 May at the Bolshoi Oktyabrsky Concert Hall in St Petersburg and 25–28 May at the Rossiya Concert Hall in Moscow – were about more than music, as he told *Goldmine*.

'This was a test of our skills, our musicality, and beyond that, our ability to communicate in this wonderful language of music to an exotic other language,' he said. '[Security guards] were sitting at the end of the rows, so if anybody got overexcited, they would make sure they didn't go anywhere. But then they disappeared, and they allowed the concert to take its natural course. And of course, people did get very excited. They listened fervently; they wanted to take every moment of Elton's music into their soul.'

Live, Cooper comes close to being as energetic as Elton himself – or even more so, given that the boss is mostly confined to a piano stool while Cooper stands up, smacking the crap out of his percussion with a variety of sticks. In 1994 and 1995, on the co-headline dates with Billy Joel as well as Elton's own shows, Cooper earned his salary every night with a seven-minute drum and percussion solo after 'Saturday Night's Alright for Fighting'. This would lead into an audience chant, climaxing with a nine-beat attack on a gong before Elton launched into 'Pinball Wizard'. Ray had performed a similar solo on tour with Eric Clapton in 1990, reportedly going so far as breaking his instruments as part of the act.

'What I was there for, I think, was to add colour to the drama. I think that's one of the reasons [Elton] asked me to go along with him,' he told *Goldmine*. 'There's something very wonderful, something very interesting in two people making music together; there's a dialogue that's happening . . . Elton didn't need me to keep time. He's one of the most perfect timekeepers in the world. His left hand on the piano is always, always, always in time.'

Note that the 1995 dates were billed as an 'Evening with Elton John and Ray Cooper': even Bernie Taupin didn't get headline billing of that stature. Not on the stage. The reason for this seems, reasonably enough, to be that the two musicians are very close friends. When the gifted blues guitarist Stevie Ray Vaughan tragically died in a helicopter crash in 1990, along with members of Eric Clapton's band, Elton was distraught, especially so because Ray Cooper was playing with Clapton at the time. 'After a lot of tearful pleading, they let me find out: Ray was okay,' Elton later recalled, revealing the depth of affection he felt for his loyal percussionist.

For some decades, Ray Cooper has also been an occasional actor in films such as Robert Altman's *Popeye* (1980) and Terry Gilliam's *Brazil* (1985) – but his most enduring role will always be as the extravagant sidekick to Elton John, a part that he's played for over fifty years.

COSTUMES

Elton's dressing-up box

'Look, I'm not Mick Jagger,' Elton John once told the *New York Times*, 'tearing from one end of the stage to the other. I'm always bloody stuck at the piano, aren't I? Clothes have always had to be part of the show that I put on. They made me memorable.'

Well, the clothes and the music. You take his point, though. Although one might point out that he often wears outrageous costumes off stage too, but then why not? Isn't that what all the coolest stars do too, in music, in movies, on TV and stepping from their limos? As he once said: 'I could never go on stage in denims.' Adding, 'I think performers are all show-offs anyway, especially musicians. Unless you show off, you're not going to get noticed.'

Elton's crazy costume ideas haven't always worked, such as in 1973, when he decided to invade the stage at a Stooges' gig in Atlanta wearing a gorilla suit. He was taken aback when the band's outrageous singer Iggy Pop – who was, it was later explained, tripping on LSD at the time – screamed and ran away rather than laughing along with the joke. One of the other Stooges then grabbed Elton and threw him bodily from the stage.

This did not deter him one bit. If anything, Elton's love of dressing up became almost an obsession. He soon engaged the costume designer Bob Mackie, a Hollywood tailor from the old school who had famously done a feathers-and-furs job on Cher. Elton was soon sporting a sequinned white bomber jacket made by Mackie, adding tasselled knee-high boots and appliquéd denim for good measure. He could do formalwear too, of course, as evidenced when he received a star on the Hollywood Walk of Fame in 1975 and showed up to the ceremony in a golden golf cart, wearing a similarly gold silk suit, out of which abundant chest hair bristled.

Live, Elton was all about making as strong a visual impact as possible. It was partly the era – glam rock may have faded but rock was not about to return to bushy beards and double denim any time soon – and partly his love of fashion and a genuine desire to simply put on a show. As he once said, 'I do like my rock stars to be a little larger than life. I don't mind the earnest ones at all, but I do like a bit of individuality.' Hence one of his most famous stage outfits – the Mackie-designed crystal-covered baseball outfit and blue cap that he wore at LA's Dodger Stadium in October 1975. Just to make it crystal (*ahem*) clear, the name 'Elton' was emblazoned on his back in capital letters. Later that year, he wowed Wembley Stadium in a sequinned, flared jumpsuit, topped off by the massive glasses he wore, shaped like ELTON, with lights flashing around them – powered by a battery pack that squashed his nose and rendered him unable to sing properly.

Another memorable stage outfit that presumably felt like a good idea at the time was the Donald Duck costume that Elton wore in September 1980 in front of 500,000 fans in Central Park, New York. The duck feet meant that he could barely walk so that operating the pedals on the piano must have been a challenge too: meanwhile, Donald's ample posterior meant that sitting on the piano stool was also tricky, causing Elton to laugh all the way through 'Your Song'. 'Once again, Bernie's tender ballad of blossoming young love was decimated by my choice of stage wear,' he recalled, ruefully.

By the time Elton was wearing wigs by necessity, he had also long since incorporated them into his growing wardrobe of outlandish stage accessories. In Australia in 1986, he wore a mohawk augmented by a Tina Turner-style spiked mane. Another notable outfit on that tour was a white sequinned suit plus a powdered wig, white make-up and a fake beauty spot, with Elton resembling an insane, glammed-up Mozart. Or possibly Marie Antoinette.

By the '90s, Elton had toned things down a little, sartorially speaking, despite the full scarlet leather suit he wore on stage in Paris in 1994, the garish, Yohji Yamamoto-designed blazers and capes he wore in Las Vegas some years later, and the sequinned tuxedo with pussy-bow blouse that he sported at the Grammy Awards in 2018. Lately, he's become a fan of floral jackets designed by Gucci's creative director Alessandro Michele for the Farewell Yellow Brick Road tour, a sign that maybe, just maybe, he's edging into a slightly more dignified old age. Over the years he has auctioned many of these outfits to raise money for his charitable foundation. You can see a nice jumble of these bizarre items on the cover art of *Reg Strikes Back*.

Of all Elton's colourful and eccentric costumes, the one we will always remember is the silver-and-white outfit festooned with fur that he wore at his fiftieth birthday at the Hammersmith Palais in

London, in April 1997. Dressed as King Louis XIV, Elton wore a wig that was 3 feet tall, decorated with a Spanish war ship and cannon. Brilliantly, the costume was so massive that he had to travel to the event in the back of a removal van – which got stuck in traffic for an hour and a half, making him fashionably late (full pun intended).

'CROCODILE ROCK'
Elton's snappiest tune

It's a mark of Elton John's versatility that he can excel at sombre songs and cheerful ones with equal ease. One of the most famous and best-loved examples of the latter is 'Crocodile Rock' from 1973's *Don't Shoot Me, I'm Only the Piano Player*, which became his first American number-one single.

Any critical analysis of this song is tricky, because on the one hand it is nostalgic, bittersweet and wonderfully referential of times gone by. On the other hand, it's schmaltzy, cheesy and potentially annoying if you happen to hear it more than once on any given day. Even Elton is sick of it, he says, swearing that he'll never play it again now his Farewell Yellow Brick Road tour is complete. If it had been released by any average sheepdog-permed Kenny, Jimmy or Scotty from the '70s, 'Crocodile Rock' would have been dismissed long ago as a novelty single.

All that said, the song has undeniable charm, especially if you were an adolescent in the '50s, 'when rock was young', as Bernie's lyric goes, as evidenced by the multiple gold and platinum sales it's earned over the years. Its key features are a cheerful Farfisa organ and Elton's falsetto, its laa-la-la-la-la-laa topline melody, both of which were once-heard-never-forgotten, as the old music biz maxim goes.

The song's main selling point, though, and the reason why tears still well up in the eyes of Elton's longest-serving fans whenever he launches into it, is its poignant look back at simpler times. To when 'me and Susie had so much fun'. To when, as Bernie so deftly put, 'crock rocking was something shocking'. Only Bruce Springsteen can take the listener into a bittersweet, long-gone past with quite this much facility.

A fair bit of hot air has been spouted over the decades over the provenance of 'Crocodile Rock'. An often-told tale has Elton besotted with a song called 'Eagle Rock' by the Australian band Daddy Cool, which sold a million copies in 1971. He heard the song while touring down under the following year and a photo taken at the time reveals Bernie Taupin wearing a Daddy Cool badge. Still, a visit to YouTube confirms that the two songs aren't particularly similar.

More seriously, a lawsuit in 1974 was settled privately between Elton (and Bernie) and a representative for the songwriter Buddy Kaye, whose 1969 song 'Speedy Gonzales' contained a falsetto section that was close to identical to that of 'Crocodile Rock'. Don't bother listening to 'Speedy Gonzales', though, because it's awful – and in any case Elton shrugged all this off in the liner notes of *Don't Shoot Me, I'm Just the Piano Player* when it was reissued in 1995. Of 'Crocodile Rock', he sniffed: 'I wanted it to be a record about all the things I grew up with. Of course, it's a rip-off, it's derivative in every sense of the word.'

Meanwhile, drummer Nigel Olsson has confessed how much he dislikes the song but enjoys playing it when he sees how much audiences love it.

In a 2013 interview with *Rolling Stone*, Elton described 'Crocodile Rock' as 'the song that probably changed the critics' opinion of me. It was a really blatant homage to "Speedy Gonzales" and all the great '50s and '60s records that we used to love, like Danny and the Juniors' "At the Hop". My career wasn't about "Crocodile Rock" – it was just a one-off thing – but it became a huge hit record, and in the long run, it became a negative for me, because people said, "Oh, fucking 'Crocodile Rock.'" I'd never started off as a hit writer, and I didn't know what a hit was, and it's evidenced on my first four albums. *Rolling Stone* reviewed it and gave it two stars, and I said, "Oh, fuck off." It was a great fucking pop record. Shut the fuck up.'

For the most fun, check out the rather wonderful clip of Elton performing the song live on *The Muppet Show* in 1978, along with the 'house band' Dr Teeth and the Electric Mayhem, fronted by keyboardist-vocalist Dr Teeth (whose over-the-top dress sense was said to be very influenced by Elton's own), drummer Animal (see the Who's legendarily combustible Keith Moon), bassist Floyd Pepper, guitarist Janice, sax player Zoot and occasionally trumpeter Lips.

In February 2016, when Elton appeared on *Carpool Karaoke* with host James Corden, the pair both donned coloured feather boas and zany sunglasses while belting out 'Crocodile Rock'. Elton leaned over and wisecracked, 'This reminds me of *The Muppets*.' But it wasn't anywhere near as good – or as funny – as that!

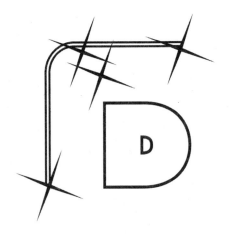

Dee, Kiki

Always on the bonk

In 1975, Elton John and Bernie Taupin were on holiday in
Barbados and decided to write a duet specially for Elton and his
friend, singer Kiki Dee. 'She's got a great voice,' enthused Elton
at the time. 'She just needs her confidence built back up again.'
Dee agreed: 'I think a lot of performers are like that,' she said.
'I saw that Elton had a shy side as well.'

Having signed the singer to his new label, Rocket Records,
Elton wanted to give her career – and his new label – a
commercial boost. What better way than having the world's
then most prolific hit-writing team craft a song for her – with
added publicity in the form of Elton himself also appearing on
the record?

They came up with two songs, one called 'Don't Go Breaking
My Heart' and another titled 'I'm Always on the Bonk'.

'I don't know who I'm fucking, I don't know who I'm sucking,
but I'm always on the bonk,' ran Bernie Taupin's lyrics in the latter.
The song was discarded soon after they sobered up. (Thankfully,
not only for us but also for Kiki Dee, who desperately needed a hit
but perhaps not *that* badly.)

Kiki – real name Pauline Matthews – was born in Sheffield in the same year as Elton, 1947; also like him, she began her career in sessions, singing cover versions of hits for BBC Radio. Because of the 'needle-time restrictions' the BBC were forced to labour under in the '60s, their output consisted of a great many such 'homemade hits'. But while she was much in demand, Pauline found it difficult to break out as an original artist, even after a name change to the more chic-sounding Kiki Dee. In 1963, she signed to the Fontana label and issued the first in a series of underperforming releases. Eleven miss singles in five years, not even her perky 1964 version of '(You Don't Know) How Glad I Am' – an American top-ten hit that year for the actress and singer Nancy Wilson – could halt her losing streak. Then, in 1970, her fortunes appeared to have taken an unexpected upswing when she became the first white British female performer to sign to the venerable Motown label, home of Marvin Gaye, Diana Ross, Stevie Wonder and the Jackson 5, to name just a few of their in-house legends.

Promoted as a 'blue-eyed' soul singer, Kiki had the attention of the critics but, sadly, very few others. One album, *Great Expectations*, and one single, 'The Day Will Come Between Sunday and Monday', both first-class recordings, both flops. By 1972, she was without a record deal or much of a career. Which is when Elton John decided that he alone could rescue her.

Success finally came in 1973, after Elton had signed Dee to his newly launched Rocket Records label. A delightfully atmospheric cover version of 'Amoureuse' – the French equivalent of the English adjective *amorous* – by the Parisian singer-songwriter Véronique Sanson (with English lyrics translated by future Elton co-writer Gary Osborne), appealed to Beaujolais-quaffing Britons, and finally took Kiki into the UK top twenty.

She followed up with 'I've Got the Music in Me', a pedal-to-the-floor blues rocker written by Kiki's keyboardist Tobias

'Bias' Boshell, which took her back into the UK top twenty the following year. Elton took her to America to open for him on tour and she was prolific as a backing singer on his 1975 *Rock of the Westies* album, with true stardom finally arriving with the afore-mentioned 'Don't Go Breaking My Heart', a chart-topper in the UK and US in 1976.

Ironically, given the song's huge international success – and the equally huge revenue stream it generated for Bernie as the co-writer, he insists he always hated 'Don't Go Breaking My Heart'. As Taupin told *Page Six* in 2019, 'I hated it, and it was the biggest single we had in Europe . . . But Elton always ignores me when I say I don't like a song. He always knows better than me.'

Dee supported Queen at Hyde Park in front of 150,000 people, also in 1976, and made a strong return five years later with the top-twenty single 'Star', written by Doreen Chanter of the British duo the Chanter Sisters, also ad hoc backing vocalists with Elton, Bryan Ferry and, later, Meat Loaf. Her 1981 album, *Perfect Timing*, was a moderate success and, like Elton, she gained her biggest audience ever when she performed with him at Live Aid four years later. When, in 1987 the BBC1 chose 'Star' as the theme tune for the revived talent show *Opportunity Knocks*, it also revived her own career.

That was about as good as it got for Kiki Dee, whose career since has been largely confined to singing on Elton's albums, recording and touring with the guitarist Carmelo Luggeri and appearing in musical theatre. She also guested on the final Alan Parsons Project album, 1990's *Freudiana*.

In 1993, Elton came to Kiki's rescue again when he included her on his *Duets* album. Their selection, the Cole Porter classic, 'True Love', a top-ten UK hit in 1956 for Bing Crosby and Grace Kelly, was also released as a single and hit number two. And of course her cameo with him on the Farewell Yellow Brick Road tour reminded the world what a great talent she still is.

Details of Dee's personal life are fairly scarce, although we know that Elton's guitarist Davey Johnstone was an old flame from her twenties and that she defeated uterine cancer in middle age. As she told the *Daily Mail* in 2013, 'While many childless women come to rue their decision post-sixty, when all their friends are delighting in grandchildren, I feel quite the opposite . . . I am perfectly happy with the delights and challenges of my career. There really are some of us who don't need any more to feel fulfilled.'

Despite her impressive twelve-album, forty-single catalogue, Kiki Dee has mostly remained in the shadow of her mentor, career-wise – although that, one might reasonably argue, is not necessarily a bad place to be.

Desert Island Discs
Going for a spin

Hailed as one of the greatest radio shows of all time, *Desert Island Discs* is the longest-running programme on British radio and the second-longest-running radio programme in the world, after the *Grand Ole Opry*.

The brainchild of 28-year-old broadcaster and producer Roy Plomley, the first episode was recorded at the bomb-damaged BBC Studios in west London on 27 January 1942 and aired two days later. It featured Plomley interviewing the Austrian-British comedian, actor and musician Vic Oliver and the format has remained largely unchanged throughout the years. Including the familiar swooning theme music, Eric Coates's 1930 composition

'By the Sleepy Lagoon', which has remained a constant since the very first edition of the show.

Built around a simple but clever premise: that each celebrity guest – 'this week's castaway' – discusses the eight recordings – 'discs' as they were still for most of its eighty-year existence – that they would bring with them if they found themselves, like Robinson Crusoe, stranded alone on a desert island. The idea: that each of the eight songs the castaway chooses should facilitate significant memories from their life.

Since that debut episode, there have been more than 3,000 castaways and four successors to Plomley, who hosted the show until his death in 1985: veteran BBC TV and radio presenters Michael Parkinson, Sue Lawley, Kirsty Young and, currently, Lauren Laverne.

John McEnroe revealed how when he arrived in London for his first Wimbledon in 1977, the summer of the Sex Pistols singing 'God Save the Queen', he thought the punks he saw walking down the King's Road were 'freaks' before the dawning realisation that, as he put it on the show, 'those are the people that rally behind me.' Keith Richards spent most of his episode extolling the virtues of all the black music (Chuck Berry, Aaron Neville, Etta James) that the Rolling Stones had adopted for their own music. Some are more obvious, like Thom Yorke of Radiohead explaining how a certain Talking Heads album changed his life. Some – most – appear as if out of the wide blue yonder. The author Michael Lewis reckoned that his wife, former MTV presenter Tabitha Soren, would rather he get caught in a sex-tape scandal than force her to listen to favourites of his, like Chicago or Dire Straits.

Guests accustomed to trotting out the same old lines are suddenly veered off course as a particular track reminds them of things they hadn't thought about for years. In one famous episode, Tom Hanks' famously ebullient public persona cracks as he recalls a tempestuous childhood triggered by an old jazz tune. 'What have you done to me?' he asks, as he begins to weep.

As well as showbiz personalities, *Desert Island Discs* is renowned for featuring politicians, scientists, sports stars, humanitarians, army generals, famous dancers and chefs, retail giants, from rags-to-riches to the manor born.

Besides the eight songs, guests are allowed to choose one luxury item to take with them and one book other than the Bible (or their preferential religious text) and the complete works of Shakespeare, which every castaway is automatically gifted.

'I probably wouldn't have taken either of those,' quipped Elton, when he appeared on the show in June 1986. He wasn't being deliberately rude, it was just an honest reaction and one shared, if truth be told, by the majority of listeners to the BBC in the '80s.

Presenting in that era of *Desert Island Discs* was Michael Parkinson, whose celebrated Saturday night talk show on BBC One, *Parkinson*, had afforded him over a decade of interviewing close-up many of the biggest stars in the world, across all fields of endeavour. He was a heavyweight. Where Plomley had been genial, deferential, scripted and scrupulously self-censored, 'Parky' as he was known to friends and associates, actually wanted to know what the person he was talking to thought about things – and why.

While that approach could go either way, it worked well for 39-year-old Elton John. In truth, he talks so fast, breathless at points as he hurries to fit it all in, the lines running through his mind. He sounds like he's out of his head. But he is engaged by Parkinson in a way no mere music journalist had ever managed. Just like the rest of us, Elton had grown up watching Parky lock horns with Muhammad Ali, Orson Welles, Peter Sellers, Sir Laurence Olivier and George Best; he couldn't help but take this seriously.

Elton described himself as a natural introvert who forced himself to become an extrovert long before he became a singer: 'In my teenage years I found that I was more or less overweight, quite a bit. And I had a strict upbringing, I was not allowed to have a drop-handlebar bike or a pair of Hush Puppies.'

Parkinson chuckles along but it's just Elton adding gloss to a sad story.

He talks about the outrageous costumes of the early '70s as him rebelling against his years tormented into conformity. How he has kept every single costume he ever wore. The giant chicken costume that weighed 300lb and 'all the electric glasses'. Hats that weighed so much he could barely walk, glasses that weighed so much they trapped his nostrils and forced his voice into a nasal twang. How as an only child he always took care of his toys and how his collections of various things could get out of control sometimes. Buying things on a whim like a decommissioned tram carriage in Australia that he had shipped home to England then couldn't figure out how to get it to his Old Windsor home without horrifying the neighbours.

'At the time these were normal things,' Elton explained, 'but looking back, I must have been out of my mind.'

The eight 'discs' he chose to play on his episode of *Desert Island Discs* in 1986 are as follows:

Pink Floyd, 'Shine on You Crazy Diamond'
Nina Simone, 'I Put a Spell on You'
Edward Elgar, 'Enigma Variations (Nimrod)'
Rolling Stones, 'Let It Rock'
Christian hymn 'Abide with Me'
Thelonius Monk, 'Mysterioso', performed by Carla Bley & Kenny
    Kirklin
John Lennon, 'Stand by Me'
Wham!, 'Wake Me Up Before You Go Go'

The disc he would save in the event of all the others being washed out to sea was Elgar's 'Enigma Variations'.

Parkinson sounds surprised. 'Really?'

'Yes,' says Elton, 'because it's just the most wonderful piece of music.'

Having turned his nose up at being landed with both the Bible *and* the complete works of Shakespeare, the book Elton decided he would take with him to his desert island was Anne Rice's gothic novel, *Interview with the Vampire* – the first in what we now know of as Rice's *Vampire Chronicles*. It leads him to say how he would have loved to have scored the music for a stage musical version of the book but when he looked into it, the rights had already been acquired by someone else. Interestingly Elton also said that he would like to score a stage musical one day – but only one. Famous last words . . .

In the long history of the show, it is always the castaway's choice of luxury item that draws the most comment. It's where the guests get a chance to be creative. For his luxury item, the Danish chef René Redzepi asked for a day of snow. In the past, special dispensation was given to Princess Michael of Kent who wanted her pet cat as her luxury item. *Monty Python* and *Fawlty Towers* star John Cleese was allowed to take Michael Palin with him, on the condition that he was dead and stuffed.

Pianos have been one of the most popular choices over the years, so you might think Elton would be tempted to follow suit. Oh no! What he chose as his luxury item was a solar-powered telephone so he could find out how his beloved Watford were faring without him: 'I'd have to keep in touch with the club, obviously.' Plus a solar-powered phone would mean he could 'keep up on the gossip. Yes, I'm still alive but who's doing what to who and what's happening? Because everyone likes a good gossip.'

DIANA, PRINCESS OF WALES

Elton John may have been said to suffer his share of drug-induced delusions of grandeur over the years, but despite the knighthood, the CBE and the half-billion-dollar fortune, he's never got so full of himself that he feels at home with a member of the Royal Family. He has some choice anecdotes about hanging out at the House of Windsor – such as the time he witnessed the late Queen Elizabeth II repeatedly slapping Viscount Linley on the cheek, then winking mischievously at Elton before walking off – but, as he accurately notes, they're an odd bunch.

During his early-'70s heyday, it was known that both Princess Margaret, the Queen's more 'bohemian' younger sister, and the Queen Mother, known to 'enjoy the arts' while cradling a large G&T, were both huge Elton John fans. It was said he had each new album sent personally to the palace. But that didn't mean he got invited into the royal parlour as a friend.

Lady Diana Spencer was the exception. They first met in February 1981 at Prince Andrew's twenty-first birthday ball at Windsor Castle, where Elton had been booked to provide the evening's main entertainment. Fourteen years his junior, Lady Diana, as she still was then, had arrived early and Elton came across her alone and chatted with her. Her found her surprisingly easy to talk to, a rarity for anyone connected to the Royals, especially for someone as embedded as Diana was about to become when she married Prince Charles at St Paul's Cathedral that summer.

While waiting for the crowd to arrive, it is said Elton and Diana danced the Charleston together for twenty minutes. They continued gossiping throughout the night and parted as long-lost best friends. Adventures followed over the years, one notable occasion being when Elton hosted Disney head Jeffrey Katzenberg, the now-divorced but still titled Princess Diana, George

Michael, Richard Curtis, Richard Gere and Sylvester Stallone at Woodside. Gere and Diana spent the evening in adoring mutual conversation, irritating Stallone, who – Elton speculated – fancied a bit of Rocky-meets-Royal action. Stallone ended up storming out after squaring up to Gere, saying, 'I never would have come if I'd known Prince fuckin' Charming was gonna be here . . . If I'd wanted her, I would've taken her!'

The Elton/Diana friendship ran until 1996, when they fell out over a book by Gianni Versace called *Rock and Royalty*. She had apparently agreed to write the foreword but changed her mind, it was assumed under pressure from the Royal Family. In response to a complaint from Elton on behalf of Versace (their mutual friend), she wrote him a severe letter – and that was it for some time.

The friends reunited in 1997 after the murder of Versace the following year. Diana was photographed comforting Elton at the funeral. She apologised to him and they made plans for lunch to discuss her assistance with AIDS charities. Sadly, the meeting never took place.

THE DIVING BOARD
Swimming in the deep end

By 2013, when *The Diving Board* was released, the music business had changed almost beyond recognition from the one Elton John first entered nearly a half-century before. Few of the major rock stars left from the golden era of the '60s and '70s even made albums any more. The Rolling Stones had released one new album, *A Bigger Bang*, in the past sixteen years and even though it went to number one in America, no one came to their shows to hear any of those songs (no one could even name any of those songs). Rod Stewart had spent the past decade relying solely on albums of ancient covers. David Bowie hadn't released a new album for over ten years.

Their reasoning was simple: people didn't buy albums any more, people didn't buy *records* any more. The real action was now all in touring. There were still some artists, however, still intent on creating new music, even though they understood albums were no longer a financial driver. Elton John was one of those. He didn't need to be – his compilations and live albums, his soundtrack and stage music work, his collaborations and cameos all brought money in, kept the profile out there. Touring-wise, he was making vastly more money now than he ever had before.

Elton didn't need to ever make a new album again, he just wanted to. Him and Bernie both. Unrestrained by label heads looking for a good fourth quarter, no longer thinking in terms of hit singles or pleasing anyone but themselves, he and Bernie came up with another intensely personal collection. Produced in LA by T Bone Burnett who had overseen *The Union*, who now urged him to revisit the piano, bass and drums format of his earliest years, the result, Elton said, was 'the most exciting solo record I've done in a long, long time.'

Elton was sixty-six years old, Bernie was sixty-three and they were still making great music. Indeed, they were so caught up in the dream, the creation of *The Diving Board* was a tortuous process. Initially written in just two days, it would take over a year for Elton to finally sign off on it. It was announced that it would be released in 2012. Then it was announced that release had been put back to early 2013 – and that the title of the album had been changed from *The Diving Board* to *Voyeur*. Then it was announced that the release had been put back to September

2013. Elton wasn't happy, was writing more songs. And then it was announced that the title of the album was back to *The Diving Board*.

The material was heavy, full-on, the feeling of 'My Quicksand' or 'The Ballad of Blind Tom' was carnival, a musical box. Music for grown-ups. City elders. There's a wonderful playfulness too in 'Take This Dirty Water' and 'Mexican Vacation (Kids in the Candlelight)', pop gospel in excelsis. Even the songs that thud a little benefit from this bold new inventiveness Elton and Bernie had discovered, which allowed for the audacious 'The Diving Board', the defiant 'Oscar Wilde Gets Out' and, best of all, the imperious 'Voyeur', a classic John Huston movie in seven verses.

It really was a new time we were living in and Elton John was starting to really enjoy it. No need to worry any more about 'loathsome videos', either. They just sent a black-and-white film clip to YouTube of Elton and the band performing the song live. To this day, most people are not familiar with *The Diving Board*, but it rewards patience, a unique and powerful piece of work.

Was it a hit? Well, it went to number three in the UK charts and number four in the US charts. But that didn't mean anything any more. It sold 60,000 copies in Britain, maybe 250,000 in America. But those who got it, *really* got it. In America, *Rolling Stone* gave the album a four-star review. Elton had 'regained his sense of musical possibility and taken a brave, graceful jump.' Elton's original champion and friend, Robert Hilburn of the *LA Times*, wrote of *The Diving Board*'s 'finely crafted and deeply moving' songs that evoked the past in 'fresh and revealing' ways.

DODGER STADIUM
Elton hits a homerun

In October 1975, Elton John was by any measure the biggest pop star in the world. His latest album, *Rock of the Westies*, was released that month and become his sixth album to go to number one in America and his second in a row, after *Captain Fantastic and the Brown Dirt Cowboy*, to do that in its first week of release. A landmark not even the Beatles or Elvis Presley ever achieved.

To mark the occasion, Elton performed two sold-out shows on 25 and 26 October at the 56,000-capacity Dodger Stadium in Los Angeles – home to the LA Dodgers baseball team – where the only other rock act of the modern era to perform there had been the Beatles in 1966. Tom Watson, the mayor of LA, declared 20–26 October 1975 to be Elton John Week. On 23 October, Elton received a star on the Hollywood Walk of Fame. He was obliged to show up on a gold-painted golf cart with a comically enormous pair of illuminated glasses and an absurdly camp bow tie glued to the front of it. Wearing a lime-green Bob Mackie suit and matching bowler hat, he threw himself into it, charmed the pants off everybody, then took off back into his limo.

There was a reception party on John Reid's yacht, *Madman*, for the release of *Rock of the Westies*. Elton had his manager charter a Boeing Pan Am 707 and fly in an entourage of family, friends and various media types and Rocket Records people especially for the occasion. Reid arranged for a documentary film crew to be on the plane too, fronted by British TV chat show host Russell Harty. Elton met the plane at the airport at the head of a convoy of Rolls-Royces and Cadillacs.

With the whole party gathered at his secluded Beverly Hills compound the day before the first Dodgers show, Elton chose just that moment for another half-hearted attempt at suicide. Having swallowed a handful of Valium, he hurled himself fully clothed into the swimming pool. He later claimed he had no intention of actually killing himself and that it was just another cry for help. He'd recently become heavily involved with cocaine, he'd also sacked Nigel Olsson and Dee Murray – an impulsive action that disappointed many fans – and assembled a new band whose first show had been the *Captain Fantastic* fiasco at Wembley Stadium four months earlier. He still hadn't formally come out as 'bisexual' even though everyone who knew him already knew he was gay. He was twenty-eight and although career-wise he was in full top-of-the-world mode, he didn't know where he was any more, just that the only place left to go was down. Of *course* he'd decided to commit suicide on the eve of the biggest shows of his life – how *fabulous*, darling! Waiting for the biggest crowd of onlookers to assemble by the pool first before taking the very public plunge.

'To be honest,' Bernie Taupin told the *LA Times* in 2022, 'it wasn't that big a deal. Just our boy putting on a dramatic show for friends and relatives. He was very good at that!' Maybe so, but Elton's very real addiction issues with drugs, food, sex and shopping had become overwhelming. The only time he felt in control, he said, was when he was on stage. Sure enough, that's exactly where he found himself a day later when he walked on stage at Dodger Stadium to a standing ovation, dressed in a spangly LA Dodgers baseball uniform, with his name and the number 1 on the back, looking like the happiest, luckiest man in the world. He stood on the stage and swung a baseball bat as the packed stadium dutifully went crazy.

Backstage, as well as Elton's dozen-strong entourage, there was the reigning US Open and Wimbledon women's champion tennis player – and gay equal-rights activist – Billie Jean King, who Elton had become friends with after meeting at a party in LA in 1973, which led directly to his fourth number-one hit in America, 'Philadelphia Freedom'. There was 71-year-old Hollywood legend Cary Grant and his grandkids. Also, Cal Worthington, whose 'My Dog Spot' TV commercials – which always featured live animals such as a lion, bear, elephant, camel, penguin, hippopotamus and a tiger, all named Spot, anything except an actual dog – made his car dealership the most famous in California. Elton had arranged for Cal to make an appearance on stage, accompanied by a lion.

Billie Jean King was dragged on stage too to sing backing vocals on 'Philadelphia Freedom', clambering onto Elton's piano as he played, and stayed on for the final couple of numbers of the set. Even Bernie Taupin made a rare on stage appearance, dressed all in white, a baseball bat in one hand, tambourine in the other. They were joined by comic-actor and gameshow panellist Charles Nelson Reilly – the first openly gay performer on American TV, famous for his double entendres and almost as well-known as Elton for his outsized glasses – followed by the 45-strong Rev. James Cleveland Southern California Community Choir. Even the backstage security team was obliged to dress up in pink satin jumpsuits and feather boas.

The two Dodgers' shows were more than just concert performances, they were a carnival, a marvel, a cavalcade of music and pageant. For 'Don't Let the Sun Go Down on Me', the twentieth song of the show, played just as the sun was actually going down behind Dodger Stadium, almost all of the 56,000 crowd held their cigarette lighters aloft. During 'Goodbye Yellow Brick Road', Elton purposely changed the line 'It'll take you a couple of vodka and tonics' to 'It'll take you a couple of tequila sunrises' in fond recognition of California's signature cocktail in the '70s. 'Elton was so happy that day,' Billie Jean King would recall. 'Everyone was so happy. I remember hanging backstage with Cary Grant and his daughter like it was yesterday.'

Elton cried after the first concert was over and again the next day after the second show. Almost a half-century later, stadium shows have become commonplace, the natural habitat of gigantic artists out to enshrine their legends. But the Elton John 1975 Dodger Stadium shows were not a victory lap: they were the zeitgeist.

DODGER STADIUM, 2022

'It's been a long journey'

Finally, then, fifty-two years after his first-ever American shows, in the city that made his name, Los Angeles, and at the very same venue where he had crowned his '70s heyday with two spectacular shows in 1975, Elton John returned to Dodger Stadium for three nights in November 2022, to officially say farewell. The event dominated Los Angeles that weekend, front-page news, backstage gossip. Getting in on the feelgood factor, the LA Dodgers baseball team donated $1 million to the Elton John AIDS Foundation. And every baby boomer in LA was ready to celebrate.

Elton *was* LA in the '70s: the music, the lifestyle, the endless number-one hits. The fact that he had survived, come back stronger, was also *very* LA. A real-life happy-ever-after Hollywood ending. If you'd been there for *Goodbye Yellow Brick Road* and you were here tonight, nearly fifty years later, for the Farewell Yellow Brick Road tour, it said something about your life, not just Elton's.

From the first *bomp!* on his piano that signalled the overture to 'Bennie and the Jets' to the last moment hours-that-felt-like-minutes later, when an animated Elton was shown on the giant screens walking towards a heavenly Yellow Brick Road, this was a night no one, least of all the celebrated performer himself, would ever forget. 'Tonight is a very special night, a very emotional night for me,' he said after 'Philadelphia Freedom', the second number of the final 24-song set. 'It's been a long journey.'

Seated at his grand piano, resplendent in bedazzled jacket and tails, his deep-rose glasses similarly sparkling, it seemed scarcely believable that this would really be Elton John's last ever show on American soil. But this was the reality the audience was being asked to accept, however reluctantly.

'We are making history tonight,' Elton announced cheerfully. 'The first-ever global stream on Disney-plus. And hello, Dodger Stadium!' Cue: pandemonium.

Still recovering from a hip injury that forced this part of the tour's postponement in September 2021, Elton moved with some difficulty across the stage, but he no longer minded what anyone thought about that. At seventy-five, he had long since come to terms with simply being himself and in that vulnerable moment appeared even more human and heroic. Something made even more tantalising when Elton paired up with his musical guests, beginning with American alt-country star Brandi Carlisle, clutching a gold microphone, who took the late George Michael's spot alongside Elton on 'Don't Let the Sun Go Down on Me'. Followed by Kiki Dee, now retired but still sprightly, her voice as good as ever, who joined Elton for a bopping version of 'Don't Go Breaking My Heart'. 'We decided to re-enact that incredible moment,' said a beaming Elton. As did the crowd.

Of the twenty-four songs, all the expected classics were in evidence – eighteen huge hits from 'Your Song' to 'I'm Still Standing' to 'Cold Heart', but mostly the gold-standard songs of his '70s highs. To his credit, he also made room for deep-dive moments, including 'Border Song', 'Have Mercy on the Criminal', 'Take Me to the Pilot' and 'Levon'.

There were some unexpected musical excursions, as on 'Rocket Man', stretched out into an eleven-minute freeform extravaganza. Or, as American commentator Bob Lefsetz put it: '[Elton] lifted us up like a Saturn V rocket.' Plus some neat chef's-kiss additions. On the way into the shows, everyone was given what looked like an Apple Watch. Nobody knew why – until they all lit up during 'Tiny Dancer'. No 1975 cigarette lighters required here in the twenty-first century.

The band, including Davey Johnstone, Nigel Olsson and Ray Cooper, augmented by Elton's usual high-end team of musos, were all dressed somewhat incongruously in dark sunglasses, white shirts, black suits and ties, all playing immaculately. And Elton's voice was . . . well, definitely *his* voice – something almost unique in these tech-savvy times where anything 'live' can be 'tweaked' to sound like whatever you want. Not Elton John, whose voice – once so honeyed and self-assured and now so much older and wrung out – he still allows to be heard without the safety net of 'production'. No, he can't hit all the notes any more, but boy does he bring new meaning to them. The truth that only age and experience, triumph and loss, wisdom and hope can authentically confer. Elton's voice isn't what it was. No longer perfect, it is no less beautiful for that.

Backstage, the VIP area was even more sparkling than Elton's glasses. Those walking a pre-concert red carpet included Paul McCartney, Mick Jagger, Lizzo, Jude Law, Joni Mitchell, Billie Jean King, Heidi Klum, Angela Bassett, H.E.R., Donatella Versace, Miles Teller, Kirsten Dunst, JoJo Siwa, Connie Britton, Christopher Lloyd, John Stamos, Raven-Symoné, Taron Egerton and Courtney B. Vance.

The show ended on the crest of an emotional wave. First encore, a deliciously cuddly duet with the panther-sleek Dua Lipa on their hit remix 'Cold Heart', which had the same night won an American Music Award for Best Collaboration. For the final-curtain encore, Elton appeared in a long shimmering-silver Dodgers' robe with the number '1' on the back, harking back to the legendary 1975 shows. He had retrieved his original Dodgers' costume from the Hard Rock Cafe earlier in the year, but it was now just a little too 'snug' to fit him.

Then Elton brought Bernie Taupin on stage. 'If it wasn't for him, I would not be standing here,' he declared. 'We've been writing together since 1967, and we . . . love each other more than we've ever done before.' He paused to hold Bernie's arm aloft. 'He's amazing.'

Up next was hubby David Furnish and their two sons, Elijah Joseph Daniel and Zachary Jackson Levon, then just nine and eleven years old respectively, who waved excitedly to the audience amid deafening applause. Elton said that he had brought them out 'to show you why I am retiring.' Adding simply, 'I want to spend time with my family. I'll be seventy-six by the time I stop touring next year,' and the whole stadium melted.

Finally, as he was left alone again at the piano, Elton had one last thank-you to make: to his American fans.

'Thank you all for dressing up,' he said, with a smile. 'It makes me so happy to see when you wear the most fantastic costumes. I became successful first in America and you bought the singles and the albums . . . the cassettes, the CDs – and, more importantly, you bought tickets to the shows, which I love more than anything . . . I want to thank you for that because you made me. Without America, I wouldn't be here. Thank you for all the years of love and generosity.'

Then, as he prepared to play the last song of the night, his final song to America, 'Goodbye Yellow Brick Road', he said simply: 'I wish you health and love, prosperity.'

As the last piano chords rang out into the night, Elton discarded his silver robe to reveal a tracksuit. Then he stepped out onto a lift that raised him up the stage. 'Be kind to each other,' he said. 'And farewell.'

DON'T SHOOT ME I'M ONLY THE PIANO PLAYER
A teen idol pin-up as well as a respected musician

From the moment in 1968 when album sales first officially overtook sales of singles, the division between those modern musical acts considered 'album artists' – superior creatives who relied on their own songwriting and musicianship to craft great new music – and 'single artists' – lesser pop chart entities who often didn't write their own material or even play on their own records – was clearly mapped out.

The fashion was for the 'album artists' to view hit singles as cherries on the cake, almost accidental occurrences, as if the very idea that they would deliberately contrive to create a commercial hit song was offensive. Indeed, by 1973, when Elton John released *Don't Shoot Me I'm Only the Piano Player*, most 'serious' rock artists restricted the release of singles to just one per album, as John Lennon, Rod Stewart, David Bowie and Paul McCartney's new band Wings did. Latest chart sensations Roxy Music didn't even allow any singles on their first two hit albums and immediately after, kept it to just one.

When 'Rocket Man' finally gave Elton John his second big hit, eighteen months after his first with 'Your Song', it merely confirmed that he and Bernie Taupin were, as they saw it, 'album artists' not pop stars. Even though an edited-for-radio version of 'Honky Cat' had been a surprise top-ten hit in America, it fitted the narrative somehow that the single failed to pierce the UK top thirty. (Despite a wonderfully surreal appearance by Elton on the UK's biggest weekly music show *Top of the Pops* dressed as – you've guessed it – a giant singing, piano-playing cat, it only reached number thirty-one in Britain.)

Elton had made his point: he may now be having hits, but they were a long way from David Cassidy or the Osmonds. Pop success, deafening, lucrative and transient, was definitely not for Elton and Bernie. The moody image of Elton that stared out from the cover of *Honky Château* – bearded, earnest – told its own story of the way he wanted to be perceived, on record at least. However, live Elton John was now a very different proposition. Here, he was embracing an approximate mid-point between the cool, dark, sexually ambiguous interpretation of glam rock embodied by his friends Marc Bolan and David Bowie and the 'truck drivers in make-up' look of Slade or the Sweet. The shows were extravaganzas of excess, not least due to the presence, on the American tour of late 1972, of 'Legs' Larry Smith, the Bonzo Dog Band member who had added some tap-dancing effects to 'Honky Château'.

Legs Larry and Elton hit it off big time, spending daytime hours 'looting' (as they called it) the local shops for items of kitsch that they could drag on stage at night, where Legs Larry would appear dressed as an American Football player to tap dance during 'I Think I'm Going to Kill Myself' and then again with Bernie and Elton, all three of them in trench coats and fedoras, backed by dancing girls and a dwarf who fired glitter from a cannon while 'Singin' in the Rain' blasted out of the PA. Like you do.

The new over-the-top showmanship went down spectacularly in America, less so when Elton and Legs tried the 'I Think I'm Going to Kill Myself' routine at the Royal Variety Performance at the London Palladium. Her Majesty Queen Elizabeth II remained tight-lipped at the sight, the critics less so as they dunked their fangs into him. Perhaps it was indicative of where Elton's career was heading. His albums were selling millions in America and his tours there were sell-outs. No longer the interloper, he was now one of the US record industry's biggest stars.

The US shows fell in that weird time lag between the recording and release of a new album. As he toured the *Honky Château* material, its follow-up was already in the can. Over the summer, suffering from a bout of glandular fever that should have stopped the runaway train but didn't because he simply refused to let it, Elton had returned to Hérouville to recapture some of that glittering honky magic the Château had brought them.

On arrival, however, he told producer Gus Dudgeon that he simply couldn't face the sessions, then just as quickly changed his mind again. Even though he felt deathly ill, 'I thought, I'm going on holiday in July, and it would be nice to have it all over with by then.'

Bernie Taupin was under pressure too, writing to order in LA and sending over lyrics as soon as they were done. When Bernie got fed up with that and took it upon himself to show up in person at the Château, he arrived to an ambiguous welcome from Elton: 'He'd been phoning every night from LA and one morning, I walked out on the lawn and there he is, behind a bloody bush! In France! Nearly drove me round the bend!'

The creative marriage may have had its share of bickering, but the sparks still flew. Bernie produced more of his best work, a pastiche of '50s rock 'n' roll tunes he called 'Crocodile Rock', and then, over breakfast one morning, a lyric about a magazine piece he'd read on a Vietnam veteran who'd returned home to his small town and a hero's welcome that he'd been unable to bear, eventually leaving America to live overseas. 'Daniel' 'took about half an hour,' Bernie recalled, and once it was down, he handed it straight to Elton, who wrote the music even more quickly. The song was recorded by the end of the day.

Paul Buckmaster arrived and added string arrangements to another standout song, 'Have Mercy on the Criminal' and also 'Blues for Baby and Me'. Influence was everywhere, from 'Crocodile Rock' to Elton's hat-tip to Marc Bolan, 'I'm Going to Be a Teenage Idol', while 'High Flying Bird' was a nod to Van Morrison and 'Midnight Creeper' much the same to the Rolling Stones.

It was another strong set produced in a matter of weeks, but conscious of Elton's commercial power, the record company did not want to schedule a release until they'd wrung every last dollar out of *Honky Château*. Release for *Don't Shoot Me . . .* was finally scheduled for early 1973, preceded by the 'Crocodile Rock' single in the November, just as the US tour reached its peak.

A night out with a Hollywood legend provided the only thing missing: a title for the new album. He found it after Elton met Groucho Marx through Bryan Forbes during his post-recording holiday in LA. Although advancing in years, Marx remained a comic force and teased Elton relentlessly, announcing that his name was the wrong way round and refusing to call him anything other than 'John Elton'. Elton in mock-surrender held up his hands and came up with the phrase, 'Don't shoot me, I'm only the piano player', a line he may or may not have adapted from its original source, Oscar Wilde. To wit: 'Don't shoot the piano player, he's doing his best.'

When the album was released, its sleeve showed a young couple outside a movie theatre, the billboard above announcing, 'Don't Shoot Me I'm Only the Piano Player starring Elton John'. Groucho's contribution was acknowledged by a poster for the Marx Brothers film *Go West* plastered on the wall by the theatre.

'Crocodile Rock's success stoked Elton's teen-appeal; his UK shows in the spring of 1973 filled with younger fans. As the *Melody Maker* duly noted, he had pulled off the almost impossible trick of covering all bases: 'In the fluctuating world of pop, he has made a dramatic comeback to answer the doubters. It has turned him into a teen idol pin-up as well as a respected musician.'

DUDGEON, GUS

Minor star meets master producer

The late Angus 'Gus' Dudgeon (1942–2002) was the legendary producer of several of the most cherished Elton John albums, beginning in 1970 with the release of *Elton John*, followed by the next nine Elton albums, including all the recognised greats such as *Honky Château*, *Goodbye Yellow Brick Road* and *Captain Fantastic*, up to *Blue Moves* in 1976, the first Elton album recorded since sacking his longstanding band, and the last of his '70s megahits. There were also three Dudgeon-produced live albums and the 1971 soundtrack album, *Friends*, before a relatively brief return to the studio with Elton in the mid-'80s for *Ice on Fire* and *Leather Jackets*.

However, Gus was much more to Elton John than merely his producer. Flamboyant in personal style and utterly confident about his creative choices, Dudgeon could go toe-to-toe with Elton on any matter pertaining to songwriting, production and mixing, and often did just that. Often, his decisions over Elton's songs were better than those made by the man himself.

Of the recording of the *Caribou* album with Dudgeon in 1974, Elton later wrote: 'We were recording "Don't Let the Sun Go Down on Me". After announcing that I hated the song so much we were going to stop recording it immediately and send it to Engelbert Humperdinck . . . I was coaxed back to the vocal booth and completed the take. Then I yelled at Gus Dudgeon that I hated it even more now it was finished and was going to kill him with my bare hands if he put it on the album.'

Unaware of the drama taking place in the vocal booth, when Nigel Olsson wandered past still hungover from the night before, he stopped to listen to some of the song, then offered his own perspective in just two words: 'Number one,' he said, then toddled off to bed.

Most of all, Elton hated his vocals on it, complained they were 'sticking out like a sore thumb.' Fortunately, Dudgeon ignored his most illustrious client on this occasion or an Elton classic might have been consigned to history. A year later, 'Don't Let the Sun Go Down on Me' was nominated at the Grammys for Best Pop Vocal Performance – Male.

On the other hand, Elton's hunches sometimes overrode the producer's advice, as when the session guitarist Davey Johnstone impressed him in 1971.

'I took Gus aside and asked what he thought about Davey joining the band,' he recalled. 'Gus thought it was a bad idea. Davey was a wonderful guitarist, but he only played acoustic: as far as Gus knew, he'd never even played an electric guitar . . . It was a very persuasive argument. I ignored it and offered Davey the job anyway. If I'd learned anything over the last few years, it was that sometimes a gut feeling is the most important thing.'

This warm but combative relationship between master songwriter and master producer fuelled what are now considered most of Elton's greatest hits. Having worked his way up via Olympia Studios and Decca to the position of producer, Dudgeon had first impressed Elton with his work on David Bowie's 'Space Oddity' single in 1969 and their first collaboration was the immortal 'Your Song'. Dudgeon added the string section that helped to make the song a US top-ten hit, kicking off a mutually profitable hit-making partnership. Over subsequent years, Elton came to trust Dudgeon's judgement so much that he would often leave the studio to let the producer make creative choices unhampered.

By the resumption of their working partnership with 1985's *Ice on Fire* album, Dudgeon had also achieved worldwide success with Joan Armatrading, Elkie Brooks, Chris Rea, Fairport Convention and many other artists. He had also earned a place in the *Guinness Book of Records* as the first producer to use a sample – a taped drum loop on John Kongos' 1971 hit 'He's Gonna Step on You Again'.

Sadly, Dudgeon and his wife Sheila died in 2002 when the car in which they were driving crashed in Berkshire: the producer was later found to have been intoxicated at the time. A haunting detail of the tragedy is that the couple may well have drowned in the flooded storm drain in which their car landed after it left the M4 motorway.

At the time of his death, Dudgeon was reportedly in the midst of a multi-million-dollar legal battle in which he claimed he was owed royalties on more than fourteen Elton John albums. That did not prevent his tragic death coming as a terrible shock to Elton and everyone in his entourage who had ever worked with the producer. Nigel Olsson commented: 'Gus was a legend and will live on as one, to all of us.' Adding, 'Gus and I had always planned to work together again at some stage and it had been suggested as recently as two months [before his death] that we were going to work together in the very near future. I am lost for words and will miss him desperately.'

Dudgeon's legacy has been preserved by the Gus Dudgeon Foundation, which runs courses for aspiring studio personnel, and there is a Gus Dudgeon Suite at the University of Glamorgan. Joan Armatrading dedicated her *Lovers Speak* album to his memory in 2003 and Elton did the same a year later with the heartfelt *Peachtree Road* album.

DWIGHT, REGINALD, SHEILA AND STANLEY
Keeping it in the family

It is said that at the core of every human being who craves the validation of an audience – actors, dancers, musicians, singers and other performers; politicians, whether they admit it or not; perhaps athletes too – there is some form of psychological void. This gaping hole is most often there because there wasn't enough love around to fill it with vital self-esteem when said person was a child. Parents, especially those mentally or physically absent, or otherwise ill-equipped to raise their children, are usually the ones responsible. A particularly stark example of this might be the life of the great Reginald Dwight.

Elton John, as he revealingly became once the inadequate Dwight persona was cast aside, has often talked, and written, about the failings of his parents, even though he felt some love for them at an earlier point in his life. According to the singer, he wasn't particularly neglected by his father Stanley and his mother Sheila, but he was often the object of their temper, which left a permanent mark on him – and he consequently appears to have inherited that inclination towards pyrotechnic mood swings himself. To put it mildly.

In a sense, the odds against a perfect childhood were stacked against him. Reginald Kenneth Dwight was born on Tuesday 25 March 1947. But while Tuesday's Child, according to the nursery rhyme, is said to be 'full of grace', little Reggie's arrival coincided with a post-war Britain still coming to terms with the mess Hitler's bombs had made of it. Conceived when Stanley was on leave from the Royal Air Force, with whom he fought in the Second World War, Reggie grew up the son of one of a generation of young men mentally damaged by their experiences on the battlefield, too traumatised to be anything other than emotionally remote.

Stan and Sheila had met when he was seventeen and she was a year younger – just kids, really – and Elton later speculated that they had rushed into marriage, as young people did back then, because it felt as if the world might be about to end. He recalled how any love the couple felt for each other was soon replaced by angry rows and bitter arguments, the only relief coming when the RAF called Stan away.

The Dwight family home at 55 Pinner Hill Road in the deeply conformist London suburb of Harrow also housed Sheila's mother Ivy and her second husband, Horace Sewell, Sheila's father having died some years before. Horace, who had lost a leg in the First World War, didn't speak much and spent most of his time in the garden – perhaps, thought Reggie, to stay clear of Sheila, who alternated between seething rage and glowering silences. As a result, Reggie grew up without any male relatives in any real, present sense, living in constant fear of his domineering mother.

Sheila's sister Win – a much easier person to get along with, by all accounts – told Reggie that he was not to blame for his mother's character, as he initially feared. She had always been bad-tempered. Indeed, she remained that way for the rest of her long life. As Win described her, it seemed that a dark cloud followed Sheila around, making people afraid of her – an effect that she in fact enjoyed.

Some of Sheila's parenting choices bordered on abuse, as we would define it today. Elton later recalled 'getting a hiding' in public, while onlookers observed; he also remembered that Sheila toilet-trained him by hitting him with a wire brush until he bled, if he didn't use a potty. Ivy – a sweet lady who the beleaguered boy drew close to for comfort – was furious at this and even more so when Sheila tried to cure her son's constipation by inserting carbolic soap into his rectum.

The most damaging aspect of this experience was that Sheila could, at times, be a loving mother. Between episodes of anger and punishment, she was kind to her son. The net result was that the young Reggie inhabited a netherworld of insecurity and fear, never sure which Sheila he would encounter on a given occasion. If you want to drain your child of their self-esteem, and thus of their long-term happiness, that's how you do it: the good-today, bad-tomorrow treatment.

When he wasn't enduring or avoiding Sheila, Reggie seems to have had a pretty standard '50s childhood, with light entertainment on the wireless, Ivy's roast dinners on Sundays, and music – first on vinyl and then in the form of a piano, to which he took effortlessly. He was gifted with a musical ear and was playing hymns and family favourites within a few years.

Musical bliss was still a world away, though, and after Stan briefly moved the family to Wiltshire and then back to Pinner, things went downhill for his sensitive and bruised son. For reasons unknown, his father suddenly imposed a set of draconian rules about what to do and not to do that made the youngster's life impossible. Rules about how to eat, regulations about how to dress, punishments if Elton's football landed in the flower bed – and all without any reasonable explanation.

Almost inevitably, the boy's reaction was to develop a fiery temper, which he later theorised was either inherited or a learned response to this terrible environment. Thus, the adult Elton that his fans came to know and love began to take shape. Fortunately, he was up and out of the household by the time he was eighteen, his career about to take off in ways no one could have predicted. The task then was to try and form an adult relationship with these two highly toxic parents – something that most of us find challenging at some point or other, but which in this case must have been a Herculean (no pun intended) challenge.

Elton never really got close to his dad, who didn't understand or approve of his career and life choices, and when Stan died in 1991, he didn't attend the funeral: his passing appears not to have affected his son much, beyond a touch of understandable regret. It was a different story with Sheila, though, who hung on grimly until 2017, finally dying at the age of ninety-two. Elton tried his damnedest to reconcile with her, involving her in his life, buying her endless gifts – which she petulantly sold off – and enduring her endless sniping about his music and lifestyle when she always insisted on having the last word.

When Sheila died, Elton held a private service for her at Woodside, his expansive Windsor mansion. Standing next to Elton after the service, his Uncle Reg gazed at the departing hearse and wearily declared, 'You can't answer anyone back now, can you, Sheila?'

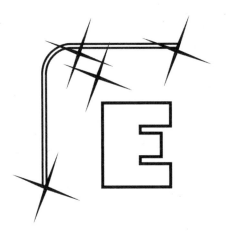

EGERTON, TARON
Kingsman becomes Rocketman

Who'd be an actor, eh? Most of them quit the stage for a life of bitter nostalgia. A small number enjoy a minor commercial hit. A tiny cohort make a decent living out of treading the boards – and a minuscule number of those actually do really well out of it.

Taron Egerton, born on 10 November 1989, in Birkenhead, on Merseyside in Liverpool, and raised in Aberystwyth, a university seaside town in Wales, is one of the lucky few, but he paid his dues both before and after fame came calling. His big ticket, and one which will probably come to define him whether he wishes it or not, is the *Kingsman* spy-movie franchise, a sort of Bond-on-speed concept in which Egerton plays a youthful talent called Gary 'Eggsy' Unwin. But he's also been in some less salubrious fare, notably the cringeworthy *Eddie the Eagle* (2016), in which he played the titular ski-jumping buffoon who became famous in the UK for being so bad at his sport. More career grief came two years later when his take on *Robin Hood* was also roundly mocked.

Still, Egerton's portrayal of Elton John in 2019's *Rocketman* was brilliant, however you assess it. The two men first met in 2017, reported *Oscar* magazine, when Elton played a small part in

Kingsman: The Golden Circle, the second instalment of the spy-movie franchise. Elton had already vetoed Tom Hardy, the original pick for the *Rocketman* lead for the simple reason, 'he couldn't sing.'

Elton and Taron bonded over Indian food and the actor began the process of getting inside his subject's head. 'I was wanting to know about his drug use and how that first started and how it evolved. And his other addictions: alcohol, eating, smoking weed,' said Egerton. '[Elton is] one of those people who just can't get enough of anything, whether it be art, work, or Class A drugs.'

Egerton neither looked nor sounded particularly like Elton in the movie, although the make-up and hair team gave it a good go, but like all the best actors, he understood that ultimately this didn't matter as much as whether he was believable as the character. 'We trust in the fact that people wilfully suspend their disbelief in storytelling and I just wanted to capture the showman in him, the anger in him, the pain and vulnerability, and trust that when it's all put together, it will feel like Elton John,' he reasoned.

The critics agreed, awarding him a richly deserved Golden Globe Award for Best Actor, a BAFTA nomination and a Grammy Award nomination for Best Compilation Soundtrack.

ELTON JOHN **AIDS** FOUNDATION

A real lifesaver

Back in his hotel suite after attending Ryan White's funeral in April 1990, Elton watched CNN's coverage of the service, staring at himself on the TV screen. Hours earlier, he had said his last goodbyes to Ryan, told him how much he would always love him, had sat at the piano and played 'Skyline Pigeon' from his very first album, because the song, with its line, 'Dreaming of the open / Waiting for the day' seemed appropriate. And now he looked at himself, 'bloated and grey', as he recalled it, exhausted, ill, not just with grief for the young man he'd watched die from AIDS a month before his high-school graduation was due, but with a cold eye on the state he'd allowed himself to get into. Drugs and booze were taking their toll: 'I looked about seventy.'

AIDS had haunted the gay community since the early '80s, but Ryan's life and death after receiving HIV-positive blood plasma as a treatment for his haemophilia and the other high-profile figures going public with their diagnoses had begun to shift opinion. That day, Ronald Reagan, who had pretty much ignored AIDS during his presidency, had put his name to a piece for the *Washington Post*, urging tolerance and understanding.

Sitting in the lap of luxury in his five-star suite, Elton thought about Ryan and how 'a kid with nothing' had done more in his short life to change the course of the still unfolding AIDS horror show than he himself, as perhaps the most famous gay pop star on earth, had contributed. By comparison, he thought, his charity singles and gig appearances felt superficial, self-aggrandising, showbizzy and insubstantial. Elton's decades-long bad habits were yet to bottom out – there would be another few months of frantic self-destruction before he would finally admit to his addictions and seek professional help – but the previously unknown Ryan White, and Ryan's incredible mother Jeanne and the work she would go on to do, were the catalyst.

In rehab, Elton learned that his recovery would create what counsellors called 'the hole in the donut', all of the spare time and energy that being sober would now offer him would need to be filled with something else. He had grand plans, learning to cook among them, but what really filled the hole was the Elton John AIDS Foundation, begun in 1992, which immediately took on the same epic dimensions as almost everything else the star had ever turned his attention to.

The $525 million the Foundation has subsequently raised over the past thirty years or so – saving an estimated 5 million lives and over 3,000 projects still currently being supported – is dizzying enough, as is the almost complete reversal of public perception of the illness and its once thought fatal prognosis and the dreadful stigma and lies that attached. Then there's the sheer swagger that Elton brought to the process. In marrying the flamboyance of his Oscar Night party and New York Gala to the cause, he made it all enormous fun and went further in shifting those perceptions of a ghettoised disease that deserved not help but condemnation. A deeply inspiring message, humanitarian and heartfelt.

They say what goes around comes around. Elton appeared to have received his karmic reward when his work with the Foundation 'indirectly' led to him meeting David Furnish and the start of the most profound relationship of his life. It's under Furnish's chairmanship that the Elton John AIDS Foundation continues to flourish – the biggest HIV charity in the world.

ELTON JOHN BAND
Without whom . . .

'It's a good time to expand the band,' Elton John told Ray Coleman in *Melody Maker* in 1972, after the announcement that former Magna Carta guitarist Davey Johnstone had joined his backing group. 'You get an inner feeling that this is the moment to do something. For the past year, too much has been focused on me. I've been lead instrument, rhythm instrument and voice. I'd gone as far as I could with three men. It was either change completely or split.'

Davey joined in time for *Honky Château*, sliding up next to bassist Dee Murray and drummer Nigel Ollson, who were somewhat taken by surprise, to say the least: 'Don't get me wrong,' Murray said, 'we both got on great with Davey from the start. He was a terrific player and great for the band. It's just that we had no idea he was coming in.'

Looking back now, it's hard not to reflect on how this sudden appointment both lifted the Elton John sound into something instantly identifiable, in the same way as that of the Rolling Stones or Queen – and reinforced the fact that Elton would still always be the one calling the shots.

For Murray, Davey Johnstone joining the band was a sign of how things had moved on since John Reid had replaced Ray Williams as Elton's manager: 'Before John was around, I'm sure Elton would have discussed the whole thing with us. Now it was as if we just weren't worth consulting.'

He went on. 'Before Davey came in, Nigel and I were getting 40 per cent of the concert money between us and Elton got 60.' Once Johnstone officially joined, the three backing musicians were expected to share 13 and a third each: 'I went to John and asked him if we could get a raise on that. His answer was no, "and if you don't like it, you know what you can do."'

In the event, that reduced share would amount to a great deal more than they had been earning before Davey Johnstone joined, as their careers skyrocketed, beginning with the release of the 'Rocket Man' single, which became Elton's first multi-million-selling international chart-topper.

'Soon as we did "Rocket Man", it was quite apparent we had something magical,' said Johnstone. 'I had no idea it was going to be as crazy as it became.'

Neither did 23-year-old Nigel Olsson, whose first Elton John session stretched back to his performance on the *Empty Sky* track 'Lady What's Tomorrow'. Nor 26-year-old Dee Murray, who made his drumming debut on the track 'Amoreena' from Elton's third studio album, *Tumbleweed Connection*. While both men had been the singer's regular live ensemble for a couple of years and were the only other musicians on stage with him during those long hot nights at the Troubadour in 1970 when the whole world suddenly shifted on its axis, neither had featured on more than just the occasional recording until then.

Both were gifted musicians – and born sidemen. Olsson, from Wallasey at the mouth of the river Mersey, was the second of five brothers. He could sing and found himself performing with small local groups then discovered his true calling when the drummer didn't turn up for one pub gig – and Nigel offered to 'go in goal' for the night on the drumkit.

The first group he appeared on record with was soulful flower-child one-hit wonders Plastic Penny, on whose only album, *Two Sides of a Penny* in 1968, he sang and played drums on one track, 'I Want You' – and who a very young Reggie Dwight and his shy friend Bernie Taupin were encouraged to submit ideas for by Dick James, resulting in the track, 'Turn to Me'.

Olsson's Elton connection was furthered when he played drums on an Island Records manufactured 'flower pop' single, 'Mr Boyd'. The group – another fabrication – called Argosy also featured a certain Reggie Dwight on piano, Caleb Quaye on guitar and an even less well-known nineteen-year-old singer named Roger Hodgson – later to become the co-frontman of '70s superstars, Supertramp.

When Argosy flopped so dropped, Olsson fell to session work, appearing on two tracks from the debut Uriah Heep album, *Very 'Eavy Very 'Umble*. And of course, one track on *Empty Sky*. When he then replaced Dave Hynes in the Spencer Davis Group, he found a real connection with the bass player, David Murray Oates – stage name: Dee Murray. They recorded one album, *Funky*, but it only got a partial release and the band faded to black.

When Dick James decreed that Elton needed a regular live band, Dee Murray and Nigel Olsson seemed the obvious solution: both could play well enough to keep up with Elton, both could use the money. Their first show as a trio was in March 1970, at the Revolution Club in London, where they played 'Burn Down the Mission' at a frantic pace until they finally felt confident enough to try something else.

They did just twelve gigs like this before they flew to Los Angeles in August for their first show at the Troubadour. Eleven shows later, Elton flew back to London to headline the Royal Albert Hall. They had three weeks 'off' in which Elton did day-in, day-out promotion for his new *Tumbleweed Connection* album, then flew back to America where he was now a rising star, for five weeks of sold-out shows before clambering back to London for a Christmas show at the Roundhouse in Chalk Farm. All the while they were honing their sound, learning to augment and expand in whatever direction Elton felt like going in. They had no guitars, they just had Elton – and themselves. It was more than enough for American audiences who stamped and cheered, and perfectly suited to the more chaste atmosphere of his English concerts. However, it was not enough for producer Gus Dudgeon, who strongly advised Elton against using them for his next album, *Madman Across the Water*. In the event, the singer managed to squeeze both Dee and Nigel onto one track, the sweeping 'All the Nasties'. The album also featured a twenty-year-old guitarist from Scotland named Davey Johnstone, who played on four of the tracks on *Madman Across the Water*.

Maybe Nigel and Dee shouldn't have been so surprised then when Johnstone 'appeared out of nowhere' in time for *Honky Château*. Davey Johnstone was the special sauce that brought the splendid colour and raw excitement that would characterise Elton John's music from here on in, that birthed the smash hits and helped create what became known as the Elton John Band.

Johnstone recalls how *Goodbye Yellow Brick Road* 'was recorded in just sixteen days, it was insane.' It was the start of a remarkably prolific period that saw six Elton albums in four years go to number one in America, three the same in the UK, along with fifteen top-ten singles. 'It was us four guys and that was it, recording everything as a band playing together,' Johnstone told me. 'We were this factory, songwriting and recording together. As soon as we recorded it and released it, we'd take it straight out on tour. In the States especially, it was just this giant unstoppable juggernaut.'

It still stings, he says, that when Elton was inducted into the Rock & Roll Hall of Fame in 1994, none of the classic '70s line-up – the Elton John Band – was invited to join him: 'A lot of fans ask why we have never been inducted. It is a good question. I don't know if they've got a good answer, honestly.'

He remains philosophical. There were even a couple of releases under the heading, the Elton John Band: 'Lucy in the Sky with Diamonds' and 'Philadelphia Freedom', which gave Elton his third and fourth number-one singles in America.

'It would have been great to have that recognition at the time but it's easier for the record company to just have Elton John.' He thinks it was probably for the best in the long run: 'I think we would have all fallen down that rabbit hole that so many people went down. We weren't angels, but we didn't get dragged into the spotlight because Elton took the heat for all that. We did a lot of music together and had a lot of fun together too. A *lot* of fun.'

Elton wasn't this big druggie in those days, that happened later on. In the early '70s, he was just this guy who dressed weird and had funny glasses.

Johnstone smiles. 'I've got to tell you. I can't say that it was terrible. Waking up with a hangover after being up for two days was a nightmare but we were young enough to be able to wake up and go, I'm going to sleep for the next day so I'm okay for what's coming up. But those were crazy times. I wouldn't change it for the world.'

He recalled once having a conversation with John Lennon, 'when we were fortunate enough to hang out with John in the mid-'70s and did a lot of music together. We were talking one night about music and he said, "Well, I believe that an album is like a postcard. It's like a little postcard of where you are at the time." I continue to think that way.'

Despite the galaxy of hits, says Johnstone, 'I believe that a lot of the great work we did in those days was overlooked. Not by the hardcore fans, we still have a tremendous fan base who know us all individually.' But by the media.

When, in May 1975, just as *Captain Fantastic* was about to be released and in the wake of the two consecutive Elton John Band number-one hits in America with 'Lucy in the Sky with Diamonds' and 'Philadelphia Freedom', Elton decided to fire both Dee Murray and Nigel Olsson, it seemed like the singer must have lost his mind. Certainly, both Murray and Olsson thought so. The most recent American tour, which had culminated with a fantastic Thanksgiving Day show at Madison Square Garden in New York – the legendary occasion where Elton was joined on stage by John Lennon – had featured the singer's most spectacular stage show yet, his name along with those of the band – Davey, Nigel, Dee and newest recruit Ray Cooper – spelt out in huge neon lights above the stage.

Both were taking much-needed holidays at the time Elton made his decision to fire them both – by phone. A decision the singer was to bitterly regret in later years. Dee Murray was scuba-diving in the West Indies when he received Elton's call. 'I could tell right off he was embarrassed about something,' recalled Murray. 'He said, "I've decided to change the band. I think you, Nigel, and I have gone as far as we can together.'" He told Murray that he had already called Olsson and given him the news. Both men were confused, then devastated, then simply aghast.

Years later, Elton would reveal that he had been wrestling in his mind with the idea of changing the band since the US tour ended: 'When I got back home afterwards, I was depressed for about two weeks. I didn't know – I thought I was just unhappy. Then I realised I had to change the band.'

Only Davey Johnstone from the original *Honky Château* line-up was spared – though he, too, would be gone within three years. What sparked this sudden remarkable decision? The two main culprits, it seemed, were restlessness and boredom. Conditions doubtless exacerbated by the singer's increasing immersion in cocaine and booze – and loneliness.

With *Captain Fantastic* already recorded but not slated for release until early summer, and his contract with DJM coincidentally about to expire, Elton found the first few months of 1975 despairingly void of the thrusting ever-onwards momentum of the past five years. Instead of enjoying the thoroughly well-deserved break, however, he used the time to fret and paw away at every existing relationship, professional and personal, in his life.

With his *Greatest Hits* compilation, released in November 1974, having topped the charts in Britain (for seven weeks) and America (eleven weeks) and selling even more copies than any of his pre-existing hit albums, Elton John was now officially the biggest rock star in the world. But with no tour to keep him occupied, no new album currently in the works and little to do but relax – something the easily bored, endlessly restless singer had never been any good at – he began to worry about the whole thing somehow suddenly crumbling to dust. He had also noted with interest the recent trend for some of the biggest singers in rock to shed their established backing bands in order to expand their musical repertoire – and to keep more of the money for themselves. David Bowie had achieved worldwide publicity after his public 'retirement' from the stage of London's Hammersmith Odeon in June 1973 – essentially a ruse to unburden himself of his backing group, the Spiders from Mars. Meanwhile, Ian Hunter had gone solo, leaving his band Mott the Hoople in disarray, the group he had spent years making an overnight success. Steve Harley had relaunched Cockney Rebel, minus any of the original members and renamed it Steve Harley and Cockney Rebel. Most telling, perhaps, his old sparring partner Rod Stewart had finally left the Faces after one last hit single, 'You Can Make Me Dance' in November 1974, before also departing the UK for a new life – new band, new girlfriend, new hair – in Los Angeles, where Elton was also now stationed.

With the Elton John Band officially no more, a host of new faces were hired not just to fill the gaping holes left by Murray and Olsson's departures, but to build a bigger, more varied collection of musicians. Drawing from the past, he brought in drummer Roger Pope and guitarist Caleb Quaye, both of whom had featured on his earliest recordings. Looking to the future, he hired bassist Kenny Passarelli, a young Latin American with Afro hair, who had co-written one of the year's biggest US hits, 'Rocky Mountain Way', with Joe Walsh. There was even a second keyboardist, an American synthesiser expert named James Newton Howard, whose work featured on a current US top-ten hit for Melissa Manchester.

The new Elton John Band – though it was never to be called that again – made its inauspicious debut at the disastrous Wembley Stadium show in June 1975, where Elton 'premiered' the *Captain Fantastic* album. The first Elton John album featuring the revamped live line-up, *Rock of the Westies*, which followed just a few months later, was a disappointment. Not the new band, who really cooked, but the formulaic material.

Elton's next album, *Blue Moves*, in 1976, was another double and expanded the musical horizons even further, featuring no less than eighteen session musicians, including twelve backing vocalists, four strings and brass arrangers, two full orchestras, a choir plus an ordained reverend choirmaster. And Elton himself. As the law of diminishing returns suggests, it all added up to something rather less than the sum of its expensively recruited parts.

The first Elton John album not to go to number one in America since *Madman Across the Water*, five years and eight number-one albums before, *Blue Moves* also produced just one hit single, the achingly bittersweet 'Sorry Seems to be the Hardest Word', which barely dipped a toe in the UK top twenty and became his last top-ten single in the US for seven years.

Elton announced his retirement from live touring in an offhand sort of way at the culmination of a charity show at Wembley Arena in November 1977, in aid of The Variety Club of Great Britain Children's Charity and The Goaldiggers Football Charity. The band had already been dismantled; the Johnstone-Passarelli-Cooper-Quaye-Howard line-up performing for the last time as the Elton John band during a seven-night residency at Madison Square Garden in August 1976.

Of course, the story of the *real* Elton John Band didn't end there. Nigel Olsson and Dee Murray, who continued working together with a variety of artists, would both rejoin Elton for his 1980 album, *21 at 33*. When they took their places on stage with the band at Elton's landmark concert in New York City's Central Park in September that year, more than 400,000 fans on the Great Lawn stood and applauded.

There would be more comings and goings, some more memorable than others, but Johnstone has been Elton's musical director since the '80s and Olsson has been playing on the Farewell Yellow Brick Road tour. Dee Murray died, heart-breakingly, of a stroke in Nashville in 1992, aged just forty-five. He had privately fought skin cancer for some years. Elton put on two tribute shows at the Grand Ole Opry, a Nashville shrine, to help raise money for Dee's stricken family. Nigel Olsson was there. 'I think about him every single day,' he said. 'Brilliant bass player. Wonderful guy. Dear, dear, dear friend. A musical genius across the board.'

'I'm actually making a documentary that I've been compiling with Dave Murray's widow, Annette Murray, who's still a dear friend of mine,' Davey Johnstone later told me. 'We've got a lot of old footage that we've collected from all those great years. Great old, super-eight footage and old photographs, stills, and wonderful things. Great stories. All about the unsung heroes as it were, all the aspects that went into making Elton the star he is today.' He said he expected the documentary to be completed in 2023.

Like any other real band, from the Beatles and the Stones to the Sex Pistols and Queen, the Elton John Band not only played like brothers, they even looked like them too. 'That's the way we considered it ourselves,' said Johnstone. 'Dee and I, we actually looked alike in so many ways on stage, and Nigel who's still my dear brother. That's what we called each other. Obviously when we lost Dee back in the early '90s, that was such a sad thing. But we were such brothers.'

Where the three original Elton John Band members – the ones that helped create and define one of the most identifiable sounds in popular music history – were more fortunate than other superstar rock bands of the era, Johnstone suggested, was that they didn't feel obliged to live up to a certain image away from the stage.

'Because you had a certain image of, say, the Stones, or Rod and the Faces, there was also that really dark side of their music and their lives. We were able to kind of slip under the radar with that.'

Musically, however, the Elton John Band, capital letters or not, remain huge on anybody's radar.

EMINEM

'I didn't know he was gay'

The music world was completely caught off guard when Elton John gave his very public backing to Eminem, live on TV at the 2001 Grammy Awards.

The 28-year-old American rapper (real name: Marshall Mathers) was then enjoying his first globe-straddling success with his third album, *The Marshall Mathers LP*, which went to number one in seven countries, including Britain and America, and sold over 25 million copies. It also birthed two number-one singles in 'The Real Slim Shady' and 'Stan', which ably demonstrated his versatility and expertise as a lyric writer: the former full of the comic-book intensity that became his trademark.

The latter though was something else entirely. The based-on-a-true-story tale of fictional character Stanley 'Stan' Mitchell (voiced by Eminem), a deeply troubled obsessive who claims to be Eminem's biggest fan. Built around a reconfigured sample of little-known British singer Dido's song 'Thank You', the track is an epic by hip-hop standards, peaking with the suicidal death of Stan who drink-drives off a bridge with his girlfriend locked in the trunk of his car. Dido, who appears in the masterful video as Stan's girlfriend, also sings vocals on the track.

You didn't have to be a staunch Eminem fan or even a lover of rap and hip-hop to find 'Stan' compelling; you just had to be someone who recognises greatness in music, whatever the genre. Listed in *Q* magazine as one of the three greatest rap songs of all time, 'Stan' has been described as 'a cultural milestone'. In *The Guardian*, in reference to 'Stan', the award-winning author Giles Foden compared Eminem to the Victorian poet Robert Browning, famous for his dramatic monologues.

Yet at the same time as furthering hip-hip's reach beyond ghetto-demographics, Eminem was regularly called out for the levels of violence, misogyny and homophobia, even hate, in his lyrics. A seemingly clinching example comes from the very same album as 'Stan' on the closing track, 'Criminal'. Specifically, the second verse that, among many other questionable references to trans- and homosexuals, ends with: 'Pants or dress / Hate fags? The answer's "yes".'

Imagine then the shockwaves that went through the Staples Center in LA, in February 2001, as that year's Grammys host Jon Stewart of *The Daily Show* introduced the outspokenly homophobe Eminem onto the stage – along with his pianist and co-singer for the night, the outspokenly gay, AIDS charity advocate Elton John.

But what a fantastic performance. Eminem sitting on the edge of his single bed, stage right. Elton to the left behind his electric keyboard, the stage dancing in shadows, a huge screen behind them flashing thunder and lightning, you can almost feel the rain. Elton unveils an unexpectedly mellifluous piano overture, which adds a whole new weight to an already heavy piece. Eminem is live and is nervous but very intense. Elton is also live and is magnificent, his playing bringing a more human dimension to the piece, 'Bennie and the Jets' beefed up for the new century. Singing Dido's part and singing it exceptionally well, his voice no longer that of an overachieving twenty-something but one of deep feeling borne of experience.

When, at the end of a brilliantly executed performance, Elton and Eminem came together on stage to embrace then hold their joined hands aloft, it was seen as a statement. If Elton says this guy is better than his image, maybe he deserves a chance. And for Eminem fans, hey, this old dude is cool.

Quizzed about his relationship with the errant rapper by British talk-show host Graham Norton, Elton was effusive in his praise. 'We became friends,' he told Norton. 'He's an amazing guy, I just adore him.'

Their Grammy performance was the most memorable and remarked on of the night. A symbolic moment. According to later reports, however, Eminem claimed he didn't even know Elton John was gay ahead of meeting him. 'Of course, I heard of Elton John,' he told *MTV News* in 2004. 'I didn't know he was gay. I didn't know anything about his personal life, I didn't really care. But being that he was gay, and he had my back, I think it made a statement in itself saying that he understood where I was coming from.'

On their moment of handholding, he said: 'It was more so just a statement, period.' He added: 'If you really think that about me [being homophobic], you really don't know Marshall. You really don't know me.'

Eminem would go on to upset people with his lyrics and he would more than once repeat the same homophobic mantras, yet Elton has remained his friend. When Eminem needed to seek help with his addiction to opioids, Elton was the first to answer the call and was instrumental in his recovery as his AA sponsor.

'When I first wanted to get sober, I called [Elton] and spoke to him about it,' Eminem recalled in *The Guardian* in 2009. 'He's somebody who's in the business and can identify and relate to the lifestyle and how hectic things can be.' Elton, he said, understood the pressure and any other reasons that you want to come up with for doing drugs: 'I reached out to him and told him, "Look, I'm going through a problem and I need your advice."' He revealed how Elton would call him every day during the early days of his recovery from wherever he was in the world. They are still friends today.

The story of Eminem sending Elton and David Furnish a saucy gift to mark their civil partnership in 2005 was first revealed in Elton's interview with Graham Norton. 'I got this package from Eminem and it just shows you how homophobic he isn't.'

When they opened the box, said Elton, they found 'two diamond-encrusted cock rings on velvet cushions.' As Norton and the studio audience roared with laughter, Elton quipped: 'I have to say, they have remained unused.'

EMPTY SKY

'The first song Bernie and I got excited about that we wrote'

Empty Sky was the first official Elton John album. At the time of its original release in June 1969, Elton remembers thinking *Empty Sky* was 'The greatest thing I'd ever heard.' Containing 'Skyline Pigeon', which he later described as 'the first song Bernie and I ever got excited about that we ever wrote,' what was at the time the greatest event in both Elton's and Bernie's lives turned out to be a damp squib, certainly from a sales point of view. Few if any bought it.

However, reviews in the hard-to-please UK music press were encouragingly positive. You may not have heard much about the strangely named Elton John, but you were reading about him a lot suddenly. But with sales so slow, it was decided not to release *Empty Sky* in America. Nevertheless, word was beginning to seep through there, too. *Cashbox* decided to review the album regardless of its non-US release, with writer Eric Van Lustbader – better-known now as the best-selling thriller writer, including eleven novels in *The Bourne* publishing franchise – predicting big-time American success for this complete unknown.

Of course, this is still 1969 so the sound effects are in full force, the psychedelia – emanating largely from Bernie's spaced-out lyrics – able to accommodate full-spectrum rock orchestration, the propulsive and cinematic. There is even some meta-dynamics at play when at the end Elton sings, 'I want you to shoosh' and the band is faded out and replaced with soft piano while he improvises in the manner of the day, 'Get down with it, baby' and similar, before the band are faded back up.

Recorded 'on the run' whenever the DJM basement studio was free for a couple of hours, with in-house engineer Steve Brown producing, the rest was uneven but intriguing. There was 'Vahalla', a melodramatic ode based on Bernie's fascination with Norse mythology. Given what Elton later described as 'Leonard Cohen-esque'.

'Western Ford Gateway' sounded like John Lennon-meets-The Band, rustic musicianship and lyrical abstraction being its thing. 'Hymn 2000' was Olde-English whimsy, an aural black-and-white movie. Rich lyrical themes. Dour flutes and organs. You had to hand it to this new lyricist Bernie Taupin, he wasn't afraid to turn his verses to anything he happened to be thinking about. On 'Lady What's Tomorrow' the subject is ecology, as sung by Peter Sarstedt. 'The Scaffold' is much harder to nutshell. Bernie's lyrics are bleak, perhaps ironic, but Bible black. Much easier to get along with is 'Sails' – good rocking gone *baaad*.

Best of the bunch is 'Skyline Pigeon'. The song had originally appeared as a single not once but twice a year before Elton's version. Through DJM, the singer Guy Darrell released it first as a solo artist, then soon after as a member of the short-lived Deep Feeling. Neither sent the tingles like this: 22-year-old Elton John at the harpsichord, alone in the darkened studio, then adding an organ track. No band. No fancy production. Just bespectacled, bashful Reggie Dwight singing and playing his heart out.

The final track, 'Gulliver Hay-Chewed', is suitably monumental, the musical execution keen and spirited. It's still 1969, remember, so there's a Beatles-ish 'interlude' about three minutes into the seven-minute finale, followed by waves of reprised moments, rocking, elegiac, embarrassingly foppish in places, seriously cool in others.

As an interesting historical footnote, *Empty Sky* featured several musicians who would figure more prominently on Elton's albums in years to come, among them Caleb Quaye, who as well as electric and acoustic guitar also supplied the atmospheric congas; drummer Roger Pope, who would later record with Kiki Dee before rejoining Elton's band for the 1976 *Blue Moves* album. And a certain young drummer named Nigel Olsson, who makes his first appearance on an Elton session on 'Lady What's Tomorrow'.

Although largely overlooked at the time in place of the albums that immediately followed, when, in 1974, at the height of Eltonmania, MCA discovered they had a whole unreleased Elton John album in the vaults, they immediately arranged to issue *Empty Sky* for the first time in America, along with a snazzy new cover by Belgian painter and sculptor Jean-Michel Folon, to replace the original David Larkham picture of a wincingly young-looking Elton.

Released in January 1975, it quickly rose to number six on the US charts. Listening to *Empty Sky* now is to discover an unexpectedly delightful collection of musical styles, including some stealing from the Stones on the chattering percussion and spare piano that heralds the title track, 'Empty Sky', an eight-minute opus. A true epic, it would not have sounded out of place on any of his greatest albums from the '70s.

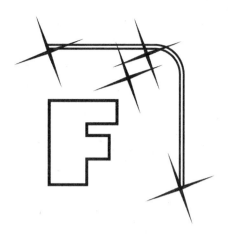

FAREBROTHER, FRED
Step in the right direction

'Derf was marvellous, a gentle man,' Bluesology drummer Mick Inkpen once opined. 'We took advantage of him something rotten. We had no way of getting to gigs, so it was a question of begging him for lifts. I called him Derf because I thought it was his real name! It didn't occur to me for ages that Reg was having a joke.'

We learn a lot about Elton John's stepfather Fred 'Derf' Fare-brother from this quote, not least that he was completely different as a parent to Stanley Dwight, Elton's biological dad. Where Stan was emotionally distant, Fred was warm and jolly, taking instantly to Elton's comedy reversal of his first name. Where Stan was unable to understand, much less enjoy, Elton's career and musical output, Derf joined in enthusiastically, helping out wherever he could. Most of all, he was kind-hearted, interested and present, which is more or less all that is required of any father.

We don't know much about Derf's former life, overshadowed as his story is by Elton and to a lesser extent, Elton's mother, Sheila. However, we do know that he was a handyman painter and decorator and that he had four children from his former marriage, which meant that money was always tight. He began his romance with Sheila after Stanley had departed to begin a new family, although the couple didn't marry until a decade later.

He and Elton got on well and built a close relationship, with the boy happy to refer to him as 'my dad' even though he still maintained a distant relationship with Stanley. As well as endlessly ferrying Elton around in his van, Derf performed an invaluable service for his stepson in getting him a gig as a pianist in a pub called the Northwood Hills Hotel. After each set, in which the budding star played a mixture of '60s rock 'n' roll and wartime singalongs, Derf would take an empty pint glass around the pub and ask for tips. These often added up to £15 a week, over £400 in today's money – a vast sum for a teenager. Elton was able to buy a Hohner Pianet electric piano and a microphone, thus taking an important step forward in his career.

Later in life, Derf was equally helpful: in 1970 he evacuated Elton and Bernie Taupin from the former's girlfriend Linda's house and offered them alternative lodging at the family home. When Elton later bought Woodside, Derf put up shelves at the new house; he and Sheila were regular house- and dog-sitters there when the prodigal son was away on tour, which was most of the time back then.

Elton repaid Derf by buying a house for him and Sheila to share and commemorating their parts in his real-life story on the *Captain Fantastic* album. Derf was also the beneficiary of Elton's heightened sense of fashion: he once gave him some scarlet 6-inch platform-heel shoes, which Derf wore to work on a building site, shrugging off the piss-taking he received from his delighted workmates as a result.

Derf died in 2010, seven years before Sheila, but he made the most of his place in Elton's life. Once over dinner with Elton, Yoko and John Lennon, Derf took his false teeth out and put them in the former Beatle's drink, just for a laugh. Nice chap.

FAREWELL YELLOW BRICK ROAD
Going back to my plough

By 2018, Elton John had had more farewells, official and other-wise, than Frank Sinatra and Status Quo combined. For the past twenty years, he had averaged 100 shows a year every year, non-stop. He still released records, or whatever they were calling them now, his classic hits were still everywhere and he still showed up in great form on TV. It didn't feel quite real that in the middle of it all the singer would feel the need to officially announce his retirement from touring.

Until suddenly it did. Elton John's Farewell Yellow Brick Road world tour – it was announced in January 2018 – would commence in September and would run for three years. Well, it was something for the fans and the media to talk about. But did he really mean it? No sooner had the announcement been made than Elton began a sold-out 27-night run at Caesars Palace in Las Vegas that would take him all the way to May, followed in June and July with two shows at the Black Sea Arena in Georgia. You might say Elton planned to work right up to the day of his retire-ment. Or pre-retirement. Or whatever this actually was.

Why now though? The clue was in something Elton told *The Guardian* in 2016: 'It's all about the school holidays now,' he said referring to his sons Zachary, then seven, and Elijah, five. 'I'm hurtling towards seventy and I've made a promise to David [Furnish] and to my sons that I really don't want to be schlep-ping around the world at seventy-two. I don't want to do tours anymore that take me away from my children.'

He would be seventy-one by the time the Farewell Yellow Brick Road tour officially began at the 8,500-capacity PPL Arena in Allentown, Pennsylvania, on 8 September 2018. And he was determined to go out with a bang. It later emerged that arena show designers STUFISH Entertainment Architects, who had previously worked production magic for the Rolling Stones and Lady Gaga, had begun work on the tour as far back as 2015. The studio's chief executive, Ray Winkler, had first worked with Elton in 1999. He and David Furnish, who took on the mantle of creative director, collaborated closely to create a pop-baroque, rock-opulent, very Elton John type show.

When it was unveiled for the first time, some thought the stage set resembled a tilting piano, yellow bricks framing a giant screen. 'The metaphor,' Winkler explained, 'is that he is walking down that yellow brick road towards his retirement and the sunset of his life.' Elton would sit at his grand piano, centre stage, the band galleried behind him, while new memory-triggering, some mindboggling, videos played on giant screens around the arena. Footage curated for specific songs, like the pictures of humdrum British life in the '70s for 'I Guess That's Why They Call It the Blues', were linked with previously unseen film of Elton together with John Lennon; Elton with Billie Jean King; Elton classing up *The Lion King*. 'These were personal items to Elton,' said Winkler.

His stage wardrobe now included a couple of dozen one-off Gucci outfits. Each night he would pick three different ones for the show but that was his only preparation ahead of the performance. Paul McCartney would put a towel over his head and inhale from a bowl of steaming hot water to clear his larynx, then gargle with salt water. Rod Stewart now swam regularly to improve breath control and lung capacity. Elton John's routine was even simpler: 'I get up, have breakfast and go for a walk in the pool. At my age that is the best thing I can do. I walk sideways and do about six miles a week.'

By the start of 2023, Farewell Yellow Brick Road was now officially the highest-grossing tour of all time and by its conclusion would reportedly net Elton over $1 billion. Elton was also named biggest earner ever, his reported take-home pay from the recent Oceania leg of the tour a not insubstantial $817.9 million (around £665 million), breaking the previous record held by Ed Sheeran for his 2019 Divide tour, which reportedly earned $775.6 million (around £630 million).

But twenty-something Ed was only out there for two and a half years and 260 shows. Seventy-something Elton was out there in the end for over five years – including the two-year gap created by the pandemic – across 330 shows. This may have been Goodbye, Elton John, but he was working harder than ever. By the tour's end, it was estimated that Elton would have spent more than 900 hours at the piano singing and playing. It was perhaps inevitable that so long a tour would also place the spotlight on a string of ailments, normal for a man in his mid-70s, but in this case with the added burden of being very much visible to the public eye.

In February 2020, he had been forced to cut short a gig in Auckland, New Zealand, when pneumonia temporarily robbed him of his voice. He was back a week later, only for Covid to strike. When Elton returned to the stage in 2021, another run of shows had to be rearranged after a hip replacement. 'I'm in pain most of the time,' he revealed. 'I can't move sideways [and] I don't want to go on stage and give less than 100 per cent.'

In January 2022, two shows in Dallas, Texas, also had to be postponed after Elton was diagnosed with Covid-19. There was more concern in June that year when a masked Elton was photographed being pushed in a wheelchair and 'looking frail', according to the *New York Post*, during a tour stop in Germany, ahead of his pre-recorded performance at the Queen's Jubilee concert that month.

He immediately poured cold water on the resulting speculation via his Instagram page. 'The tabloids ran a silly story about me "looking frail",' he said. 'The true story is I'm in top health and playing and singing at my very best [and] loving every minute of it.' He claimed the reason he was in a wheelchair was purely to rest. 'After another rousing 2.5-hour show, we arrived at Leipzig airport just before curfew, to find part of the airport had closed. It was an extremely long walk to get to the plane, so my team kindly laid on a wheelchair so I could rest my hip after doing the show. That's all, folks.'

With such a huge back catalogue of classic songs, the 24-song setlist Elton adhered to most nights inevitably left out some favourites. What, no 'This Train Don't Stop Here Anymore'? But that's a perfect song for his farewell show! There was also tutting from some Elton purists that 'Mona Lisas and Mad Hatters' was only performed occasionally. Part of a 'deep cut' section that included 'Levon' and/or 'Have Mercy on the Criminal'.

Everybody else, however, had their best night out at a show for years, wall-to-wall Elton John hits on their final parade, beginning with 'Bennie and the Jets' and ending with 'Goodbye Yellow Brick Road'. His most universally loved hit, 'Your Song' was included every night. It was estimated that by the tour's end Elton would have sung and played 'Your Song' 2,404 times during his career: 7,401 minutes of 'Your Song' live. I hope you don't mind . . .

So, is this really the end for Elton John? It's still hard to believe. In 2023, it was reported David Furnish admitted that Elton was already eyeing up more work. 'It's really important to make a distinction between Elton retiring from touring but not playing his last public performance,' he said. Nigel Olsson, who first played drums on an Elton John album back in 1969, put it more succinctly in the *LA Times* when he said, only half-jokingly: 'Now we're on the final farewell tour, somebody asked me, "What are you looking forward to, after the tour?" And I said, "The start of the next tour!"' Saying out loud what everyone else was secretly thinking, he added: 'I'm hoping it's not a farewell tour.'

FLOGGING IT

The most exclusive shop in the world

One thing you could never *ever* accuse Elton John of is being tight with money. If he had it, he spent it. On himself, on others (many others). But mainly on himself. And why not? He'd earned it all the hard way and what use was money anyway if you couldn't treat yourself? Hence, the properties, the cars, the clothes, the private planes, the limos, the drugs. In 1988, however, searching for a way forward after deserved victory in his libel case against *The Sun,* and with his marriage to Renate Blauel now officially dissolved, Elton decided to fling open the doors of his four-storey mansion in Windsor – and flog the lot. More than 2,000 items of his personal possessions were put up for sale in a massive four-day auction at Sotheby's.

Hundreds of bidders from all over the world vied for whatever they could get their hands on. Album artwork, tour itineraries, jewellery, stage costumes, furniture, paintings. Dozens of pairs of Elton's trademark weird and wacky glasses attracted some of the most intense bidding. The cheapest pair went for around £1,200. The Hard Rock Cafe in Los Angeles paid almost £15,000 for a battery-operated pair that lit up and spelled E-L-T-O-N. A Wurlitzer jukebox named after the *Captain Fantastic* album raked in over £25,000 and the super-sized fibreglass Doc Marten boots Elton wore in the movie *Tommy* (1975) went for about £16,000 to a rep from Doc Martens, who said they'd be used for 'exhibitions and marketing'. The auction was expected to bring in about £4.5 million but the grand total came to a little over £7.5 million – a significant portion of which went to his Elton John AIDS Foundation.

There would be more Elton-sanctioned auctions in the future, some to raise money for charitable causes, others to simply be rid of what he saw as unnecessary encumbrances now he was sober. In June 2001, Christie's of London held a special live auction for a swathe of luxury classic cars from Elton's own personal collection. Twenty classic cars were put for sale, beginning with comparatively modestly priced vehicles like a 1986 Ferrari 421 Sports Coupé (estimate: £15,000–25,000; price realised: £42,300) and a 1975 Bentley Corniche Convertible (estimate: £25,000–35,000; price realised: £49,350). All the way up the scale to a 1993 Jaguar XJ220 (estimate: £130,000–150,000; price realised: £234,750) and a 1973 Rolls-Royce Phantom VI Limousine (estimate: £110,000–150,000; price realised: £223,750).

He was reportedly hoping to fetch a final price of £1.9 million but the Christie's auction raised almost twice the initial pre-sale estimate. 'When the bidding kept going up and up, way above the estimates, I was both thrilled and surprised,' said Elton, who followed the sale from Atlanta, Georgia, where he was touring. 'There's obviously a lot of money to be made in second-hand cars,' he quipped. He added that it was practical considerations that had motivated his decision to sell so many fabulous vehicles. 'I'm away so much and they don't get driven. I'd rather people had pleasure out of them.'

His obsession with beautiful cars began, he explained, the day in 1971 when he was able to swap his Ford Escort for an Aston Martin. 'It's a collection that I've really loved collecting and it's hard . . . I'm sad about it going but you have to cut ties loose.'

Two years later, a bed once belonging to Elton was put up for auction. According to the auctioneers, Fellows, the Art Deco-style double bed was originally sold in a 2003 Sotheby's auction entitled *Elton John and His London Lifestyle* after Elton sold off almost all the furniture in his Holland Park home in order to bring in a more contemporary style. The bed, with a stepped headboard flanked by two bedside cupboards, was expected to fetch between £300 to £500. Also for sale at the auction were a pair of Versace Rosenthal

Wild Flora ice pails, printed with lilies entwined around classical columns, expected to fetch from £300 to £400. Elton eventually put around 400 lots under the hammer, all items from his house, including fake leopard-skin sofas and artwork worth hundreds of thousands of pounds. Speaking at the time, he said: 'I wanted to have the opportunity to display more contemporary work in one of my UK homes, but, as my house in Windsor has a very traditional style, the obvious choice was to remodel my Holland Park home.'

In 2011, the Elton John AIDS Foundation auctioned six important works of contemporary art at Sotheby's. The sale held in New York included Keith Haring's untitled 1981 ink-on-paper drawing depicting three men. Estimated at $50,000–60,000. There were also works by New York artist Jeff Koons, British artists Tracey Emin and Howard Hodgkin as well as Cecily Brown and Jim Hodges. Proceeds were all earmarked for the foundation's initiatives. The auction was part of a series of art-related events to mark the foundation's twentieth anniversary in 2012.

In 2017, Christie's in New York auctioned off 120 different items including property and rare photographs belonging to Elton. The sale reportedly raised over $3.7 million, again dedicated to the Elton John AIDS Foundation. Then in 2020, the Royal Mint announced an exclusive new collection of Elton John Coins. As they explained on their website:

> We are delighted to announce a special charity auction to raise money for the Elton John's UK Charitable Foundation. Fifty years on from the release of his *Madman Across the Water* album, we celebrate this great and original artist with a one-off piece of art. This exclusive commission features a replica of the reverse design for the Elton John 2020 UK coin on one side and the titles of some of his best-loved songs in a spiral motif on the other, including 'Rocket Man', 'Goodbye Yellow Brick Road' and 'Crocodile Rock'.

With the bidding starting at £12,000, this unique medallion will be auctioned on an online timed auction. Bids can be placed from 21 April until 6 May 2021 and all profits will go towards supporting the Elton John's UK Charitable Foundation.

Bernie Taupin also got in on the act. In 2018, he offered 198 items for sale via Julien's Auctions house in New York. There were pages of handwritten lyrics, many with musical notations by Elton, including 'Your Song'. Awards received over the years, gold and platinum albums from around the world, some hand-painted lyrics of 'Tiny Dancer' and 'Candle in the Wind', citations of achievements, twenty-plus sculptures, knives, trophy belt buckles, vintage T-shirts, tour memorabilia, plaques, some hand-painted lyrics of 'Don't Let the Sun Go Down on Me', previously unseen photographs, a neon sign, some money clips and a lighter, the lyrics to the 'Candle in the Wind 1997' tribute to Princess Diana, on typed sheets with alternate lines handwritten, even the leather chair Bernie wrote many of his most famous lyrics in.

An extraordinary treasure-trove for the serious collector, you didn't have to break the piggy bank either. Many items were estimated in their hundreds, most in their low thousands. The two most expensive items were the original working lyrics to 'Empty Garden (Hey, Hey Johnny)', the eulogy to John Lennon, asking price: $28,125, and the original working lyrics to 'I'm Still Standing', asking price: $25,000. Lower down the scale, you could bid for Bernie's personal Elton John's Greatest Hits chart plaque, asking price: $128. A portion of the proceeds were earmarked by him for The Wounded Warrior Project and the Elton John AIDS Foundation.

Furnish, David

'It's very important one partner doesn't lose themselves in the other'

Being married to a celebrity when you aren't famous yourself is both a bonus and a burden. On the one hand, you get all the benefits of your significant other's fame and fortune; on the other, your identity is compromised because you are no longer an individual – you are regarded as an adjunct, a hanger-on, a trophy partner. To survive and prosper under those suffocating conditions requires unusual strength and confidence, which is why celebs often hook up with other celebs – it's just easier, less tricky questions.

This applies doubly in the case of Elton's husband David Furnish, the talented but previously unknown Canadian who married one of the most famous men in the world. For many it would have been an insurmountable challenge, but with his welcoming smile and unruffled demeanour and no doubt patience of a saint, David has managed to make it look easy. It's hard to think of a happier-looking 'showbiz couple'. Certainly, Elton looks happier than he's ever been in his life.

Born on 25 October 1962, in North Scarborough, a middle-class district of Toronto, David is the son of Gladys and Jack Furnish, a director at the Bristol-Myers pharmaceutical company, and has two brothers, John and Peter. Like his future husband, fifteen years his senior, Furnish's early life was dominated by a private inner struggle with his sexuality. Arts and theatre were his passions rather than sport and, in the homophobic '80s, that meant undergoing schoolyard cruelties. 'We used to get teased. We were sort of the "art fags",' he told the *Toronto Star*. 'Nobody ever said, "Hey, it's okay to be gay". It was always, "Oh, they're gay" as though it was like the worst thing in the world that could happen to them.'

Furnish found friends in drama class at his high school, Sir John A. Macdonald Collegiate, where he acted in productions of *Godspell* and *Pippin* alongside the future *Will & Grace* star Eric McCormack. He worked hard, in and out of school, saving for college with a series of mundane jobs, with his funds matched by his father. At the University of Western Ontario, where he enrolled on a business studies degree, he was determined to excel. 'People who partied their first year away were the ones whose parents paid for everything,' he remembered. 'It was my money, I worked all those years, all those jobs. I studied really, really hard, rather boringly.'

Between his second and third college year, he came out to his astonished parents, who were deeply distressed. 'I remember my mom saying: "I love you and I support you, but all I look at is a life of unhappiness, isolation, prejudice and illness . . . I think you would be a wonderful father and it breaks my heart to think that you will never have that available to you".'

Uncertain of his feelings, he dated both men and women into his late twenties. He landed a plum job at the advertising agency Ogilvy & Mather, who transferred him to London in 1989 at his request: he did well there, becoming the company's youngest director of account services. Four years later, a certain bored rock star was looking for company one weekend and fate took an unexpected hand.

'I was rattling around the house feeling thoroughly sorry for myself,' remembered Elton, 'when I came up with an idea.' Newly clean from drugs and sick of talking to people about addiction, he called a friend and asked if he could bring some people over to Woodside for dinner. In due course, said friend rolled up the drive plus four mates, one of whom was David Furnish.

A conversation about photography led Furnish to a tour of Elton's collection and a spark was kindled between the two men, who arranged to meet for dinner the following day. This went well and a relationship was soon up and running.

Before too long, Furnish quit his job at Ogilvy & Mather, where he was managing accounts for Sunpat peanut butter, Rowntree's Jelly and Gale's honey, because it didn't square with Elton's schedule. In any case, he was keen to move into film-making and journalism, and once his name became known, he started writing for *Tatler* and *GQ*. To his credit, he understood the importance of keeping his feet on the ground and his own identity solidly intact.

'It's very important in any relationship that one partner doesn't lose themselves in the other and that's very easy if you're involved with a celebrity,' he once told *The Guardian*. 'They get so much attention and so much deference anyway, it would be very easy to just get swept up into being their other half. But the person that Elton fell in love with – well, I had my own career, my own identity. The worst thing I could do was sacrifice that.'

By 1995, Furnish was a film-maker, albeit one focusing the camera on his partner, with the excellent *Tantrums & Tiaras* (1997) TV documentary. Since then he's racked up a further dozen or so credits, with his best-known productions *Gnomeo & Juliet* (2011), *Billy Elliot the Musical Live* (2014) and of course *Rocketman* (2019). More significantly, he is now chairman of the Elton John AIDS Foundation and deeply involved in his partner's business, not without causing some mild ripples along the way. As Elton explained in 2016, 'My businesses have been badly run for the last five or six years, [so] he's come in, had a look at what's gone on, pruned a few people away, made it a leaner, meaner machine. We've made some changes and some of them haven't been very popular, because people don't like being gotten rid of, which is quite right. On a human level, I understand that people are hurt; on the other hand, they needed to go.'

On 21 December 2005, it became legal in the UK for same-sex couples to enter into civil partnerships and Elton and David did the deed that very day with a ceremony at Woodside. When, in 2013, parliament passed the Marriage (Same Sex Couples) Act, which introduced civil marriage for same-sex couples in England and Wales, Elton and David chose their ninth anniversary in 2014 to convert the partnership into a marriage. An occasion so grand Elton had one table set aside solely for the Beatles and their families. The couple have two sons, born through surrogacy: Zachary (born 25 December 2010) and Elijah (born 11 January 2013) and everything suggests that they're a happy, fulfilled family.

Have there been problems along the way? Of course, just as there are for everyone in a marriage. Furnish sought treatment for an alcohol problem in 2014. As Elton later wrote, the combination of being constantly in the public eye, frequent flying when he was always very nervous of doing so and the effort of looking after two boisterous kids was the root cause.

Still, Elton and Furnish seem to be in it for the long haul. As the latter told the rapper 6Lack in a 2018 webisode devoted to the subject of love, 'Here's a crazy thing in our relationship. We started a tradition that was not about technology, but every Saturday, we gave each other an anniversary card, because we met on a Saturday . . . You write about the week that's passed and the week that's coming, and you connect, and you tell each other that you love each other. I think seeing the handwriting on paper and feeling the person's humanity through that, and the fact that we religiously do it every Saturday, has been a very powerful bonding thing for us.'

GIFTS

The giver that just keeps gifting

Who enjoys buying things most? People who had nothing when they were young. Now, Elton John's background is not one of abject poverty – it was more the standard postwar experience, where you didn't have much because there wasn't much to be had – but gifts were few and far between, by necessity. To say that he made up for this when he started earning money is something of an understatement.

The money that Elton has spent over the decades on presents, whether for his loved ones, staff members, friends and acquaintances or just for himself, is – by his own admission – literally incalculable. He recalled shopping trips in Los Angeles in the '70s and '80s for which the excess baggage charge at the airport for all the stuff he'd bought to bring home cost more than the plane ticket itself.

Back in England, he filled his homes with rare antiques, collectable art, fabulous clothes and baroque furniture, curios and knickknacks of every description, as well as motor vehicles that were as impractical as they were expensive and unnecessary. Famously, he was among the first to own one of Clive

Sinclair's silly C5 tricycles in the '80s, as well as a 240mph McLaren F1.

Elton's friends also benefited from his extreme buying habits. As he explained, 'The whole point of being in this business and being blessed and being successful is that you're able to do things for your friends or your family, which means that they can have something special in their lives, too.' He gave a country cottage to his chauffeur, Bob Halley, and his wife, Pearl.

Elton favours unusual gifts. He once bought a cuckoo clock with a wooden penis that popped in and out every hour and gave it to John Lennon. His on-off chum Rod Stewart received an original Rembrandt, although this was scarcely reciprocated. As Rod once told *The Guardian*, 'For Christmas I bought [Elton] a pop-up fridge from Harrods. It cost me £600 – a lot of money in the '70s. We swapped presents and he said: "Oh very nice, dear, thank you". He gave me a Rembrandt painting! I've never felt so stingy.'

The present-giving went the other way, too. As a Christmas present in 2021, Ed Sheeran had a large marble penis delivered to Elton and David's English country mansion. Perhaps the best gift of all, however, came from the aforementioned Rod the Mod. In the '80s, when Elton's hair loss began to attract unwanted tabloid attention, Rod sent him an old, helmet-shaped hairdryer of the kind that women used to sit under in high-street hair salons. In return, Elton sent him a Zimmer frame covered in fairy lights.

All this extravagance couldn't last forever, it seems, and Elton has dialled it down in recent years. The fun might have gone out of it when his mother – the recipient of a great many valuable gifts from her son over the years, from jewellery to platinum discs – flogged the lot.

Now that he's a father, Elton apparently tries to rein in his spending. He and David Furnish maintain a one-gift rule at

Christmas, keen to show their sons Elijah and Zachary that life isn't all spend, spend, spend. This is healthy behaviour: Elton once revealed that therapists had told him over the years that his gift obsession was addictive, a view which he rejected. To an extent, we agree with him: most of us, were we in his position, would shower our loved ones with presents. Sometimes generosity is a good thing, even if it's taken to extreme levels. However, the act of giving someone a gift is a thrill in itself, especially when it's done spontaneously – an example being the cars Elton ordered for his Aunt Win when he heard she was depressed. It boosts the giver's self-esteem, as well as supplying an illicit thrill at the spending of so much money. In the case of our self-despising, deprived-childhood hero, they're a reliable way to feel good. Perhaps no one ever gives a gift for wholly unselfish reasons?

GLASTONBURY

Once more with feeling

When Elton John swanned onto the Pyramid Stage at Glastonbury at around 9 p.m. on Sunday 25 June, it wasn't just the end of the 2023 festival, it was the end of one of the greatest, most colourful, certainly most successful eras in British pop. Elton's last ever show on British soil.

Or was it?

'It's emotional for me because it may be my last ever show,' Elton told the 100,000-strong crowd, many of whom cheered and laughed as they instantly picked up on the word 'may'. By that point, it was an open secret that Elton could be 'considering offers' for future performances.

Be that as it may, this was a fitting send-off for the Rocket Man. For the first time on the Farewell Yellow Brick Road tour, the singer shuffled the setlist, beginning not with 'Bennie and the Jets', but instead with his fabulously frenetic version of the Who's 'Pinball Wizard'.

Indeed, everything about this 'final' performance suggested that we ain't seen nothing yet when it comes to an Elton John show.

The only slightly disconcerting aspect was the lack of big-name guests. In the week leading up to Glastonbury, there had been talk of Dua Lipa and Kiki Dee repeating their guest appearances at Elton's final show in America. Along with hints that Eminem night be there, too, or even Britney Spears. Or at least Ed Sheeran.

Instead, Elton surprised everyone by first bringing on Gabriels singer Jacob Lusk, who joined him for 'Are You Ready for Love', not usually included on the farewell tour. Followed by little-known Nashville-based singer-songwriter Stephen Sanchez, who rather incongruously sang his own song 'Until I Found You'.

Better known was his next guest, Japanese and British singer, actress and model Rina Sawayama, who sang the Kiki Dee part on 'Don't Go Breaking My Heart'. Then there was the appearance of Killers singer Brandon Flowers, who came on and did a splendid duet on 'Tiny Dancer' while simultaneously looking like a televangelist with a new set of pearly-white dentures.

Other than that, it was business as usual: an extraordinary confection of immortal pop hits unrivalled by any other British singer-songwriter.

As Elton said in the run-up to the show: 'You've got to keep people interested.' Putting the setlist together for Glastonbury, he said, was 'a bit like having sex. You start off really well, then you chill out a little bit, then towards the end of the show all hell breaks loose.'

A bit like his yellow-brick-road career, you might say.

GOODBYE YELLOW BRICK ROAD
Hello, gold and platinum highway

The release in 1973 of the subsequently hugely successful *Goodbye Yellow Brick Road* double album marked the high point of the golden years, both for the record industry and, most especially, for Elton John. As the '70s began to unfold, the size and scale of this new empire became ever more apparent. The music business was now an albums business. Artists that sold albums became the industry figureheads, rather than those who had hit singles. The improvements in home hi-fi equipment meant that musos, songwriters and producers willing to stretch out and explore new concepts and soundscapes intersected with a record-buying audience desperate to travel with them from their poster-strewn bedrooms.

In 1973, the year in which Elton released *Don't Shoot Me I'm Only The Piano Player* and his landmark double album, *Goodbye Yellow Brick Road*, was an astonishing one to be alive and buying records. Within twelve short months came Pink Floyd's *The Dark Side of the Moon*, David Bowie's *Aladdin Sane*, Led Zeppelin's *Houses of the Holy*, the Rolling Stones' *Goats Head Soup*, Stevie Wonder's *Innervisions*, Marvin Gaye's *Let's Get It On*, the Who's *Quadrophenia*, Mike Oldfield's *Tubular Bells*, Lou Reed's *Berlin*, Emerson, Lake & Palmer's *Brain Salad Surgery*, Black Sabbath's *Sabbath Bloody Sabbath* and Bruce Springsteen's debut, *Greetings from Asbury Park, NJ*, all game-shifting albums still being played and loved half a century later.

By 1972, Elton really was the Rocket Man, in space up there alone. It was one thing to have your songs turn into hit singles in

Britain and Europe, quite another to now be an enormous star in America. Elton and Bernie Taupin's songs were now considered in the same realm as Lennon and McCartney – and were just as popular. The endlessly outrageous 'funny' glasses, glittery mile-high shoes and general air of honest self-effacement made Elton John one of the family in the same way that the Beatles had been, and far more obviously fabulous contemporaries like Bowie, Bolan and even Rod Stewart never could be.

At the same time his live shows were becoming bigger and more spectacular. His regular band, soon to be formally named the Elton John Band, were tighter than anybody else's and much more versatile. They had their own recognisable sound now, but would do almost anything with it, as Elton really began to demonstrate on *Goodbye Yellow Brick Road*. He was still only twenty-five, but this would be his peak. And he never really got time to enjoy it and he sensed that but didn't know yet what to do about it.

In documentary footage by the renowned British film-maker Bryan Forbes, his neighbour in Virginia Water, Elton's mum Sheila looks into camera and says of her son: 'I never expect him to be over the moon at any time. He's just not that nature.' Confiding: 'He's had darker moods since he made it in the pop world than he ever did before . . .'

The documentary was to tell the life stories of Elton and Bernie, and it was to be called *Elton John and Bernie Taupin Say Goodbye Norma Jean and Other Things*. Released in 1973, you can find it online. It's well worth a look.

In his voiceover, Forbes says of Elton: 'Sometimes [he's] as unyielding as the diamonds he wears on his fingers, sometimes [he is] plunged into self-critical gloom . . . As much an enigma to himself as to his friends . . .'

The one thing Elton clung to like a life raft, relied on and was certain of was his talent. That was unshakably present. He may have found himself hurtling down a path everyone told him wouldn't hurt a bit, but he was making the work that would define his creative life.

As the album format assumed its pace as the ultimate form of musical expression in the '70s, the best records took on their own character. This was still the age of albums made to be listened to as Side One and *then* Side Two. Musical books, with explosive starts, big finishes, a short intermission. Followed by the Second Act, leading up to the ultimate pay-off at album's end. Everything about the package had to match the impact of the music so that the music blended seamlessly with the lyrics and the eye-catching artwork into a single immersive experience.

And something else happened, too. The really big, meaningful records had their own origin stories, their own sense of time and place. Led Zeppelin retreated to the Welsh mountains to make *Led Zeppelin III*, an album that dripped with the atmosphere of ancient, rainswept hills; the Stones got high on drugs and decadence in a French villa for *Exile on Main Street*, you could actually inhale the vibe from the music.

In 1972, Elton John had his *Honky Château*. That's where he'd completed his two breakout albums, where he'd make the next one. When told the place was suddenly closed due to some internal dispute, he might have thrown a hissy fit but he knew he was on a schedule. He knew he had another album to deliver, but he also knew it would have to be his best yet: this was his moment, come what may. And it was dice-roll time.

With the money now rolling in too, Elton's horizons were suddenly broader. There was a studio in Jamaica, the Stones would cut *Goat's Head Soup* there. Jamaica sounded pretty good to Elton, maybe the change he needed. Cool, vibey, different, a place of sun and palms, mountains and sea, the kind of place where shit might come together . . . or maybe fall apart in a way that made the magic happen.

Musos weren't the only ones thinking that way. As Elton and the travelling circus that accompanied him flew in, George Foreman fought Joe Frazier in the 'Sunshine Showdown' for the boxing heavyweight championship of the world at the National Stadium in Kingston. In a fight partly financed by the Jamaican government, Mean Big George cleaned Popular Guy Joe's clock in round number two to become the undisputed champ and violence hung like smoke over the city.

Elton and crew were booked into Kingston's Dynamic Sounds studio, home also for Toots and the Maytals and where the Stones would record their next number-one single, 'Angie'. They arrived the day after the world title fight to find every hotel in town rammed to the rafters with boxing people, the atmosphere still simmering from the brutal beating handed down to Frazier by Foreman. Worse, Elton had been booked into a hotel that was miles away from the rest of the band and when they got to the studio, they found themselves in one of Kingston's most notorious neighbourhoods. The building that housed Dynamic was ring-fenced with barbed wire and had armed guards standing watch.

Far from the freewheelin' herb-scented vibe he'd pictured making music in, Elton didn't leave his hotel for the first three days. Instead, he worked his way through the stack of lyrics that Bernie had given him to read. Here came his moment, that confluence of events that resulted in something unpredictable yet wonderful, a pure flow of music that, over those three short days, left him with twenty-one songs.

On a small electric piano, just him working alone, he came up with 'Bennie and the Jets', 'Candle in the Wind', 'Goodbye Yellow Brick Road', 'Saturday Night's Alright for Fighting', 'Funeral for a Friend' and so many other songs and passages that would live as long as music was listened to.

As the fight crowd finally dissipated, Elton finally made it out of the hotel and into the studio but the place was a write-off. The equipment was dated and the gear that producer Gus Dudgeon had ordered still hadn't arrived. The studio piano was a dog, any lingering sense of good vibes firmly crushed by the armed guards that stood watch outside of the barbed-wire walls. Jamaica was going through a period of political instability, a war between the conservative JLP and the socialist PNP that was in the process of turning parts of the capital into no-go zones.

The decision was made to get out of town and regroup in New York, but even escape proved nervy, their various hotels disputing payment, threatening to impound cars and who knew what else? Some of these people had guns.

When Elton and crew finally got to New York, there was at last some good news. The financial dispute in France had been settled, and they could return to their French home-from-home to record. The Château had never looked or felt better, it shimmered in the early spring sunshine. Bryan Forbes returned with his documentary crew and the footage crackled with the positive energy that had been so conspicuously absent in Kingston. With all of the songs written, and with Elton and the band honed sharp by endless recording and touring, they got all the material down in just two weeks.

The double album was another staple of the glistening new empire that the record industry was building, a statement of artistic success and extra consideration. No longer a three-minute throwaway, the pop song was a vehicle for greater expression. Albums – especially *double* albums – were grand statements. *Goodbye Yellow Brick Road* would open with the eleven-plus minutes of 'Funeral for a Friend'/'Love Lies Bleeding', an epic, mostly instrumental overture for what was to come. As he wrote it, Elton had been imagining the kind of music he would want at his own funeral and the melancholy that he captured was perfect for offsetting the wild, thumping, bawdy tunes that followed.

Bernie was pushing at his boundaries too and it showed in 'Social Disease', 'All the Girls Love Alice', 'Dirty Little Girl' and

'Jamaica Jerk-Off', lyrics populated by ingénues, alcoholics, prostitutes and teenage lesbians. The control of tone and mood was absolute. Elton could switch from that wildness to something as broken-hearted and beautiful as 'Candle in the Wind' and make it totally believable (the song, in both of its incarnations, may seem over-familiar now, but imagine hearing for the first time, 'All the papers had to say was Marilyn was found in the nude . . .'). To bring material so varied together and make it coherent, to feel as though it couldn't happen any other way, was the work of a supreme artist.

Everyone around him felt it. Elton knew it. As the finished tapes arrived at the record company, the thought of a double album suddenly appeared viable. The material was there, the moment was right. Everyone from the Beatles to the Stones, Dylan and the Who had done one (sometimes more than one). Holding Elton back was the thought of his younger fans having to lay out the extra money for a double. In the end, he made the right decision. The Beatles, he pointed out, 'did the *White Album* and now we'll have our double too.'

In 1973, surrounded by the most extravagantly presented, supremely talented, original music makers there would ever be, status was everything. There were simply too many brilliant singer-songwriters to try and measure yourself against in any meaningful way. The only way that truly counted was artistic status, all-time career-highs and the best way to achieve that in 1973 was with a double album. Better still, a double album with a concept. *Goodbye Yellow Brick Road* was designed to leave behind for good the simple singer-songwriter image of pre-glam yore and lift Elton and his hot new band up into Zeppelin and Bowie territory.

Of course, it also had to have a great album cover. Gatefold sleeves adorned with images sympatico with the music, they had to be both clear and indisputably far out. The illustrator and children's novelist Ian Beck created the *Goodbye Yellow Brick Road* cover image of a stack-heeled Elton stepping from a broken-down urban street and into a poster with its yellow brick road winding towards the horizon and a sun that was either setting or rising depending on your worldview.

Heralded by his first single, the gloriously raucous 'Saturday Night's Alright for Fighting', Elton proved he could rock as authentically as the Who – if he wanted to. Released in June 1973, 'Saturday Night . . .' was not the huge chart-topper that 'Daniel' and 'Rocket Man' had been – Elton John would remain the ultimate balladeer – but it was a great rock song and slipped immediately into the pantheon. Elton would never sound so nasty again.

When it was released in October, *Goodbye Yellow Brick Road* became his second album to top both the UK and US charts. America's number-one album for eight consecutive weeks and eventually the biggest-selling album of 1973, it remains the biggest-selling and most universally acclaimed Elton John album ever. Among its many gems, from the exquisitely bittersweet 'I've Seen That Movie Too' to the gorgeously swooning album closer, 'Harmony', this was an album so good it could afford *not* to release these tracks as singles.

It was the cathedral-like title track however that crowned the album in more than just name. The song 'Goodbye Yellow Brick Road' was Elton John and Bernie Taupin at their purest, their most heightened. Autobiographical for Bernie, metaphorically for them both. A song that elegantly puts the case for leaving behind the easy-sleazy life 'where the dogs of society howl' and 'going back to my plough'. At the time it was released it seemed like just another superior Elton ballad – up there with 'Daniel' if not quite 'Your Song' – but there was more to it than that, its endless layers gradually revealed over many years. Tellingly, on his Farewell Yellow Brick Road tour, it became the song Elton performed last every night, elegiac and suspenseful.

The accompanying Yellow Brick Road tour was conducted from a private Boeing 747 provided by Elton's American record company, MCA. Now the Rocket Man's life was to hit even giddier heights.

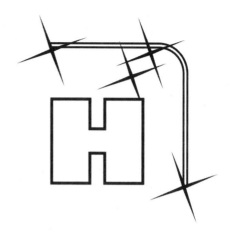

Hair

Hair today gone tomorrow

The significance of male hairstyles in the shaping of rock 'n' roll cannot be underestimated. Long before Elvis Presley was proclaimed the King of Rock, he was the acknowledged King of Hair. Jet black, voluminous, gleaming with Brylcreem, it quickly became known as 'the Elvis cut' – a slick twentieth-century version of the pompadour style originally named after Madame de Pompadour, eighteenth-century mistress of the French king Louis XV.

Before Elvis rebranded the look in the '50s, it was known, variously, as a quiff, a ducktail, a jellyroll, and was uniformly sported by rockers and greasers, leather-jacketed young men of questionable repute. James Dean had a version of it, as did Jerry Lee Lewis. Little Richard turned his gelled and powdered pompadour into a tonsorial bonfire. But it was Elvis who made it a quintessential component of his rebel rocker image. A sure sign the party had started and the old folks weren't invited.

Similarly, in the early '60s, when the Beatles became as famous for their hair as their hits, which they grew down to the collar (shriek!). Newspaper editorials warned worried parents about allowing their children to abandon the short-back-and-sides traditionally favoured by male barbers. Schoolboys were punished and sent home if their hair even touched the tops of their ears. The taunt, 'Get a bloody haircut, son!' rang through the streets.

Then came the Rolling Stones and suddenly the previously-thought benign world of male hairdressing was turned upside down. Hair now sped past the collar and out in all directions. It became about morals. By 1967, things were out of control. 'Get a bloody haircut' was replaced by 'I can't tell if you're a girl or a boy!' But it wasn't just pop stars growing their hair down their backs, it was now practically every male below the age of thirty. The hippies were the first to actually commodify hair as a generational dividing line. Long hair symbolised youth, rebellion, freedom. Short hair represented the man, the rules, choking conformity.

By the early '70s, when Elton John became a star, long hair alone was no longer even news: it was what you did with it. Like Rod Stewart, who developed his signature erupting-volcano hairstyle, overgrown to the point where it became a stylishly crooked hood. Or David Bowie with his Ziggy Stardust hairstyle: a proto mullet taken to the next dimension, shockingly red and completely different from all the other pop stars.

Keith Richards also developed a new 'do', simply by not combing his dark tangled hair, or washing it much, cutting it himself with a pair of kitchen scissors, staring into the bathroom mirror rolling-stoned out of his hairy mind. Then there was Robert Plant, with his golden ringleted lion's mane that shook gently as he roared into the microphone. And Marc Bolan, with his 'corkscrew hair' that he sprinkled glitter onto.

Those who didn't have any particular thing going on hair-wise simply relied on keeping it long. With the exception of Hot Chocolate singer Errol Brown, there were literally no baldies in the pop charts. Or if there were, like Art Garfunkel, they kept it hidden it under an old school wig. Elton John was the only major star of the early-'70s rock scene that quite noticeably didn't have great hair. Or, eventually, *any* hair.

No one of course was more aware of this than Elton himself. He had been horribly self-conscious of his prematurely thinning hair from a teenager when he first began to notice his forehead beginning its retreat. His mother Sheila would remind him that baldness ran in the family, predicting he would be bald by the time he was twenty – Elton had been insecure about his hair ever since. The fact that he was short, wearing glasses and 'carrying a bit of timber,' as Ozzy Osbourne once wryly observed, could be addressed with the right shoes and the most sparkly trousers and the right drugs to keep you off the nosh, but his increasing baldness was the one enemy Elton could not find a way to defeat.

He had put up a heck of a fight over many years. First came the traffic light hair dye, then the delicate combovers, then caps and hats, the costume headwear. Then two hair transplants in Paris in the late '70s that promised much and offered little. After Elton got sober in the '90s, it was 'pieces' that prompted derision in the media. After his appearance at the Freddie Mercury Tribute Concert at Wembley Stadium in 1992, one review observed that it looked as though he was singing with 'a dead squirrel' on his head. Other comments were less kind.

The much-improved wig he wore in 1997 when he sang the new version of 'Candle in the Wind' at the funeral for Princess Diana was much easier on the eye. Elton looked almost whole-some, the cut and colour perfectly suited to his face.

Up to the present day when Elton's lengthy, sometimes painful but ultimately worth-it 'hair restoration' is not even remarked on. These days he is happy to discuss his coiffeur without embar-rassment. He had considered simply shaving off all his remaining strands and going completely bald, he told Chris Evans, and only changed his mind when he decided it would make him 'look like Shrek'.

HERCULES

My kingdom for a horse

''AROOOLD!'

''ARROOOLD!!'

That cry, unmistakable to successive generations of British television viewers as the catchphrase of Albert Steptoe, rag-and-bone man of London's insalubrious Shepherd's Bush and star, along with his high-minded son Harold, of the BBC sitcom *Steptoe and Son*, was deeply familiar to Elton and many others. During the show's early-'70s peak, more than 28 million Brits tuned in to Harold's attempts to escape both his father and his apparent fate.

Perhaps Elton identified with that theme more than most. On 7 January 1972, he legally changed his name in a final decisive break from his own early life, though in truth, by then the switch was less symbolic than practical: he'd grown fed up with having to explain why the name on his cheque book didn't match the face that the cashiers and shop assistants now recognised so readily from the TV and newspapers.

'I'd always thought middle names were slightly ridiculous, so I did the most ridiculous thing I could think of and took mine from the rag-and-bone man's horse.'

Hercules was that horse and so Elton Hercules John it was.

A few months later, Elton and his manager and then-lover John Reid moved into a new property located in the millionaire retreat of Virginia Water in northern Surrey, an upmarket enclave bordered by Windsor Great Park and the Royal Estate that includes the Wentworth golf course and the surrounding network of lush and quiet private roads and residences.

They looked first at a house owned by the Who's drummer Keith Moon, but 'The Loon' had left his mark via a series of bullet holes in the walls and a white Rolls-Royce abandoned at the bottom of the swimming pool. Instead, they settled on a split-level home at number 14 Abbots Drive, its own pool happily Rolls-Royce free, and having paid the handsome sum of £50,000 (the modern-day equivalent of almost £1 million) for the purchase, they promptly renamed the house 'Hercules' in honour of the fresh start that they were making.

Giddy up, 'Arooold!

HOMES

Where Elton's heart is – whichever one he's in

Before 1972, Elton John was skint like the rest of us and lived with his then-partner John Reid in a one-bedroom flat in the Water Gardens development near the Edgware Road in London. Once the money started rolling in, though, he and Reid purchased a three-bedroom bungalow with a swimming pool and a loft converted into a games room in Virginia Water, Surrey.

This was the house Elton named Hercules, after his adopted middle name. Nearby neighbours included Bernie and Maxine Taupin, as well as Sheila Dwight and her new husband Fred 'Derf' Farebrother, so a social life was assured. Keith Moon and

Ringo Starr used to turn up at all hours of the night, too, so life was never boring.

By 1974, Elton had become phenomenally wealthy, thanks to the *Goodbye Yellow Brick Road* album, and raised his residential game by upgrading to the Woodside estate in Old Windsor, Berkshire, which is still his primary residence today. He paid £400,000 for the property, a sum equal to £4 million in 2023, and spent many years replacing its vile modern decor with a traditional look. The property has eight bedrooms, many acres of gardens, tennis courts, a library and an eighteenth-century orangery where Elton's grandmother lived for some years. However, a chap can't be expected to make the gruelling twenty-minute journey from London to Windsor all the time and, quite reasonably, Elton snapped up a town house in the capital's Holland Park area in 1992. He filled the place with a collection of blond wood furniture, inspired by similar items owned by Freddie Mercury, although he sold much of it off in 2003.

A year after acquiring the London house, Elton bought a luxury condo in Atlanta, Georgia, reportedly on the thirty-sixth floor of a high-rise building. Friends expressed surprise that he didn't opt for a bolthole in New York City or Los Angeles but as he explained at the time: 'I like that southern hospitality. Everyone is incredibly courteous and friendly.' The 6,000-square-foot space looked out over lush treetops and old houses in Atlanta's Buckhead neighbourhood. Elton is said to have had the white walls repainted thirteen times to get the right reflective surface. Two smaller rooms were turned into one for a dining room with parquet de Versailles-patterned floors laid throughout.

At some point in the '90s, Elton also purchased a lush '20s-era villa in Nice, France, painted pink, where he reportedly kept large art and china collections, and which has been estimated as being worth around £15 million. Prince Harry and his wife

Meghan used the home for a private holiday with their son Archie in 2019.

'After a hectic year continuing their hard work and dedication to charity, David and I wanted the young family to have a private holiday inside the safety and tranquillity of our home,' Elton tweeted at the time.

It's not just homes for himself to live in, either. Following the death, in 2010, of his beloved stepfather Derf, Elton bought a two-bedroom home in England for his mother Sheila, located along the beautiful Sussex coast, replete with conservatory and separate summerhouse. The cost: £650,000. After Sheila passed away at the age of ninety-two, he sold the property in 2018 for £950,000.

In 2012, he and husband David Furnish found their California dream home, buying a 5,000-square-foot mansion with kidney-shaped swimming pool, palatial gardens and cinema room in Beverly Hills. They wanted to make room for their growing family, Elton explained. Which may also explain his purchase of a seventeenth-century palazzo with stunning views from its Gothic windows, on the island of Giudecca in Venice, Italy.

In 2021, he also acquired the neighbouring mansion for a reported $8.5 million. According to public records, this property comes in at 5,343 square feet and features five bedrooms, four bathrooms, two pools and sweeping hilltop views.

'Everything is centered around the art,' Elton told *Architectural Digest* magazine in a March 2013 interview. Paintings by Keith Haring, Damien Hirst and Philip Taaffe adorned the walls, along with other striking pictures and photographs. 'Certainly, there was a family slant in the art we chose,' Furnish said at the time. 'We focused on things that are colourful and positive and celebrations of life.'

HONKY CHÂTEAU
Bags packed pre-flight

Elton John was twenty-four years old, in love with his handsome twenty-two-year-old manager John Reid, living with him at their new house in Virginia Water, in leafy Surrey. He had changed his name by deed poll, leaving the last of Reg from Pinner behind. The Elton John origin story was over, the main act about to begin. He'd loved making the album *Madman Across the Water*, even if the critics had been sniffy and the British fans slow to embrace it. Recorded in just four days, as he allowed in his autobiography, *Me*: 'It's not particularly commercial.'

One significant contribution to the record came from a tall and skinny acoustic guitar and mandolin player from Edinburgh called Davey Johnstone, who had come in via Gus Dudgeon and Bernie Taupin. Elton was impressed both by Johnstone's playing and his taste in music. He had made up his mind: Davey was in.

The brainwave to record in France came from the Rolling Stones, who had rented a villa on the Côte d'Azur, where they made the bulk of perhaps their last truly great album, *Exile On Main Street*, using a mobile recording studio. Word came down that Elton might be able to use it too, but just when he'd got enthused by the idea of a cross-channel jaunt, it fell through. That left Gus Dudgeon casting around. Luckily, he stumbled on a place just 30 miles or so outside of Paris that the Grateful Dead had recently made a record in, a half-ruined château in the countryside near the village of Hérouville, with a built-in studio.

Elton flew out to take a look with Gus and was immediately enchanted: 'It was in the middle of nowhere, with a swimming pool, tennis court. You could record in a room with a thirteenth-century chandelier, overlooking nothing but fields.'

It seemed the perfect setting, inspiring and beautiful but also cut off from distraction and temptation. Everyone had their own room, comfortably furnished but hardly five-star, and came together for meals in the grand hall, provided by a live-in chef. They could stroll across the courtyard to the studio and once work was done for the day, laze by the pool or walk in the grounds when it was warm enough and get down with the vibe. They could also visit the château's vineyard and enjoy the local wine.

All of this in combination seemed to supercharge Elton and Bernie Taupin. The latter arrived in France with some ready-polished gems, including a lyric that had come to him as he drove along the motorway towards his parents' house one evening. He'd been thinking about a short story he'd read called *The Rocket Man*, part of Ray Bradbury's famous collection, *The Illustrated Man*. That story had inspired a song that Bernie liked, too, also called 'Rocket Man', by the US psychedelic folk band, Pearls Before Swine.

It percolated in Bernie's subconscious and chose that motorway drive to come right to the front of his mind. The lines, 'She packed my bags last night, pre-flight / Zero hour 9 a.m.' came to him suddenly, which he liked more and more as he thought about them, but he was still two hours from home. He had to repeat the words over and over until he arrived and ran inside his parents' house, yelling for a paper and pen.

Once the lyrics were finished, the song took the notion of Bradbury's story, explained Bernie, 'which was about how astronauts in the future would become sort of an everyday job. So I kind of took that idea and ran with that.'

Elton as usual wrote quickly, working out the song on the piano in the same room where the band was having breakfast one morning. He decided 'Rocket Man (I Think It's Gonna Be a Long, Long Time)', as it was eventually titled, needed that soaring yet plaintive chorus that Elton magicked out of deep space and like the tune it was often compared to, David Bowie's 'Space

Oddity' (also produced by Gus Dudgeon), it caught the mood of the Moon landings and the Apollo missions that were a feature of the age, reflecting the essential strangeness of man travelling to other planets and the vast reaches beyond.

Metaphorically, as a generation of '70s post-hippy drug users later claimed, the song could just as easily be heard as a metaphor for a long-term cocaine habit. The references to being 'high as a kite by then' and how 'lonely out in space' it is, being the rocket man 'burning out his fuse up here alone'. However, Elton's over-reliance on the drug was still some years away.

The rest of the *Honky Château* album was cheerfully eclectic, full of Elton's disregard for anything other than his muse. In 1971, while others tied themselves in knots worrying over style or concept or theme, he simply reacted to what Bernie Taupin had written, discarding an idea if he had to force it or rewrite more than a couple of times.

The record was a blend of the penmanship honed over the past five years and the confidence that the recent addition of major success brings with it. The opening track – and second US hit single – 'Honky Cat' called for Dr John-style New Orleans jazz boogie; 'Mona Lisas and Mad Hatters' for Don McLean-style balladry and wit; 'Susie' for Leon Russell-style blues-funk, and Elton and the band were good enough for both and plenty more. Davey Johnstone brought texture as well as toughness, his tastefully evocative slide guitar playing on 'Rocket Man' adding to the song's ghostly allure.

As Charles Shaar Murray noted in his review in the *NME*: 'Elton John is still growing, still playing, still creative and he's still better than James Taylor and Leon Russell put together.'

The album was also indivisible from its birthplace. The château was immortalised in its title and the record dedicated to Catherine Philippe-Gérard, the young Frenchwoman who ran the studio and to whom Elton had quickly grown close. By the time the album was released in May 1972, its first single, 'Rocket Man', was already a major hit on both sides of the Atlantic, ushering in the peak years of Elton's early career.

But if the music strongly signalled where Elton would be going in the rest of the decade, the image was still somewhere off-message. The beige cover of *Honky Château* featured a black-and-white headshot of Elton, cool shades on, soulful beard across his chin – the classic '70s singer-songwriter look – and yet he would soon be redefining flamboyance on the stages of North America. The contrasts and contradictions in his personality and in his artistry ran deep and were now flowing out, trailing the birth of a new kind of star, an astronaut in the rarest air, a rocket man about to head out and never ever come down.

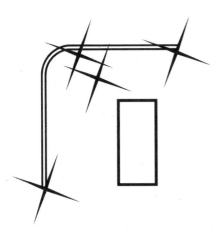

I'M DILL DANDIN'

Bring your own mask

It's safe to assume that the phrase 'I'm dill dandin'' had not been much used before 18 April 2020. After that point, though, these unusual words became the focus of intense hilarity – both among Elton John's fans and far beyond – thanks to his participation on that date in a concert called One World: Together At Home.

The live-streamed gig, split into two online and TV segments, was organised a few weeks into the coronavirus pandemic, ostensibly intended as a display of togetherness – as well as a nifty way of finding out if money could be made out of online events at a time when all live gatherings were banned, resulting in the termination of the Farewell Yellow Brick Road tour, among countless others. In the end, it reportedly made around £40 million for the World Health Organization, answering that question unequivocally, and leading to a sequence of big-name streamed gigs into 2021, when venues were allowed to begin opening again.

Elton played fifth on the TV bill, after Lady Gaga, Stevie Wonder, Paul McCartney and the country singer Kacey Musgraves, delivering a surprising rendition of 'I'm Still Standing' from the garden of his Beverly Hills mansion. Seated at a grand piano in front of a basketball hoop, he began by thanking frontline health workers before launching into a uniquely spirited performance.

The problem is not his energy levels, which are impressive for a 73-year-old, nor the limited range of his vocals, which makes him struggle to hit the song's higher notes: the issue is that the words are literally unrecognisable. He genuinely does sing 'I'm still standing' as 'I'm dill dandin'', while the rest of the lyrics come over more or less as gibberish.

Elton's followers were mystified. As the *Mirror* newspaper wrote, 'Fans were left uncomfortable and highly concerned after his worrying performance . . . several fans replied expressing their concern, with many advising him to go to a doctor and ask for help.'

Fortunately, the rest of Elton's pandemic was spent more profitably, not least with an album called *The Lockdown Sessions*. Released on 22 October 2021, most critics agreed this collection of duets was the best thing Elton had done in quite some years. As he accurately put it at the time, the music was 'really interesting and diverse, stuff that was completely different to anything I'm known for, stuff that took me out of my comfort zone into completely new territory . . . Working with different artists during lockdown reminded me of that. I'd come full circle: I was a session musician again. And it was still a blast.'

The most-talked-about track was the album's lead single – a slinky duet with the dance diva Dua Lipa on 'Cold Heart (PNAU Remix)' – which became a UK number-one hit. The tune, a slick club anthem that slyly combined parts of Elton's songs 'Sacrifice' (1989), 'Rocket Man' (1972)', 'Where's the Shoorah?' (1976) and 'Kiss the Bride' (1983), made him the first solo artist to have top-ten singles in the UK in six different decades.

It seemed that Elton John was very much still standing, pronounced correctly or otherwise.

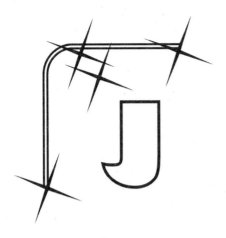

JACKIE

I'm gonna be a teenage idol

The most popular weekly teen/pre-teen magazine/comic for girls in Britain in the '70s was *Jackie*. Fashion tips, advice about boys, true-love story black-and-white photo strips, advice about boys, pictures of pop stars . . . and advice about boys. It had everything – and it was in colour. And unlikely as it sounds, it played its part in the Elton John story.

Elton met twenty-year-old Nina Myskow, then Jackie's girl-about-town fashion writer, in his early days at Dick James Music. Though he would definitely not have looked at home among the endless pictures of Donny Osmond and David Cassidy that then populated *Jackie*, Nina took an interest in Elton: 'He was funny and entertaining to be with – and depressed about his career.'

When 'Your Song' finally gave Elton a hit in 1971, Nina arranged for him to star in one of the romantic *Jackie* Life Story strips. 'Elton loved posing for the drawings,' she recalled.

When Nina joined *The Sun* as their chief pop writer just as Elton's star was rising highest in the '70s, they both adjusted quickly to their new, more exulted statuses and stayed friends throughout her subsequent career as TV panellist, reality TV personality and writer. Nina was one of the people who advised Elton during his ugly and protracted, if eventually successful, high court case against *The Sun* in the early '80s. She was there again, too, in the tabloid-frenzy surrounding his 1988 divorce from Renate Blauel.

Nina recalled how Elton had confided in her that he had considered seeking psychiatric help, before deciding, 'I think I should overcome my own problems.' He added that as part of the divorce settlement, Renate had taken ownership of a seventeenth-century cottage in Godalming, Surrey.

Renate had chosen the cottage, Elton told Nina: 'Because she liked its name. It was called Cobblers.'

JAMES, DICK
Tin Pan Alley titan and father figure

Elton John's career, now into its seventh decade, has been long enough to see the music industry change its stripes – economically, politically and in every other way – to the point where the business practices of his early days have little resemblance to those considered commonplace today. The way in which young musicians are treated is just one of those ways and Elton knows this from experience, as we'll see.

In 1967, the music publishing business in London was dominated by Dick James, a classic '60s figure. Born Isaac Vapnick in 1920, James was the son of Polish-Jewish immigrants who had worked his way up the music industry ladder over decades of effort, initially as a singer. In 1955, he'd made an impact with the theme tune to one of the most popular children's TV shows of the era, *The Adventures of Robin Hood*, which gave him a top-twenty hit. Further success eluded him, however, and in 1962 he set up as a music publisher in Denmark Street, the London version of New York's famous Tin Pan Alley.

James's big breakthrough came in 1962 when his friend, EMI in-house producer George Martin, persuaded him to take on the publishing contract of the then-unknown Beatles. Although the band had enjoyed one minor hit single, 'Love Me Do' – one of the first original compositions by Lennon and McCartney, which had reached number seventeen – James initially mocked Martin's suggestion with the words: 'Liverpool! So what's from Liverpool?' However, when the group's manager Brian Epstein played him the Beatles' new single 'Please Please Me', James immediately saw the potential and moved swiftly, creating a company he called Northern Songs specifically to handle Beatles' material, splitting the revenue 50:50.

Much as this sounds like a rip-off of Lennon, McCartney et al., the deal was typical for the time and in fact James was generally regarded as an honest, trustworthy man. Northern Songs went on to make vast sums for its owners, while James soon added other companies including Jaep, a partnership with Brian Epstein that published Cilla Black, and acquired half of Gralto (the Hollies), Pacermusic (Gerry and the Pacemakers), Cookaway Music (home of hit-makers Roger Greenaway and Roger Cook) and Page One (the Troggs). Dick managed to do all this with the help only of his accountant Charles Silver and his son Stephen James, who would eventually take over most of the administration after his father retired, particularly of DJM, named for Dick James Music, soon to be the publishing home of Elton John and Bernie Taupin.

In the late '60s, Stephen persuaded his father to establish a recording studio in the DJM suite, now located in the prestigious New Oxford Street. It was here that Elton John was busted one night by DJM's office manager Ronnie Brohn, caught jamming in the studio with the in-house engineer and guitarist Caleb Quaye, after hours and without permission. Informed that some guy called Reggie had been recording demos on his premises, Stephen asked to hear the music and was impressed enough to play the tapes for his father.

Quaye was told to summon Reggie and his songwriting partner Bernie Taupin to come and meet the boss and in late 1967, the two young songwriting hopefuls found themselves waiting in an office anteroom, shaking with nerves. Both men expected a serious reprimand, which made it all the more astonishing when James quizzed them about their future ambitions and, liking what he heard, offered to handle their publishing – for his usual 50 per cent cut.

On 7 November 1967, the two youngsters signed to DJM: in both cases a parent countersigned, as they were under twenty-one. The agreement assigned DJM world copyright on a minimum of eighteen songs, written over the next three years, said period to be renewable. James gave them an advance of £100 to share between them – around £2,300 today – to be recouped from future royalties of 10 per cent of recorded sales revenue and 50 per cent of live and broadcast income. In addition, James paid Reggie £15 and Taupin £10 per week as a retainer, also recoupable: the former got more money because he played the piano and sang, as well as writing the music.

Nowadays the terms of a publishing contract would be more generous, but you can't really compare the two scenarios because recorded music income is pitiful these days. Indeed, Reggie was delighted with the DJM deal, because it allowed him to quit Bluesology and move a step closer towards fulfilling his dream of becoming an independent songwriter.

There were downsides, of course, largely down to James being a 47-year-old – considered practically a senior citizen in those days – who couldn't understand Reg's desire to be a hip singer-songwriter with prog and jazz leanings. He insisted that his new signings write commercial pop music that they could hopefully sell to mainstream chart regulars such as the Hollies and Dusty Springfield.

It was with that thought in mind that his DJM label unwisely chose the anodyne 'I've Been Loving You' as the first solo single by the now-renamed Elton John. Even more unwisely, DJM overhyped the song, with adverts claiming that Elton was '1968's great new talent – you have been warned!' When the song failed to get anywhere near the charts, it was back to the drawing board for the wily Dick James. Indeed, the single was swiftly withdrawn and did not reappear until the *Rare Masters* box set in 1992.

Significantly, Elton later confessed that he had written the song – music *and* lyrics – on his own. That he only included Taupin's name in the credits to try and earn Bernie his first songwriting royalties. A cunning plan that failed spectacularly when the record flopped.

Sadly, for Dick James and Elton, his second single, 'Lady Samantha' – the first genuine John/Taupin song ever to see the light of day – suffered the same fate. As did his third single, 'It's Me That You Need'. It did become a minor hit in Japan, reaching number thirteen, where it became Elton's only hit in Japan until the release over a quarter of century later of the 'Candle in the Wind 1997' single.

Tellingly, none of these tracks made it onto the first official Elton John album, *Empty Sky*, recorded 'on the run' in the DJM basement – between sessions being paid for by other artists – with in-house engineer Steve Brown producing. Issued by the DJM label in June 1969, it also missed the charts by miles, despite containing 'Skyline Pigeon', which Elton later described as 'the first song Bernie and I ever got excited about that we ever wrote.' Nonetheless, Dick James decided to dig deep into his pocket for Elton's second, self-titled album, stumping up £6,000 (the equivalent today of over £125,000) for what everyone considered to be a make-or-break release.

Elton appreciated the leap of faith, although he speculated that James's hand might have been forced by the sudden enthusiasm of Island Records' new A&R executive Muff Winwood, former bassist of the Spencer Davis Group. Muff knew a sure thing when he saw one, as evidenced by his subsequent successes with Sparks, Traffic, Mott the Hoople and a great many other '70s superstars.

Sensing an opportunity, Muff approached Elton about the possibility of signing to his label in the wake of the dismal showing for *Empty Sky*. The relationship between Elton and DJM remained strong, however, not least because of the unbreakable bond that had developed between the singer and his publisher, akin said observers to that of father and son. As with any such relationship, the pair didn't always see eye to eye. Elton was enraged in 1970 when, after refusing to play in America for fear of losing momentum in the UK, an offer to play Stateside that he liked was turned down by James.

Jeff Beck was keen to use Elton, his bassist Dee Murray and drummer Nigel Olsson as his backing band on that year's US tour. Although he was only offering the musicians 10 per cent of his takings, Elton would be given a solo spot and the audiences would be huge. One had only to consider the effect such a collaboration had had when Rod Stewart had been the singer in the original Jeff Beck Group before leaving in 1969 to join the Faces and launch his own solo career. However, James declined the opportunity, earnestly declaring, 'I promise you now that in six months' time Elton John will be earning twice what Jeff Beck does.' While he wasn't too far out in this prediction, Elton was furious and observers from that time suggest that the rot set in between the 'father and son' from that moment.

Elton eventually parted ways with DJM in 1974, setting up his own Rocket Records label. His manager and then-lover John

Reid, who had worked for James, was concerned that his client had been unreasonably treated by DJM and as the years passed, he slowly assembled enough evidence to take legal action.

Reid's case hinged on the bane of all contracts: unspecified deductible costs. Essentially, after DJM, its administrators and overseas personnel had taken their cut of Elton and Taupin's income, the two songwriters were only paid £15 each from every £100 each they earned. As Elton later described it, these terms may have been standard in the '60s, but that didn't mean they were right.

A precedent for the eventual court case had been established in 1972, when a ten-year-old contract between a songwriter and a music publisher was deemed unfair, and after the books at DJM were audited – much to James's annoyance – the way seemed set for legal action and the case eventually began in late 1985.

Reid's legal position was that Elton and Bernie, young as they were in 1967, should not have been asked to sign away half of their revenue and all of their copyright. Furthermore, he claimed that they should own a larger chunk of the £200 million that their DJM-published music had earned in the intervening years. Reid also pointed out the large deductions that DJM's overseas sub-publishers had taken from the business revenue.

The James team defended themselves robustly, correctly pointing out that they had sunk large sums of money into Elton at the start of his career when his records sold nothing. Over the hearing, which took over fifty days to deliver, witnesses including Sheila Dwight and Muff Winwood were cross-examined about Elton's early business affairs. For his part, Dick James – apparently none the worse for recent heart trouble leading to bypass surgery – painted a picture of a young musician with whom he had enjoyed a paternal relationship, with never a hint of financial skulduggery.

Elton, Reid and their team were seeking copyright in the 144 songs published during their six-year contract with DJM, plus unreleased song masters, payments of the difference between what had been paid and what they should have been paid, plus compound interest of a decade or so. Estimates were that a verdict against DJM would cost Dick and Stephen James as much as £30 million, causing James Senior untold stress. He was deeply hurt that his former protégé would treat him in this way, feeling as if his surrogate son had rejected him after years of mutual regard.

The High Court eventually found in favour of Elton and Reid, but it was a pyrrhic victory. Elton was awarded less than £1 million, revealed Stephen James, but – according to his biographer Philip Norman – subsequently covered Dick James's legal costs to the tune of £6.8 million.

Three months later, James died of a massive heart attack at his St John's Wood home, succumbing before he could be taken to hospital. Years later, after Elton had written of his distaste for the legal action and his affection for his deceased mentor, Stephen told the *Mirror* newspaper: 'There is no doubt in my mind [that Dick] would have lived longer if it wasn't for the stress of the court case.'

Elton himself carries this sadness for life. As he wrote in his autobiography, *Me*: 'I loved Dick. It was really ugly, really sad. That wasn't how the story of Dick and [me] was supposed to end at all.'

JOHNSTONE, DAVEY

The musical moderator

'My mother used to say moderation in all things and I didn't listen to her,' Davey Johnstone told me in 2022. 'There was no moderation at all in those days, we were completely nuts.'

Johnstone's wolfish smile belies his septuagenarian status. With his long arctic-blond hair and rakish scarf-and-tinted-glasses, he actually looks better than he did when he was a gawky twenty-year-old providing the eerie lost-in-space guitar effects on 'Rocket Man'.

From Edinburgh, Johnstone began playing guitar when he was ten, after his older sister, Annie, noticed him playing his violin sideways: 'So she got me a guitar for Christmas.' As a teenager, he became a noted presence on the Edinburgh folk scene: 'When I was fourteen, I was playing in bands whose other members were twenty-five.' Among those he played with were legendary guitar-sage Davey Graham and innovative folk-rock legends Bert Jansch and John Martyn – and a very young banjo player from Glasgow named Billy Connolly. 'This was before he became a world-famous comedian,' Johnstone smiles. 'Billy was just my mate who I used to jam with in pubs.'

Lured to London with the promise of making records, he joined progressive folk group Magna Carta and helped make ends meet by taking on session work, principally acoustic guitars, mandolin, sitar and dulcimer. Hired by producer Gus Dudgeon to play on Bernie Taupin's eponymous 1971 solo album, it was Bernie who introduced Davey to Elton.

'I thought Elton was a very shy, quiet kind of a guy, which he certainly was and can still be,' says Johnstone. It wasn't until he began touring with him that he discovered that, as he puts it, 'Elton is the hugest diva on the planet. He has always wanted to be a star and that's what he is, a giant star. He has a lot of different sides and his attitude is he is who he is and screw everyone.'

This last said with a conspiratorial wink. For the mid-to-late '70s was 'when a lot of substances had become the norm . . . We'd have people like Ringo and Keith Moon visiting during rehearsals. Waking up with a hangover after being up for two days was a nightmare. Those were crazy times, but I wouldn't change them for the world.' Back then, 'All the excesses were considered the trappings of a successful rock 'n' roll band. You went to Tramp, or Rags and you'd bump into Queen, because they were also managed by John Reid, and hang out with everyone else who was in town that night.'

Cocaine was discussed as though it was vintage champagne: 'It made you something of a connoisseur, especially on a night off, because we'd take anything.' Even though Elton would make occasional half-hearted attempts to slow down, 'our behaviour carried on through the '80s', says Johnstone. He recalls one show in Dublin in 1986 as typical of the time: 'We were partying a lot. It was pretty insane. A couple of friends from Def Leppard came along. They were hanging out in the suite where there was all kinds of stuff going on. We got a call from the front desk saying sorry, but you have drunk the hotel out of Guinness. Pretty spectacular, drinking a Dublin hotel out of Guinness.'

Johnstone recalls he and Elton chatting with Def Leppard singer Joe Elliott. 'He said, "How often do you guys do this?" Elton and I turned to each other and shrugged, "Every night." It was great fun, but it was getting pretty knife-edge dangerous by that point. You don't realise the harm you're doing to yourself. The more you drink, the more you do blow, or if you're on your twenty-fifth joint of Afghani [hash] mixed with everything else, that could be super dangerous. There's nobody to tell you, maybe you shouldn't do that, because people don't want that to stop, you are the life and soul of the party.'

Soon after, 'came collapse time.' Johnstone knew he was in trouble 'when I found myself saying, "I can't go on stage without a bottle of vodka." When I first stopped my fear was: will I be able to perform without that? That's crazy thinking. I'm just glad I'm still around. I'm just grateful I was given that shot, that God shot. That punch in the head saying, Jesus Christ, wake up, man. If you really want to carry on and do this for the love of music, then stop all this other shit.'

Johnstone says he 'stopped all that nonsense' in 2009: 'Getting older, I decided I got to really look after myself and plus the schedule we're on with Elton, which we've always been on, it's been really nonstop. It's crazy. So I had to kind of take myself away from that. I still love the idea, especially of draft Guinness and good Scotch whisky, but I don't imbibe any more. The only thing I imbibe now is tea,' he says, showing off the teapot he now carries on tour. 'I always carry a toaster with me too.' He duly holds up the bag he carries his toaster in.

The fame and riches took a toll in other ways too. After two broken marriages, Johnstone met his current wife, Kate, a Danish fashion coordinator, at one of Elton's famously outrageous parties in Paris in 1989. Davey affectionately describes her as 'my third and final wife. We've been together for thirty years, so I got it right on the third attempt.' His first wife, singer-songwriter Diana Johnstone, 'was a Cornish girl. We had Tam, my first son, who's a wonderful musician and videographer. With my second wife, Rosa, we had Jesse and Daniel, and Jesse's the most incredible drummer. And with Kate, we were fortunate enough to have four amazing kids.'

Tragedy struck in 2001, when the couple lost their nine-year-old son Oliver. The easy smile freezes momentarily. Johnstone was in Chicago, on Elton's co-headline tour with Billy Joel. It was his fiftieth birthday and Kate had joined him on tour to celebrate: 'I got the call during a concert. Our kids were being looked after by nannies, who were wonderful. But Oliver got away from them. He was a bit of a mischief-maker and he went into the pool, hit his head on the side and drowned. It's the most earth-shattering thing that's ever happened in my life. My wife and I had to pull together in order to survive that.

'To this day, it's not an easy time to experience the anniversary of his birthday or the anniversary of his passing. But those are the kinds of things that happen where you say, well, what are you willing to do? I could have just topped myself and been really selfish about it. I had to get together with my wife and sit down and decide to get through this like a real person and not some idiot full of self-pity and drink myself to death.

'The way we keep Oliver's memory alive is we talk about him all the time. Every year on his birthday, we set off balloons that we write messages on. So, he's a blessed boy.'

Elton's album, *Songs from the West Coast,* released later that same year, carries a dedication to Oliver.

These days Johnstone is Elton's musical director, the most consistent presence in his band this past half-century, playing on dozens of albums and over 4,000 concerts. Along the way he has also worked with Rod Stewart, Alice Cooper, Meat Loaf, Stevie Nicks, John Lennon and many more, including movie scores with James Newton Howard and Hans Zimmer.

He says he feels 'truly blessed' to still be working and friends with Elton. 'The only thing that's missing really are the hard drugs and the hookers and groupies,' he says, reaching for his teacup. Moderation personified.

JUMP UP!

The gayest hassar in town

Spring 1982 was a giddy period of both success and calamity for Elton John. In May, his beloved Watford FC had secured promotion to the top flight of English football for the first time in their history – six years after Elton had successfully taken over ownership of the club. Just a few weeks before, however, he had released his sixteenth studio album, *Jump Up!* – which Bernie Taupin later described as 'one of our worst . . . a terrible, awful, disposable album.'

It's only redeeming feature, according to Bernie, was the track, 'Empty Garden (Hey Hey Johnny)', his personal tribute to John Lennon, which he had written the day after Lennon's fatal shooting in December 1980. Elton had also considered composing a tribute to his dear friend but felt it would be 'clumsy' to do so – until he saw Bernie's lyrics about a gardener who 'weeded out the tears and grew a good crop' and how awful it was that 'one insect can damage so much grain'. However heartfelt, it was, in truth, a maudlin tune that failed to make the UK charts when released as a single. (It limped to number thirteen in America.)

More successful was the track, 'Blue Eyes' that Elton had co-written with his new lyricist Gary Osborne. 'Blue Eyes' would become his first top-ten single in the UK for nearly five years. A song of yearning performed at a near-standstill tempo, it also gave Elton his first top-ten hit in America for some years. The video for the song – originally written about Elton's then lover Vance Buck – was filmed in Australia on Sydney's famed Bondi to Bronte coastal walk and dedicated to Elizabeth Taylor (though her eyes were more violet than blue).

The rest of the album wasn't quite as bad as Bernie Taupin made it sound but suffered partly due to the mishmash of co-writers Elton now worked with – including Taupin, Osborne, and feted Andrew Lloyd Webber lyricist Tim Rice on the confusingly titled 'Legal Boys'. A song about vulture-like divorce lawyers, it sits oddly here. Although Elton would work brilliantly with Rice in the future on *The Lion King* and *Aida*, this sounds like a stray from one of Lloyd Webber and Rice's lesser masterworks.

Although certified gold in America, the album was small beer compared to the multi-platinum chart-dominating '70s. The fact that it reached into the top twenty in the UK and US, however, offered some satisfaction for a singer now foundering to find a place in the new pop decade.

Further indications of that malaise can be detected in the gatefold sleeve, featuring pictures of Elton's friend and lover Vance Buck, luminary of New York's underground nightlife, who Andy Warhol had introduced him to in 1978 – alongside, somewhat incongruously, pictures of Gary Osborne's then five-year-old son, Luke. The cover shot of Elton conspicuously sans glasses, in blue, jauntily angled fedora, grey suit with bullhorn shoulders, is equally random: a lunging attempt to look *au courant* that ironically has the opposite effect. There were two slightly different cover shots of *Jump Up!* but they both felt the same.

To promote the album, Elton set out that summer on his first full British tour for over five years. Onstage, he now performed in a hussar tunic with gold epaulettes, dashing sash, frogged breeches and knee-boots with tassels, topped off by a mitre-shaped cap. And of course, no glasses. Like the plain-Jane typist who finally throws off her glasses and wows the handsome young boss.

The *Daily Mirror* ran a feature spread with the headline: 'THE GAY HUSSAR!' There were other sniggering digs about homosexuality in the barely 100-word caption. Nothing seemed to go quite right for Elton that year. After a catastrophic performance at London's Hammersmith Odeon, where he was still remembered fondly for his annual Christmas concerts there throughout the '70s, *The Sun* reported stage-door fans witnessing Elton coming out of the venue after the show, still in his bizarre costume and banging his head 'at least six times' on the bonnet of his Rolls-Royce.

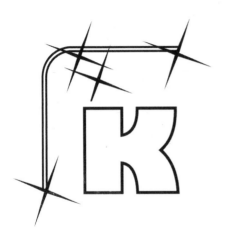

KNIGHTHOOD

Arise Sir John . . .

It was an extraordinary moment, even in a life overflowing with them. A Tuesday in February 1998, less than six months after the funeral of Princess Diana, and Elton John was at Buckingham Palace, decked out in sober morning dress and accompanied by partner David Furnish and his mum Sheila Dwight and her husband, Fred 'Derf' Farebrother. The Investiture was hushed and full in rightful reverence for the proceedings being observed.

The Lord Chancellor looked at his cue card and called the newest Knight of the Realm forward to receive the touch on his shoulder from the ceremonial sword of Her Majesty Queen Elizabeth II.

'Sir John Elton . . .' he boomed.

Apparently, the decades of global superstardom hadn't quite penetrated everyone's psyche. If Elton was nervous, the Lord Chancellor's unwitting transposition took his mind back to a signed film poster that he'd once been sent by Groucho Marx, which Groucho had signed 'to John Elton from Marx Groucho'.

That unexpectedly awkward hurdle navigated, Elton knelt before the Queen to receive his knighthood, awarded for Services to Music and Charity. His achievements in both were worthy of the honour and yet it was also a measure of how far both artist and nation had travelled. In the early '70s, it would have been almost inconceivable that so transgressive a musician as Elton John would find themselves accepted into the heart of the establishment.

'My joy at receiving this great new honour is immeasurable,' Elton proudly gushed to the waiting media hordes outside. 'They don't come much bigger than this.' His words were heartfelt. In order to be at the palace, he had flown in from Los Angeles and was then flying almost immediately on to Australia. Because, he said, 'This is not the sort of thing you put off. There is no way I would miss this. I love my country, and to be recognised in such a way . . . I can't think of anything better.'

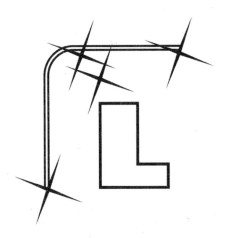

LAWRENCE, SHARON

'I'm afraid I gotta tell you – you're number one again'

Sharon Lawrence was a former journalist with the Los Angeles branch of the news agency United Press International, who had somehow drifted into music PR after becoming friends in the late '60s with Jimi Hendrix. Lawrence was thirty-five when she began working for Elton John's then American publicist Norman Winter in 1973. She had toured with the Rolling Stones, worked with David Bowie and been a marketing consultant for some of the largest record companies in the world, including MCA, Columbia and Apple. She confessed she 'wasn't such a fan' of Elton's music when she first began working for the singer but conceded that 'I always liked him very much as a person.'

Lawrence quickly became a vital part of Elton's inner circle, the kind of trusted friend he would take with him on his shopping sprees, insisting that Sharon share his largesse. When Elton went into Tower Records to buy hundreds of records at a time, he would take Sharon with him and buy her hundreds of records too. She became his confidante, the only person able to get through to him whenever he was having a temper tantrum – his 'Little Moments' as his band and entourage called them.

One of the only people who seemed able to deal with both Elton and John Reid, Lawrence was asked to run Rocket Records USA when it was launched. Now whenever Elton toured America, Sharon would most often be by his side: in the limo driving back from the show as Elton scribbled in his diary, something he did after every show in those years; backstage warding off over-zealous guests; taking his calls in the middle of the night.

One of her most important jobs, she recalled to biographer Philip Norman, was phoning Elton every Wednesday morning as soon as the new weekly pop charts were released: 'I'd call him up and say, "Well, I'm afraid I gotta tell you – you're number one again." One day when I told him, Elton said, "It's going to be terrible to be number two, isn't it?"'

For many years, Sharon Lawrence was one of the most important figures in what she called 'Elton's circle of dependence'. However, by the end of 1974, she had decided enough was enough. Elton's world had altered almost beyond recognition: cocaine and its many-splendoured associates like cases of vintage champagne, whole store's worth of jewellery, outrageously expensive cars, along with a whole new tribe of sycophants and hangers-on. Rocket Records in LA was now overrun, she felt, by people who absolutely did not have the star's welfare at heart.

'They were the ones who'd say they wanted a Porsche and half an hour later, Elton would have bought one.' Adding, 'The end for me was when I found out some people were doing drugs in the office. I said, "I want nothing more to do with this."'

Even after Lawrence ceased to be on the payroll, Elton's well-being continued to be of grave concern for her. Though she deliberately distanced herself from him now whenever he was in LA, mutual friends kept her abreast of the latest news, 'telling me about the awful things he was doing to himself.' Then, one night, around three in the morning, Elton phoned Sharon at home and begged her to come over to his latest palatial mansion in Benedict

Canyon. John Reid was out of town, he explained, and he wanted to play her his new album. Reluctantly, she got herself out of bed and into her car. When she arrived at the house, she recalled, 'He looked ghastly . . . incredibly strung up, anxious and panicky.'

Obliged to sit and listen while Elton played her his new album, *Rock of the Westies*, at deafening volume, almost begging for her approval, like most people who eventually listened to the album, she didn't think much of it. She didn't have the heart to tell him that though.

Sharon Lawrence remained friends with Elton John for years afterwards, even returning to Rocket temporarily in 1976 when Elton signed Cliff Richard to the label, promising to give him his much-longed-for US hit, which Sharon duly helped him deliver, with the single, 'Devil Woman', which reached number six in the US chart, selling over a million copies. Soon after however, Sharon went on to a successful career as a journalist, author and friend to the stars. She died aged eighty-two in October 2020.

LEATHER JACKETS
In small print: Not Real Leather

This then was the nadir, the scraping sound at the very bottom of the barrel for Elton John albums. Released in 1986, *Leather Jackets* was an album of firsts and worsts. The first Elton John album not to feature any top-forty singles in either Britain or America, although it did find the top-ten singles chart in Australia with 'Heartache All Over the World', which Elton considered the worst song he had ever recorded. 'It was pretty insubstantial,' he grimaced in 2001. Five years later, he declared *Leather Jackets* to be his least favourite of all his albums: 'Gus Dudgeon did his best, but you can't work with a loony,' he admitted to *Mojo*.

It would become the worst-selling album of Elton's career. He even hated its biker-themed cover, dismissing it as 'very butch but a total disaster. I was not a well budgie.' Still married – just about – to Renate Blauel, he confessed, 'It was just one bag of coke after another.'

Interviewed in 2000 for the VH1 series, *Behind the Music*, Dudgeon could only concur: 'There was a chance he could polish himself off. He'd go out and do some coke and it'd be all over his mouth, his nose would be running, and I'd go: "Oh God, this is just awful."'

'LITTLE JEANNIE'

Age is not a number

Like Icarus tumbling back to earth, after his astounding success in the '70s, Elton John's career in the '80s surprisingly was a much more hit-and-miss affair. His 1980 album, *21 at 33* – so-called because it was Elton's twenty-first album release (including live and compilation albums) at the age of thirty-three – would be the first in a decade-long line of *meh* albums enlivened only here and there by the stunning hit songs he was still occasionally capable of producing, beginning here with 'Little Jeannie', the lead single and Elton's first significant hit with Gary Osborne at the typewriter. His biggest single in America for four years, reaching number three, it still didn't make the UK top thirty, but the video was spun like a plate around the world and everyone still recognises the song when it comes on today.

Spelled 'Little Jeanie' on the cover of some releases, 'Little Jeannie' also featured for the first time since they were summarily fired five years before, Dee Murray and Nigel Olsson (though not Davey Johnstone, who was now working with Alice Cooper). With its gentle undulating tempo and plaintive first-name lyric, 'Little Jeannie' was a close musical companion to 'Daniel' and for many longstanding Elton fans, it felt like a welcome return to form.

The album, however, was not of the same order. Not as incontrovertibly awful as its predecessor, *Victim of Love*, but far from peak Elton. Even Bernie Taupin returning for a few songs couldn't entirely save the situation. Not with such wince-inducing fare as 'White Lady White Powder': 'I've had my face in a mirror for twenty-four hours,' sings Elton trying to sound alarmed, 'Staring at a line of white powder . . .' He and Bernie had reunited, briefly, during recording at Super Bear Studios in Nice. Elton was reaching out; he needed hits. But for once, Bernie didn't have any.

Elton also worked on material with hip new British singer-songwriter Tom Robinson, whose 1978 punk anthem 'Glad to Be Gay' had provided a significant step change in perceptions of public morality. With Tom, Elton cowrote 'Sartorial Eloquence', the second-best track on the album and its second single.

Elton also included 'Give Me the Love', a swanky, blue-eyed soul belter – part Donna Summer, part Toto – he'd written with Judie Tzuke, then the hottest new female star in Britain enjoying her first hit, 'Stay with Me till Dawn'.

In the end, Elton and Bernie cowrote three tracks and Elton and Gary cowrote three. Plus two with Tom and one with Judie. And it grew with repeated listens. The very opposite of what most of Elton's other '80s albums would do. Even 'White Lady White Powder' began to sound like the Eagles once you'd had a tequila. But 'Little Jeannie' was the standout, the only song so far of the Gary Osborne partnership worthy of '70s Elton.

THE LION KING
Elton feels the love

Elton John wasn't initially keen to get involved in composing music for *The Lion King*, having had his fingers burned with the soundtrack to the critically panned *Friends*, back in 1971. Still, when legendary stage musical lyricist Tim Rice called him out of the blue in 1992, the pitch was compelling enough to persuade him to give it a go. Rice was theatrical royalty, having co-written huge international hits like *Jesus Christ Superstar* (1971) and *Evita* (1978), with long-time collaborator Sir Andrew Lloyd Webber, and several more successful productions since.

Fortunately, the process was Elton-friendly in that Rice wrote the lyrics first, just as Bernie Taupin did, and the fact that the movie's storyline was already in place helped to make the song-writing more structured. Still, Elton later confessed that he experienced some doubts as the soundtrack progressed, primarily because of the youthful themes of the songs: the flatulent warthog role in the song 'Hakuna Matata' was particularly concerning, it seems.

The film turned out to be a triumph, fortunately, entrancing kids and adults alike. With American box-office receipts alone in excess of $300 million, it became the highest-grossing animated film of all time and the second highest-grossing movie ever, just behind *Jurassic Park*, released the year before.

Elton explained that his and Rice's intention had been to write 'ultra-pop songs that kids would like; then adults can go and see those movies and get just as much pleasure out of them.' He likened it to Disney's 1967 classic animated musical *The Jungle Book*, where he felt the 'music was so funny and appealed to kids and adults.'

The song 'Can You Feel the Love Tonight?' bagged an Oscar for Elton and Rice, while 'Hakuna Matata' was nominated in the same Best Original Song category. The soundtrack album sold 18 million copies and kept the Rolling Stones' *Voodoo Lounge* album off the US number-one spot through the summer of 1994. Keith Richards, never close to Elton, reportedly complained about being 'beaten by some fuckin' cartoon'.

In 1997, *The Lion King* was adapted into a stage musical in New York, where if anything, its success was even greater. On the opening run, it was nominated for eleven Tony Awards, winning six of them, including the most prestigious award for Best Musical, and became the most successful theatre show in the history of Broadway. It's still touring through the US, twenty-six years later, and has played worldwide as well as spinning off its own soundtrack album. The movie itself was remade in photorealistic animation in 2019.

The Lion King was perhaps Elton John's finest cinematic musical hour. The songs he cowrote and sang also repositioned him to the new generation of '90s kids and teenagers, too young to remember his '80s hits, let alone his imperial '70s catalogue. As relaunches go, you couldn't ask for more than to be associated with a cultural phenomenon of this size. Indeed, it might be reasonably argued that a single unexpected phone call from Tim Rice was partly responsible for the entire second half of Elton's career.

LIVE AID

'You bastards, you've stolen the show!'

'From Planet Windsor, here – at no expense whatsoever – is Elton John!' announced the comedian Billy Connolly from the stage of London's Wembley Stadium at 8.50 p.m. on Saturday, 13 July 1985. Moments before, news had come in that Live Aid, the show at which Elton was about to perform, was being broadcast on 95 per cent of the world's TV stations. The previous three hours had seen performances by U2, Dire Straits, Queen, David Bowie and the Who, the biggest bands in the world at the time – but despite the pressure of following them, plus the news that billions of people were watching him in close-up, Elton seemed completely confident, cracking quips and attacking the piano briskly for his first song, 'I'm Still Standing'.

Why such confidence? Simple: Live Aid, with its vast scale and star-studded cast, was simply perfect for Elton John, the same as it was for Freddie Mercury that day: the kind of event he could simply swan into and dominate with ease, having played more than a few stadiums of his own over the previous decade.

TV host Noel Edmonds offered his private helicopter to ferry Elton, Bowie, Spandau Ballet and a bunch of other musicians to the event. 'We shuttled people into London Transport's cricket ground, about 400 yards from Wembley Stadium,' Edmonds told *The Guardian*. 'On the day it was the climax of their cricket tournament, and they wouldn't abandon their game for us, so the umpires had whistles, and when they saw a helicopter coming, they blew the whistles and cleared the field for us to land.'

Live Aid production manager Andy Zweck later recalled how event organiser Bob Geldof 'had to play some tricks to get artists involved. He had to call Elton and say Queen are in and Bowie's in, and of course they weren't. Then he'd call Bowie and say Elton and Queen are in. It was a game of bluff.'

A possibly apocryphal story from that day has Elton refusing to disembark from the helicopter until its rotors had fully stopped spinning – he didn't want his wig to blow off. Once backstage, Elton is thought to have been distinctly unimpressed by the pop-up dressing rooms formed out of mouldy portacabins. Instead, he took it upon himself to set up a garden area with fake grass and a barbecue, at which he began cooking burgers for passing stars. He nipped out to witness Queen's show-stopping, career-relaunching set and is said to have shouted to Freddie Mercury afterwards, 'You bastards, you've stolen the show!'

Elton had no need to worry. His own set, the longest of the event at around thirty minutes, was delivered masterfully. Pounding through 'I'm Still Standing' followed by 'Bennie and the Jets', he entranced the watching billions with 'Rocket Man' before inviting Kiki Dee to join him on stage for 'Don't Go Breaking My Heart'.

The real heart of his set, however, was an epic rendition of 'Don't Let the Sun Go Down on Me', on which Elton was accompanied by George Michael. The duet was more signifi-cant than it seemed, as the 22-year-old Michael had just launched a solo career and his band Wham! was on the point of splitting. His guest slot at Live Aid helped to market him as a potentially successful solo act, which of course he soon became. His tacit approval by Elton John offered much-needed credi-bility by association.

Finishing up with a rollicking cover of Marvin Gaye's 'Can I Get a Witness', Elton exited the stage with a flourish. Is there any other way for him to exit a stage?

LIVE ALBUMS

We're gonna do one more and then we're gonna go . . .

In his earliest years the sheer energy and exuberance of Elton John's performances would take first-time attendees completely by surprise, having grown accustomed to the more considered musical mien of his studio albums. Especially when the live band consisted of Elton on vocals and piano accompanied only by drummer Nigel Olsson and bassist Dee Murray. But as you can hear on his first live album, *17-11-70* (titled *11-17-70* in America), that trio could summon more power and precision than most out-and-out rock bands with guitars.

In these days of streaming, YouTube and some artists putting all their concert performances online the same night of their shows, it's hard to explain to anyone that hasn't grown up with this facility just how important live albums used to be back in the '70s, '80s and '90s. Apart from expensive, illegal and often badly recorded bootlegs, live albums were the only physical mementos fans had to help them recall some of the best nights of their lives. The quality was often variable, from the utterly unbeatable – the first official Rolling Stones' live album, *Get Yer Ya-Yas Out!* in 1970; *Before the Flood* by Bob Dylan and the Band in 1974 – to the woefully underwhelming – Led Zeppelin's *The Song Remains the Same* in 1976; Rod Stewart and the Faces *Coast to Coast: Overture and Beginners* in 1974. But when they were good, they were fan-candy from heaven.

Elton John has managed to release some of the very finest examples of the form, each of his five officially released live albums showcasing entirely different eras of his career along with different musicians, different countries – and different costumes. Beginning with *17-11-70*, released in April 1971. Originally intended not for a live album but as a live radio broadcast on WABC-FM in New York, the performance took place before just a hundred people in the room and thousands of listeners at home or in their cars.

When bootleggers began putting out their own substandard versions of the recording, however, it prompted both Uni in the US and DJM at home in Britain to put out an official seven-track edition of the original thirteen-song show. Thank goodness they did as it ranks among the very best live albums of the '70s. Indeed, the singer has stated in several interviews over the years that in his view it's the best live recording of his career. So rowdy and full-on was his performance that when Elton cut his hand halfway through, he simply continued hammering away at his piano until all the keys were smothered in his blood. In the future there would be extended versions, including, in 2017, a double vinyl version that contained all thirteen songs. It really is a treasure.

The first official Elton John live album, *Here and There*, was released in April 1976, at the giddy peak of his success. Side One was recorded in 1974 at the Royal Festival Hall in London and as Elton explains at the start, 'We thought we'd do an evening of sort of nostalgia or semi-nostalgia and go back through some of our earlier albums,' starting with 'the first song that Bernie and I ever really felt excited about that we ever wrote and it's called "Skyline Pigeon".' After that, highlights include a beautifully understated version of 'Border Song' and a wonderful 'Love Song' featuring a guest appearance from Lesley Duncan. The most up-to-date the side gets is with 'Honky Cat' and 'Crocodile Rock'.

Side Two was recorded at Madison Square Garden, New York, in November 1974 on the Caribou US tour – the same Thanksgiving show where John Lennon made his historic appearance – and has a completely different, much wilder atmosphere as you might expect, opening with an uproarious twelve-minute version of 'Funeral for a Friend/Loves Lies Bleeding', before sliding gracefully into 'Rocket Man' followed by an ecstatically received

'Bennie and the Jets' and ending with a gloriously uplifting 'Take Me to the Pilot'. Again, as the years sped by longer and ever better versions of the album would emerge, first as a brilliant double CD in 1995 which contained the whole twenty-five-song set, including Lennon's surprise three-song appearance. Elton might have preferred *17-11-70* from a personal perspective, but for fans of Elton's classic superstar period, this is most definitely the best.

Cut to eleven years later and the release of the third and most ambitious Elton live album, another double, *Live in Australia with the Melbourne Symphony Orchestra*. Recorded on Elton's Tour De Force tour of New Zealand and Australia in December 1986, the show presented two halves with an intermission. The first half featured Elton and his now fourteen-strong band and focused on all the hits from 'Rocket Man' and 'Bennie' to more recent classics like 'I Guess That's Why They Call It the Blues' and 'I'm Still Standing'.

The second half of the show had the band replaced by the Melbourne Symphony Orchestra and was a much more self-absorbed and intentionally 'serious' performance. During the first set Elton had sported at various junctures a punk-Mohican and a ludicrous Tina Turner wig. During the second, he refined the gag further, arriving on stage dressed head-to-toe as a cartoonish Mozart, replete with purple powdered wig and beauty spot. Perhaps this was to disguise his nervousness at attempting some-thing as pretentious as performing with a real-life symphony orchestra. The set itself is delightful at certain moments but taken as a whole, hard to digest or indeed take too seriously. There were many versions and excerpts released over the years of both sets, but the original album focused mainly on the orchestrated set. It was all very classy – and just a little bit dull.

In 2019, there came *Live from Moscow '79*, released to mark Record Store Day – and the fortieth anniversary of the show in May that year at the Rossiya Concert Hall in Moscow. It was a special occasion indeed, with Elton at the piano accompanied only by Ray

Cooper. In common with *17-11-70*, the Moscow 1979 album had begun as a radio broadcast, this time for the BBC. Featuring prime '70s-era Elton hits, it had languished in bootleg form for several years. Released on CD, it contained sixteen of the twenty-seven numbers Elton and Ray had performed that night and apart from the wholly inexplicable inclusion of the eleven-minute-plus mostly instrumental version of 'I Heard It Through the Grapevine', it's a more than worthwhile addition to Elton's live catalogue.

His most recent live album, another double, but this time presented as a fifteen-track CD, released in November 2000, was more like it – at least in spirit if not always in execution: *Elton John One Night Only – The Greatest Hits*. Produced by the legendary Phil Ramone, who had worked with literally everyone from Burt Bacharach to Bono, Frank Sinatra to Stevie Wonder, Dylan to Streisand, and dozens of other superstars. Heck, it was Phil that recorded Marilyn Monroe's heavy-breathing version of 'Happy Birthday Mr President', which she famously sang for JFK in 1962. Phil knew that the best live recordings were the most faithful to the occasion, that perfect vocals and playing were not paramount and that vibe and good feeling were the order of the day.

Which is why one so easily forgives Elton's sometimes strained and awkward-sounding voice. The throat ops he had undergone in the '80s and the catching-up of age had conspired to deepen his voice, place it more out of his control, so that you can hear him wrestling with it, trying to make it do what it should but not always successfully. These days you would simply tweak the vocals on a computer. Even then such things were already available and in regular use. But this was Phil Ramone: there would be no 'fixing it later in the studio'. The result was a heartfelt authenticity, Elton John being true to his real voice, whether pairing up with Bryan Adams on 'Sad Songs (Say So Much)', or Mary J. Blige on 'I Guess That's Why They Call It the Blues' or, on the longer versions, Billy Joel on 'Goodbye Yellow Brick Road'.

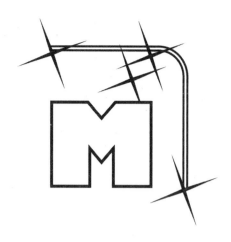

MADE IN ENGLAND
The long way home

In the three years since *The One*, his twenty-third studio album, Elton John had enjoyed a personal and professional renaissance. No longer a prisoner to his addictions, he had met David Furnish and begun what would become the most important relationship of his adult life. Indeed, the album is actually dedicated to Furnish. His career had also rebounded in spectacular style, first with the excellent *Duets* album in 1993, which spawned several hit singles and went platinum in Britain and America. Then the following year with the soundtrack to the hit Disney animated movie, *The Lion King*, which contained the classic Elton ballads 'Can You Feel the Love Tonight' and 'Circle of Life', both with lyrics by the celebrated British stage writer Tim Rice, both huge international hits: Elton's most successful singles worldwide since 'Nikita' almost a decade before.

With his life finally back on the track, in 1995 Elton released a return-to-form album with *Made in England*. The opening track and first single, 'Believe', has strong John Lennon energy circa the *Imagine* album. The lyrics are much more direct, the singing and playing equally straightforward and powerful, the overall effect one of confidence and elan. Elton was no longer seeking your approval, he was simply being himself – his *new* sober self.

The title track was also a modest hit single, anthemic and singalong, and there were a number of heart-warming ballads, in particular 'House' and 'Blessed', and a definite tip of the straw boater back to the days of soul-baring story-songs with 'Belfast'. Paul Buckmaster, making his first appearance on an Elton album since *A Single Man* in 1978, added the wistful trad-music coda, as though it were being played in an Irish pub. Former Beatles' producer George Martin, who owned AIR Studios in London where the album was recorded, wrote the horn and string arrangement on the gently lilting 'Latitude'.

Another big international hit, *Made in England* went gold in Britain and platinum in America. Suddenly it felt less like Elton John was back, more like he'd never been away.

MADMAN ACROSS THE WATER
Still waters run deep

It's easy to see why some think of *Madman Across the Water*, released at the end of 1971, as Elton John's 'progressive rock' album. Even 'Tiny Dancer', its most famous track and generally assumed to be its best, unfolds gradually over six minutes into a manicured symphony, as directed by Paul Buckmaster.

There are still hangovers from *Tumbleweed Connection*, Bernie Taupin romanticising the American Dream in ways only a non-American could on 'Indian Sunset', the lyrics clanky from half a century later, but the music cinematic and freewheeling.

Elsewhere there is straight-no-chaser rock, lightning and thunder ballads, old-timey folk and gasoline blues.

There is also a general feeling of far-out-ness. This was some of the most uncompromising, boldest music Elton had released. 'Razor Face' is made undeniable by Caleb Quaye's swooning guitar electrickery. 'Hotel Inn' would have been the best song the Rolling Stones ever recorded if they'd had what Elton had going on *Madman Across the Water*. Producer Gus Dudgeon directing the widescreen orchestra, blowing like the wind, while Elton gets down to some dark funky stuff. This was Elton John from Pinner, outdoing both the Band *and* Yes at their own games. Dazzlingly so.

Most of all, there is the title track, 'Madman Across the Water'. Originally a nine-minute epic recorded for *Tumbleweed Connection*, it had featured David Bowie's new discovery Mick Ronson on some truly wild and transcendent guitar. But it was simply too long to fit onto an album already forty-seven minutes long, the outer limits of a 12-inch vinyl record in 1971.

That version would eventually surface years later on various compilations and special editions of *Tumbleweed Connection*. The shorter-by-a-third masterpiece that became the title track of the fourth Elton John album is far more polished, better thought out, Elton's vocals less overwrought, more reflective. The guitar, now played by Davey Johnstone, making his debut on an Elton recording, is similarly defanged, but the lush orchestration and heightened sense of drama make this version definitive.

It was the most adventurous, starkly impressive album of Elton John's classic early-'70s period, yet his least successful. In an era when the Beatles had paved the way for Big Musical Statements and everyone was making long, complicated albums, even the Rolling Stones, *Madman Across the Water* fitted right into the growing pantheon. Bernie Taupin recalled being taken aback at the interpretation of the monumental title track, particularly in America, where it did make the top ten but number eight. 'Back in the '70s,' he recalled, 'when people were saying that "Madman Across the Water" was about Richard Nixon, I thought, "That is genius, I could never have thought of that."'

All it lacked was hits of which there were none, certainly not in the UK, where 'Tiny Dancer', such a pretty song, proved a little too deep and complicated as a single, missing the US top forty and flopping completely in the UK. The elegiac ballad, 'Levon', fared even worse as a single at home and only a little better in the US, where it peaked early at number twenty-five. As a result, outside of America, where it dipped its toes briefly in the top ten, *Madman Across the Water* was Elton John's biggest commercial failure since *Empty Sky* (1969). It was also, surprisingly, considered Elton's least likeable album. In the review in *Rolling Stone*, Alec Dubro compared it unfavourably to its two (in America) predecessors. He gave a high five to 'Tiny Dancer' and 'Levon' but generally considered Bernie's lyrics too confusing and the musical whole a 'difficult, sometimes impossibly dense record'. Some critics did get it, like Penny Valentine in *Sounds*, whose review hailed Elton as 'a music man of immense feeling and power'.

In the main its reputation suffered, not least when compared to the splendours that were about to follow. When re-released in Elton's *The Classic Years* collection, it was the first album not to feature any bonus tracks – a shame as the only other track from the sessions, released on the 1992 *Rare Masters* collection, 'Rock Me When He's Gone', is an undiscovered gem. A joyful hand-clapping, soul-testifying, rock 'n' blues originally written for and recorded by Elton's old mate, Long John Baldry, it would have made a rollicking hit single.

MADONNA

'That's me off her fucking Christmas card list'

Sir Elton and Queen Madge are renowned for being shameless divas. Because of this, you might imagine they would be friends, even besties. Yet for the best part of a decade, they were embroiled in a very public feud. It wasn't always this way. One of their first appearances together was during the 1995 BRIT Awards, where they were photographed backstage, Elton pulling his shirt open to reveal his chest. Madonna did the same, but revealing slightly less. They seemed to be enjoying themselves, exchanging mock insults while laughing.

Things took a turn for the worse in 2002 when Elton branded Madonna's theme track to the 2002 James Bond movie *Die Another Day* 'the worst Bond tune ever'. He claimed to be a big fan of Madonna's but felt the song would have been better suited to someone like Shirley Bassey, who is old enough to be Madonna's mum. Ouch!

Two years later, however, during the *Q* magazine awards in London, where Elton was awarded with the Classic Songwriter Award, he launched into a bitter tirade after Madonna was nominated for Best Live Act.

'Madonna, best fucking live act? Fuck off!' he raged from the stage while accepting his own award. 'Sorry about that but I think everyone who lip-synchs in public on stage when you've paid, like, seventy-five quid to see them should be shot. That's me off her fucking Christmas card list but do I give a toss? No.'

Madonna's publicist issued an official response to Elton's unduly harsh words, insisting: 'Madonna does not lip-synch, nor does she spend her time trashing other artists.' Before adding gracefully, 'Elton John remains on her Christmas card list, whether he is nice . . . or naughty.'

Elton later agreed his comments at the Q Awards were 'unfair' and said he didn't want the situation to 'escalate' as he considered Madonna his friend – 'She's been to my house for dinner.' He tried to explain the tirade away as 'something I said in the heat of the moment, and probably should not have said', adding that he would apologise when he next saw her in person. But after Madonna refused his invitation for her to perform at his bachelor party, he was overheard complaining to guests that, 'Madonna, the miserable cow, wouldn't do it.' When his comments made the gossip sheets, once again, Madonna's publicity machine swung into action: 'Madonna wishes Elton all the best and hopes married life will make him a happier person.' Meow!

Madonna had the last laugh at the Golden Globes in 2012 when during the build-up to the awards ceremony, Elton said she had 'no fucking chance' of winning Best Original Song against his track 'Hello, Hello', which also featured Lady Gaga, for the animated kids' film, *Gnomeo & Juliet*. When Madonna then won the award for her track, 'Masterpiece', from the soundtrack to the film *W.E.*, written and directed by Madonna, David Furnish waded in with a since-deleted Facebook post, about 'how these awards have nothing to do with merit,' adding that Madonna's acceptance speech was 'embarrassing in its narcissism.' Yet again, Madonna appeared to take it all in her stride, observing that Elton has 'been known to get mad at me,' but that, 'He's brilliant, and I adore him, so he'll win another award. I don't feel bad.'

Elton wasn't happy to let the matter rest there though, describing her as 'a great singer' who makes 'great pop records', but one that acts like a 'fairground stripper'. Yet again, Madonna found the high ground, telling an audience at one of her shows in Nice, France: 'I'd like to dedicate this next song to a Mr Elton John. I know he's a big fan of it, and I know he's a big fan of mine.' She smiled her million-dollar Monroe smile. 'And you know what? I forgive him. Gotta start somewhere.'

When asked about their feud some years later, Elton batted the question away, merely stating that it was 'over and done with'. They had bumped into each other at a restaurant in France – and agreed to be friends again after Elton bought Madonna dinner.

'I apologised profusely,' he said, 'because what I said should have never appeared in public. She was fantastic. She was just like, "Okay, let's get a move on."'

MERCURY, FREDDIE

'My black book is bursting at the seams!'

'From the minute I met him, I loved him,' recalled Elton John of the late Queen star Freddie Mercury – and indeed, on examining the many similarities between the two musicians, it's easy to see why they should have become such close friends. Both sang and played piano to a very high level and both had been shy kids, misunderstood by their families, who took an unorthodox path through life and reached heights that their demographic could never have understood. Both Elton and Freddie were bisexual, although they diverged in that the former eventually came out in public and the latter never did, and both were extravagant, insecure, bitchy, moody, hilarious, hugely talented people.

Other common factors were more prosaic, such as the fact that the two men shared a manager, John Reid, from 1975–78. It was during Reid's era that Queen released their literal and meta-phorical magnum opus, 'Bohemian Rhapsody', even though the manager worried that it was too long. Elton didn't get it at first either, describing it as the campest song he had ever heard and its title as ridiculous.

It seems they were destined to be friends as well as contemporaries. As the redoubtable Queen singer recalled, 'The first time I met [Elton] he was wonderful, one of those people you can instantly get on with. He said he liked "Killer Queen" and anyone who says that goes into my white book.' Adding in typically catty Freddie style, 'My black book is bursting at the seams!'

It was October 1974 and, while Elton was already the biggest-selling rock star in the world, the two men soon became fast friends, building a relationship based on clubbing and gossip. As Elton remembered, 'He was just magnificent. Incredibly smart and adventurous. Kind and generous and thoughtful, but outrageously funny.'

In 2019, Elton remembered in an interview with the comedian David Walliams: 'There's nobody like Freddie. He was larger than life. So funny, so gifted. So talented in what he wanted to do in his videos, using ballet dancing. He had such an incredible mind . . . [he] was one of the funniest people I've ever met and was so wonderful to spend time with.'

He added: 'We just used to sit there and dish the dirt, basically, and do drugs and laugh and laugh. There was a club in London on Jermyn Street that I used to go to a lot. We were there every night . . . It was just great. It was like John Lennon, hanging out with him was a pleasure. There was no attitude, it was just a laugh. For me, probably apart from Mick Jagger – who I think is probably the greatest singer in a band and entertainer – Freddie was definitely second. I mean, he was beyond belief – he really was.'

The feeling was mutual, with Freddie once saying: 'Elton's a good old cookie. I love him to death and I think he's fabulous. To me he's like one of those last Hollywood actresses of any worth. He has been a pioneer in rock 'n' roll.' He also remembered a particular occasion attended by Elton and Rod Stewart: 'They both came to my last birthday party and sang happy birthday when the cake was wheeled in. I shouted out, "This is probably the first time the two of you have sung without being paid for it!"'

As with his friendship with Rod, Elton and Freddie had pet names for each other: Elton was Sharon, Freddie was Melina. The two even performed on stage together, notably on 19 November 1982, when Freddie joined Elton on stage at Manchester's Apollo Theatre for a medley of rock 'n' roll classics: Jerry Lee Lewis's 'Whole Lotta Shakin' Goin On', Elvis Presley's 'Hound Dog' and two Beatles' songs, 'I Saw Her Standing There' and 'Twist and Shout'.

As the '80s wore on, time took its toll on both men, Elton with a crippling set of addictions and Freddie with his undisclosed HIV diagnosis. After a visit with their mutual friend Tony King, Apple Records' label manager in the US, Freddie commented that Elton looked as if he needed help. 'Coming from Freddie, no saint when it came to booze and drugs himself, that judgement should have carried a lot of weight,' noted Elton in his memoir, *Me*. An encounter that helped persuade Elton into rehab in July 1990.

Within a year, Freddie was seriously ill. His infection had evolved into full-blown AIDS and he was confined to his bed for the last few tortuous weeks of his life. Elton was a regular visitor during this fraught period. As Freddie's personal assistant Peter Freestone later recalled of Elton's visits: 'They would get together and there would just be no stopping and just talking, talking, talking, talking for hours and hours . . . Once Freddie got sick and he was at home a bit more, Elton would come around regularly, maybe every fortnight he would come around. He would sit and talk with Freddie, particularly during that last year . . . just so that Freddie knew he wasn't alone, and that really showed the genuine, deep friendship between them.'

Freddie Mercury died at the age of forty-five on 24 November 1991. At his funeral, Elton appeared with 100 pink roses bearing the message 'Thanks for being my friend. I will love you always'. The relationship wasn't quite over yet though: a month later, Elton received a Christmas present that Freddie had arranged before his death – a painting by the English impressionist artist Henry Scott Tuke, who specialised in nudes of young men and boys. The gift was accompanied by a note that read: 'Dear Sharon, I thought you'd like this. Love, Melina. Happy Christmas'.

MICHAEL, GEORGE

Wake me up before you go

The story of the friendship between Elton John and the late George Michael is often reduced in most observers' minds to two things – a triumphant hit and a bitter falling-out – but there was much more to their relationship than that. While they were two of the world's greatest songwriters and performers, the pair had serious struggles in common, namely a tendency to overdo drugs and a midcareer coming-out. One of them overcame these challenges; the other did not.

After becoming the biggest teen idol of the '80s in Wham!, George Michael went truly stratospheric in 1987 with his slick solo album *Faith* and camp-anthem single 'Faith', which went to number one in America and sold nearly 1.5 million copies in the UK, more than any of the biggest Wham! albums. He'd already had three solo number-one singles in the US on top of the three he'd achieved in Wham!. Now the double-whammy of *Faith* gifted Michael the only thing left in the world he still didn't have: recognition of his potential beyond the showbiz fizz of Wham!. *Faith* hugely aided this process and placed him firmly on the ladder to becoming an Elton John in his own right. The two were already friends, as evidenced by Elton choosing 'Wake Me Up Before You Go-Go', Wham!'s biggest zillion-seller, as the finale to his *Desert Island Discs* appearance in 1986.

'I became friends with him very early on in Wham!,' Elton recalled. 'I remember I played at the last Wham! concert dressed as Ronald McDonald for some reason at Wembley Stadium and I bought him a three-wheeler car, with him and Andy [Ridgeley], and I put their names on the front of it and put some fairy dice.'

As Elton reminisced elsewhere, 'I remember sitting in the car just off of Hyde Park, listening to a cassette of "Wake Me Up Before You Go-Go". I said, "George, that's the nearest record I've heard to a Motown record for years and years."'

By the time the two became friends, George Michael was cultivating a more adult image. This new direction was first unveiled to the public at the historic Live Aid concert at Wembley Stadium in June 1985, when Elton turned up for an unexpected and quite stunning duet with George on 'Don't Let the Sun Go Down on Me', his own 1974 hit. Michael returned the favour by performing guest vocals on Elton's *Ice on Fire* album, released later that year. Then in 1986, Elton was the star guest performer at Wham!'s farewell concert, held again at Wembley Stadium: this time the two sang 'Candle in the Wind' together, with the song's mournful message only diluted somewhat by Elton's Ronald McDonald costume.

The peak of the partnership came in 1991, when the two singers released a live version of 'Don't Let the Sun Go Down on Me'. By now, Michael had successfully repositioned himself as one of the most successful and admired singer-songwriters in the world, with *Faith* and its grand follow-up *Listen Without Prejudice Vol. 1* (1990) elevating him in wealth and prestige to a level close to that of Elton himself. His 1991 cover-songs tour had included 'Don't Let the Sun . . .', hence the duet and single, which topped the British charts for two weeks, earned a Grammy nomination and gifted Elton his first number-one single in America for many years.

Elton and Michael remained friends through the '90s, although the former's now sober lifestyle and the latter's now reliance on drugs didn't exactly mesh. Behind closed doors, George resented Elton's attempts to get him into rehab, even when an addiction to sleeping pills caused him to hit the headlines. 'I don't want to know about God, I don't want to join some cult,' he told Elton, refusing to take any further advice on the subject.

The two remained on cordial terms for a time, attending the funeral of their mutual friend Princess Diana together in 1997, but a split came in 2004 when Elton referred to Michael's problems in the press. He stated that his friend was in a 'strange place' and that there was a 'deep-rooted unhappiness' in his life, which caused the infuriated Michael to write a letter to the gossip magazine *Heat*, essentially telling Elton to shut up and mind his own business.

'Elton John knows very little about George Michael and that's a fact,' he seethed. 'Contrary to the public's impression, we have spoken rarely in the past ten years and what would probably surprise most people is that we have never discussed my private life. Ever . . . Other than that he knows I don't like to tour, I smoke too much pot and my albums still have a habit of going to number one.' Ouch!

Michael reinforced this in an interview with Michael Parkinson in 2006, claiming that Elton would 'not be happy until I bang on his door in the middle of the night saying, "Please, please, help me, Elton. Take me to rehab." It's not going to happen . . . Elton just needs to shut his mouth and get on with his own life.' Double ouch!

Although the *Daily Mail* reported that the schism had been resolved by 2011, with a source glibly explaining, 'They have been seeing each other quite a lot. The feud is finally over. George and Elton are getting on brilliantly again and everybody is thrilled', the two were never seen together in public again.

Michael's death on Christmas Day 2016 at the age of fifty-three was attributed to natural causes, but unsubstantiated rumours have circulated to the effect that the singer had grappled with heroin and methadone addictions in his final years. At this point, it's unlikely this will ever be proven or disproven.

In 2019, Elton told his friend Sharon Osbourne on her American TV show, *The Talk*: '[George] resented the fact that I had hinted that maybe he change his life a little bit and he'd be happier if he tried something else . . . The person has actually got to want it. It's like me in the end; I really wanted it. I had two alternatives: one, to die, and one to live, and I wanted to live. But that's the difference if you want it, and poor George didn't want it.'

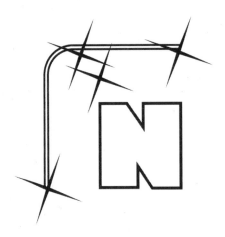

'NIKITA'

From Russia with love

One of the most memorable moments of an otherwise largely forgettable period in Elton John's career was the track 'Nikita'. Released in October 1985 as the lead single from the otherwise largely forgettable album *Ice on Fire*, 'Nikita' became Elton's biggest worldwide hit since 'Don't Go Breaking My Heart' almost twenty years before, reaching number three in the UK, number seven in America and number one in eight countries around the world.

A languid song of longing, the lyrics describe the singer's long-distance love for Nikita, a Russian border guard at the Berlin Wall that he can no longer be with as he is not allowed into the country. Although the video, shot by film-maker Ken Russell, with whom Elton had last worked on 'Pinball Wizard' from the 1975 Who movie, *Tommy*, depicts Nikita as an inscrutable fur-hatted woman, it was noted by some journalists that in Russia, 'Nikita is a man's name – something Elton said he was aware of but unconcerned by.'

Anya Major, who played the title role in the video, was a 29-year-old former athlete, actress and model, who had appeared the year before in Apple's ground-breaking '1984' commercial, spinning on her heels while wielding a sledgehammer. Elsewhere in the video, she and Elton are depicted in various 'romantic' scenes together, playing chess, going ten-pin bowling and one scene where she is wearing the colours of Watford, while Elton appears to be dressed as a Turkish shopkeeper in a fez. The video also featured Elton's own red Bentley Continental Convertible. None of which added much to the song but rewarded the singer with a video that channels around the world were happy to endlessly rotate. Safe, easy on the eye, it was an entirely '80s creation.

There was one other minor hit single from the album, 'Wrap Her Up'. Featuring Elton's new bestie George Michael on guest vocals and Kiki Dee on backing vocals, it sounded exactly like what it was: a generic '80s pop song written-by-committee (no less than six names received a co-credit on the sleeve); a sugar rush that quickly faded. Not even the return of producer Gus Dudgeon could prevent *Ice on Fire* from sounding like the other good-not-great albums Elton had released in the '80s. So, while 'Nikita' helped propel *Ice on Fire* into the top five in the UK, it became his lowest-charting album so far in the US, tiptoeing to number forty-nine.

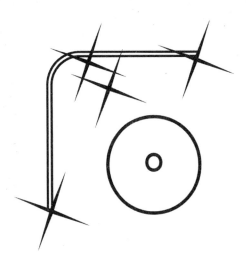

OSBORNE, GARY

Gary had his own method

In 1977, Elton John and his lyricist Bernie Taupin severed their songwriting relationship, albeit on a friendly basis, wanting to work separately for a time. But while the latter went off to work with Alice Cooper and other artists, Elton simply hired a new guy to pen his words for him, a talented singer-songwriter named Gary Osborne.

Born into showbiz royalty in 1949, Gary is the son of the late musical director Tony Osborne, a professional pianist and trumpeter who became famous as an arranger able to handle prima donnas like Shirley Bassey, Judy Garland and Eartha Kitt. 'There's no problem,' he remarked. 'You just talk back to them in the same language.'

Educated privately in Switzerland, Osborne first got involved in the music business when he was just fifteen. It began when he and his sister Jan – who later married Small Faces/Who drummer Kenney Jones – recorded one of Gary's songs together, a seductively offbeat duet by two lovers having fun pretending to be innocent, 'I'm Not to Blame'. Assisted by Petula Clark's producer Alan A. Freeman, a single was issued in 1965 under the moniker

Gary and Jan Lorraine. People liked it. Crooners of the day such as Nana Mouskouri and Val Doonican now looked to the young writer for fresh material.

Osborne was seventeen when he had his first American hit, a co-write with the established hit-maker Tom Springfield (older brother of Dusty) called 'On the Other Side', which the Seekers took into the charts in 1966. His upward trajectory turned Osborne into a dashing London 'face'. He was still in his teens when he began presenting the *Cool Britannia* radio show on the BBC World Service. By the early '70s Osborne was working for RCA (Elvis Presley's label) in its London A&R department. He then turned his hand to advertising jingles, writing hundreds of songs for brands such as Pepsi, Abbey National and Shredded Wheat.

He soon connected with the composer Jeff Wayne, who produced two albums by Osborne and the singer Paul Vigrass: the first of these, 1972's *Queues*, contained three moderately successful singles. The following year he wrote the English lyrics to 'Amoureuse', the French song which became Kiki Dee's first hit on Rocket Records and thus the Elton John connection was made.

Elton had to change his working process to accommodate Osborne, who preferred to write lyrics to music, whereas Bernie Taupin had always supplied the lyrics first. On balance, Osborne's method makes sense, it's easier to edit words to match the music rather than the other way around. On the other hand, the guy writing the music is Elton John. Some accommodation was surely available? But no. Gary had his method and Elton, spurred on by the challenge, knuckled down to the task at hand.

The two men wrote some truly world-class songs together and enjoyed their share of million-selling forever hits: 'Part-Time Love' in 1978, a likeable rom-com set to music which took Elton back into the top twenty in both Britain and America for the first time since 'Sorry Seems to Be . . . ' two years before. 'Little Jeannie' in 1979 gave him his first US top-five hit since the pop ditty with Kiki Dee three years before. Then there was the immaculate 'Blue Eyes' (1982), a tender tribute that later became an elegy for Vance Buck, Elton's former beau who died of AIDS-related causes in 1993. Although originally a love song, there's a posthumous morbidity to it that is sickly sweet – the sound of last orders at the bar, resignation, and regret, for when the moon is blue. The mood draws you in like quicksand and leaves you floating with your thoughts.

Their close friendship became equally important. On one occasion Elton called Osborne for emotional support, having been jilted by a boyfriend on Christmas Day. Left alone, as he later recalled, with only unopened presents and an uncooked turkey, the staff at Woodside having been given a seasonal holiday, the star was bereft. Gary and his wife Jenny changed their own Christmas plans and immediately came down to Windsor to keep him company – an act of generosity Elton has never forgotten.

Other occasions were more cheerful. Elton, a keen card player but with a gossipy reputation for not always paying off his gambling debts, once racked up such a loss to Osborne that Gary insisted he cough up at once.

'All right, what do you want?' Elton reportedly said.

'I want that,' Osborne replied, pointing to one of Elton's sports cars.

His debtor promptly handed over the keys.

Not everyone welcomed Elton's choice of new lyricist. The acclaimed biographer Philip Norman wrote, 'It was his personality that appealed to Elton.' Osborne's lyrics 'were bread and butter where Bernie Taupin would have provided sherry trifle.'

The songwriting partnership between Elton and Gary lasted for around five years, but although they crafted several top-drawer tunes, the hits were generally thin on the ground – certainly compared to Elton's history-making run with Bernie.

By *Too Low For Zero* in 1983, Taupin was back full-time and Osborne had moved on. He had been the main lyricist on the 1978 'album musical', *Jeff Wayne's Musical Version of the War of the Worlds*, which sold 15 million copies. Other collaborators keen to benefit from the Osborne touch included the singer-songwriter Jennifer Warnes, R&B singer Millie Jackson and veterans such as Cliff Richard, former Chicago bassist Peter Cetera and the Righteous Brothers. As recently as 2006 he was enjoying chart hits with Lil' Chris, a pop-punk artist from the reality-TV show, *Rock School*.

Osborne was in the news most recently when a legal tussle with his sister Jan over their late mother's estate made headlines. 'Gary Osborne has enjoyed a glittering five-decades long career in music,' burbled the *Daily Mail*. 'His biggest success was in writing the lyrics to Jeff Wayne's musical retelling of H. G. Wells' *War of the Worlds*, which finally scored him an Ivor Novello Award in 2011.'

Proof indeed that even a creative and personal relationship with a star like Elton John can be outshone by a sci-fi yarn.

PEACHTREE ROAD
The dark side of the street

Named after Peachtree Road, the northern part of Peachtree Street in Atlanta, Georgia, where one of his many homes was located, Elton John's twenty-seventh solo album was a decidedly low-key affair. No longer manically focused on making a hit record, his appetite for that sort of instant gratification was satiated, in the UK at least, after two consecutive number-one singles. The first, his 2002 collaboration with Britain's then hottest boyband, Blue, on a new hip-hop-lite version of 'Sorry Seems to Be the Hardest Word'. The second, the remixed and upgraded-for-the-new-century version of 'Are You Ready for Love', which went straight in at number one in its first week of release in August 2003.

Elton was on a roll and looked to be enjoying himself, not giving a damn what anyone thought about it, as long as he thought it was good. Which it was. The arrival in November 2004 of *Peachtree Road* was of an entirely different order, however. The only album on which he had sole credit as producer, *Peachtree Road* was heartfelt verging on dour.

Harking back to his earliest albums, the emphasis was on art for art's sake, with Elton and Bernie Taupin free to roam wherever it took their fancy. The opening track, 'Weight of the World', set the tone, world-weary, dry, backed up with violins, cellos, violas, a nine-voice choir and Elton's lonely piano. There's a gospel undertone to tracks like 'Answer in the Sky', shades of Bernie's beloved Americana on the country-tinged 'Turn the Lights Out When You Leave', wincingly confessional on 'My Elusive Drug' and an almost Dylan-esque focus on mortality on 'It's Getting Dark in Here'.

There were no obvious hit songs and only one track, 'All That I'm Allowed (I'm Thankful)', that touched the edge of the UK top twenty. Worldwide sales reflected that fact, with it becoming one of Elton's worst-selling albums. *Peachtree Road* remains a good-not-great album, one for the small hours, perhaps, reflecting on a chequered past . . . after everyone else has gone home.

'Pinball Wizard'

That short fat blind kid sure plays a mean pinball

Elton John has never really bothered to try and make the transition from rock star to movie star: no Elvis Presley or Harry Styles-type silver-screen ambitions for him. Still, had he ever made the effort, he might well have brought something to the world of cinema: his brief, but captivating turn in the 1975 movie *Tommy* remains magnetic to this day.

Directed by the flamboyant British film director Ken Russell, *Tommy* is an adaptation of the Who's 1969 album of the same name. Like the original concept LP – a 'rock opera' about a deaf, dumb and blind kid (in late-'60s parlance of the lyrics) who plays out-of-this-world pinball and thus achieves godhood – Russell's movie is fascinating but flawed. The plot doesn't make much sense, but the cast and soundtrack are great and the cameo appearances endlessly watchable.

Prominent among these is the Pinball Wizard, the 'Bally table king' played by Elton. A sneering, posturing brat who engages in a pinball showdown against Tommy himself – played by Who singer Roger Daltrey – Elton looms above everyone else in a pair of four-foot-high Doc Marten boots. Lip-synching to his own version of the song 'Pinball Wizard', Elton can't do much from his position atop his boots but point, pout and pretend to play a mini-keyboard attached to his pinball machine – but his is the image that everyone always remembers most clearly from the film.

Yet he almost didn't appear in the film, having turned it down a couple of times already: even then, the Who's rock-savant guitarist Pete Townshend had the singer Tiny Tim in mind for the role. Producer Robert Stigwood insisted on Elton. It was a brilliant piece of casting. The PR department spread a 'rumour' that Elton had only taken part after it was agreed that he could keep the boots afterwards. Buzz building from the get-go.

'Of course, it became an iconic scene in the movie with the fucking boots and clinging onto the pinball machine for dear life,' said Elton.

It's still the only clip they show whenever *Tommy* is referenced on TV or online.

The film version of the 'Pinball Wizard' song was released as a promo-only single in the US and didn't chart for that reason, but made number seven in the UK. It's a faster, much more energetic, all-round bigger version of the original, with Elton's high-pitched wails a world away from his modern baritone and a reminder of what a force of nature he was in his younger days.

He still plays the song today: connoisseurs consider it the best cover of a Who track ever recorded.

As for the boots? Stephen Briggs, whose company was the UK licensee for Doc Martens, paid £11,000 for them in 1988 – the modern equivalent of around £30,000. A relatively meagre outlay for a genuine piece of rock history.

PLAYBOY

Elton gets 'em off

In 1975, while living the high/low life in Los Angeles, Elton John agreed to participate in one of *Playboy* magazine's famous interviews. This was prestige stuff, the no-place-to-hide Q&A style of the *Playboy Interview*, as it was always billed, reserved only for such international figures as Martin Luther King Jr, Frank Sinatra, Jean-Paul Sartre, Stanley Kubrick and many others of the same stratospheric ilk.

Confessional, candid, taboo-breaking, the *Playboy Interview* format was renowned for its ground-breaking approach. Nevertheless, Elton managed to reveal more than anyone – even the magazine's editors – could have anticipated about the dark side of being the world's biggest-selling rock star.

Published as the cover story of the January 1976 edition of *Playboy*, accompanied by some informal Terry O'Neill photographic portraits that were as warts-and-all as the story and billed as 'a candid conversation with the unlikeliest, flashiest pop star of them all', the story began: 'Five years ago, Elton John was just another schlub like the rest of us. He was broke half the time, he was shorter even than Robert Redford, his hair was already beginning to thin, he was usually more plump than he liked and he wore glasses as thick as Coke-bottle bottoms.'

The interview was conducted, the magazine reported, beneath 'a Bedouin-style canopy' overlooking Greta Garbo's gazebo. Over several pages, Elton spoke freely – mostly – about topics ranging from his view of the tabloid papers that now followed his every move to those old warhorses, sex and drugs, to money, success and the fear of failure and most unexpected of all, his dysfunctional childhood, fraught relationship with his parents and their bitter divorce.

The magazine reported that Elton had personally earned more than £8 million in 1975, a claim he didn't dispute, while pointing out others earned more but that he got the attention because, 'I probably flaunt it more than anyone else. I spend lots on myself.'

He appeared sanguine about tabloid coverage, even that in the *National Enquirer* and the *National Star*, which had become America's best-selling tabloids through their willingness to write up the most outrageous rumours. Claiming that when he read something in a tabloid that was 'absolute rubbish' he'll think, 'How dare they print that? Then I'll turn to the next page and read about someone else and go, "Hmm, did they really do that?" I'm the first person to get sucked in.'

The magazine tiptoed around the subject of his sexuality, already well known around LA and London and other metropolitan elites, yet not yet broached explicitly in public forums, by enquiring disingenuously if Elton 'got off on the bisexuality scene', as evoked by the other English rock stars like Mick Jagger and David Bowie. His reply was equally disingenuous: 'I really don't know what to say about it,' before adeptly moving the subject on to those celebs of either gender who could still make him stare in awe when they entered a room. 'Jagger, Sinatra, Elvis, probably. Also, people like Noël Coward, Edith Piaf and Katharine Hepburn.'

When it came to a straight question about drugs, Elton was even more devious: 'I've got a completely split personality. One minute I'm up, then I change like the wind.' Rather like a cocaine addict, although perhaps the magazine didn't dare say so.

The big reveal of the interview concerned his lonely upbringing and the 'terrible inferiority complex' his physical appearance – short, chubby, bespectacled – had left him with. A situation entirely exacerbated, he suggested, by his tyrannic former-RAF father, Stanley Dwight: 'My father was so stupid with me, it was ridiculous . . . it was just pure hate.'

Elton said he had been left so isolated by his fractured childhood he had grown up 'with inanimate objects as my friends.' It was why he enjoyed spending so much of his money on gifts for himself and others and why he felt the need to hold onto possessions: 'I'll look at them and remember when they gave me a bit of happiness – which is more than human beings have given me.'

It was this section of the interview that drew the rabid attention of the British tabloid press. The *Daily Mail* tracked Stanley down to a house in Cheshire, where he told their reporter Sally Brompton that he refuted his son's various claims about missing his birth, had kept a home posting with the RAF until Reggie was fifteen months old, did not 'hate' children and certainly did not regard his son as 'a mistake'.

Stanley went on to say that his solicitor had advised him to sue both *Playboy* and/or Elton personally and that he had refused: 'I don't want to do anything that would alienate Reggie. I just don't understand why he's started saying all these awful things.' He explained that the last time he had seen Elton, he had played football in the garden with his four younger half-brothers and had slipped a cheque for £2,000 into his 'Aunt Edna's' pocket in order for her to buy the Peugeot 504 she had her eye on. However, since then Elton had withdrawn all contact, stopped phoning on Christmas Day and sending birthday cards to the boys, or even replying to their letters.

'He doesn't seem very happy to me,' Stanley told Brompton. He said the last time they had spoken he had asked his son who his friends were: 'He said Elvis Presley and Billie Jean King.' Adding sadly, 'I think Reggie has to buy his friendships.'

PUTIN, VLADIMIR
To Vlad, Love Elton

It's hard to imagine now, given the horror that he has visited upon Ukraine, that the early years of Vladimir Putin's Russian presidency were those of greater cooperation with the west. Back in 2000, he was calling for Russian membership of NATO. In 2001, he offered Russian military forces to support US troops in Afghanistan. He addressed the German Bundestag. His oligarchs were buying mansions, yachts, art, football clubs, washing dirty money, exercising soft power. However, Putin's relations with the emergent east – India and China – were less well formed. By September 2015, he was preparing to meet with then US President Barack Obama and speak at the United Nations in New York. He went on the American news magazine TV show *60 Minutes* and told of his admiration for America's 'openness'.

At home, of course, it was a different story. There, he was an unreconstructed autocrat, his power built on major muscle, decades-deep corruption, immense wealth and the fear of a former officer of the KGB, a man that hunted bare-chested on horse-back for the cameras. In 2013, he had passed a law banning 'the propaganda of non-traditional sexual relations among minors': its meaning was clear.

In 2014, Elton placed an open letter to Putin on his website condemning the 'vicious' legislation and its consequences, which he had heard first-hand during his tour of Russia in 1979. As follows: 'The people I met in Moscow – gay men and lesbians in their twenties, thirties and forties – told me stories about receiving threats from vigilante groups who would "cure" them of homosexuality by dousing them with urine or beating them up. Everyone shared stories of verbal and physical abuse – at work, in bars and restaurants or in the street.'

The story took a bizarre turn when Elton visited Ukraine in 2007 to lobby for LGBTQ+ rights and followed up with an Instagram post saying that Putin had called him and that he looked forward to meeting him 'face to face to discuss LGBT equality in Russia'. A call like that was perhaps not completely beyond the bounds of possibility: Putin had praised Elton publicly several times and acknowledged his huge popularity within Russia. But Putin's spokesman, Dmitry Peskov, was quick to deny that any call had taken place. As soon as he had done so, a pair of hoaxers well known in Russia for prank-calling celebrities revealed that they were responsible.

'We thought it wasn't likely that Putin would want to meet with him and call, at least not so quickly,' said Vladimir 'Vovan' Krasnov, who said he had impersonated Putin while his co-prankster, Alexei 'Lexus' Stolyarov, had posed as the president's spokesman, Dmitry Peskov. 'But it turned out that Elton John was really waiting for this call and so he immediately believed it really was a conversation with the people who we said we were,' he told newspaper *Komsomolskaya Pravda*. 'He said: "Thank you, you've made my day. This day and this conversation has been the most wonderful and lovely in my life."'

'It was so genuine-sounding, I had no idea,' said Elton. 'I answered the questions very studiously, so I didn't really feel bad when it came out that it was a hoax, I didn't feel like I'd made a fool of myself. And then the next day, the actual Kremlin get in touch: "President Putin is very upset about this, he'd like to call you." I was at home in Windsor, in the kitchen, when he rang. We spoke for about ten minutes.'

Elton said he remained optimistic about getting through to Putin, at least on the subject of LGBTQ+ rights: 'Do I think anything's going to come of it? I sincerely hope so, whether or not anything will happen, even if I do go and meet him, I don't know. But if you don't put your foot in the water, you'll never find out.'

According to the *real* Peskov, Putin, 'said he knows how popular a performer Elton John is. If in the future their schedules allow, he's ready to meet with him and discuss any questions that interest him.'

Despite the call, Putin continued to stress 'traditional' rights to his audience in Russia and the meeting never happened. Things would become darker after that. *Much* darker.

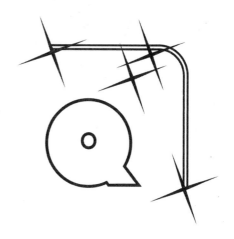

Quotes: The Bitch Is Back

What a terrible thing to say

The man who sang 'The Bitch Is Back' has never been backwards about coming forwards, as his mother might have said. Here are some of his most eye-opening quotes.

On Janet Jackson:
'You know, fucking music magazines writing a review of Janet Jackson, saying: "This is the greatest show – four and a half stars". It's fucking lip-synched! Hello! I'd rather go and see a drag queen. Fuck off!'

On the state of modern pop:
'There's so much good music out there. Much better than all the pop shit they play on Radio 1. I never liked shows like *The X Factor*; I'm glad they are on the way out.'

On sex:
'I am the most well-known homosexual in the world . . . I think people should be free to engage in any sexual practices they choose; they should draw the line at goats though.'

On drugs:
'I was more ashamed that I couldn't work the washing machine than the fact that I was taking drugs.'

On religion:
'The reality is that organised religion doesn't seem to work. It turns people into hateful lemmings and it's not really compassionate.'

On overbearing security staff at a show in Gloucestershire:
'I came here to play music. All you stewards down there – especially the woman in the ponytail – fucking lighten up, will you? These people have come to hear music and if they want to put their hands in the air, let them. This is not fucking China, so piss off! You've got a fucking uniform on and you think you're Hitler and you're not. You can piss off!'

On music videos:
'I couldn't give a fuck! I make music, I don't make fucking films. I hate fucking videos! They're fucking loathsome!'

On clubbing:
'What I want to do now is completely different to going to a gay club when I was twenty-eight and picking up a bloke. The thought of going to a club now fills me with complete horror.'

On British TV soap, EastEnders:
'We see enough misery in the newspapers every day without having to tune in to some poor cunt boiling an egg in *EastEnders* and having his fucking head chopped off because his wife doesn't like him. Oh, fuck off, there's so much misery around! Fuck off! We're addicted to misery in this country. Fucking *EastEnders*!'

On record company chiefs:
'I think most heads of most record companies are idiots. About 5 per cent are any good. They're only in it for themselves, they don't care about artists. They're all about the next fix, the next single. It's like they're having a hit of cocaine every fifteen seconds. And if somebody falls by the wayside, they're by the wayside. They're not allowed one blip. In America, most of them are idiots. They're sickening, actually. They sicken me. They're thick as shit.'

On the piano:
'I play [hundreds of] shows a year, why am I going to go home and play the fucking piano? I've got one at Woodside and one at my house in Atlanta, and I never touch them. Rufus Wainwright plays every morning when he gets up – "I have to play an hour every day" – so everyone's different, but, God, I couldn't think of anything worse. I have leisure and I have work. And I do enough work. When I get home, the last thing I want to do is play the piano.'

On the guitar:
'I've always wanted to smash a guitar over someone's head. You just can't do that with a piano.'

On fame:
'I loathe celebrity. I can't stand it . . . Fame attracts lunatics.'

On Bernie Taupin:
'I have no fucking idea how our relationship works . . . I've never had an argument with him in my life, not about work, not about personal things, nothing. And we're totally different people. I mean, he's a fucking cowboy who likes guns and I collect tablecloths and porcelain. It's very odd.'

On Rod Stewart's version of 'Country Comfort':
'It sounds like he made it up as he played it − I mean, he couldn't possibly have got farther away from the original. It was like "Camptown Races".'

On David Bowie:
'The best thing to happen to your records is for you to die . . . Obviously, no one wanted David to die, but it's astonishing how many records he's sold since − something like 2 million in two weeks. And that's CDs . . .'

On his decision to prevent Donald Trump playing Elton John songs at his rallies:
'I don't really want my music to be involved in anything to do with an American election campaign. I'm British. I've met Donald Trump, he was very nice to me, it's nothing personal. His political views are his own, mine are very different, I'm not a Republican in a million years. Why not ask Ted fucking Nugent? Or one of those fucking country stars? They'll do it for you.'

On Keith Richards:
'Like a monkey with arthritis.'

On the next Elton John album:
'Who really needs a new album from me?'

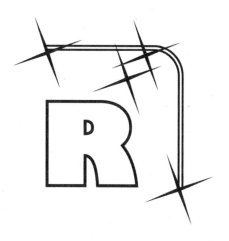

REG STRIKES BACK
Trash-can dreams

Billed as his official comeback album – his first since his throat operation in 1987 and, less publicised, his first since the disappointing *Leather Jackets* two years before – it was hoped *Reg Strikes Back* would return Elton John to the rock firmament he had spent most of the '80s tumbling from. Those hopes were dashed however, as once again Elton delivered an album hobbled by mostly second-rate material and a production so rooted in '80s studio orthodoxy it sounded workmanlike at best, just plain dull at worst.

Chris Thomas was back in the production hotseat, but without songs as strong as 'I'm Still Standing' and 'I Guess That's Why They Call It the Blues', which Thomas had previously produced, not even he could make songs as strangely convoluted as 'Japanese Hands' and 'Since God Invented Girls' climb up off the floor. As for 'Mona Lisas and Mad Hatters (Part Two)', what the connection was between this try-hard Noo Yoik funk-rock belter and the delicate original ballad remains a riddle. Yes, both sets of lyrics are about the 'trash-can dreams' of Manhattan, but only the original is worthy of repeat listens.

In America, the upbeat pop of 'I Don't Wanna Go with You Like That' became Elton's biggest solo single since 'Island Girl' in 1975, reaching number two. Nobody really knew why, only that it couldn't have been the dreadful video where he is dressed in a grey suit, grey shirt, grey tie and grey fedora. Elton was still only forty-one but the video made him look about twenty years older. In Britain, by contrast, the single tipped in at number thirty. The album didn't benefit either, scraping into the lower reaches of the top twenty in Britain and America before vanishing. As comebacks go, this one came and went back again quickly.

REID, JOHN

'Young, ambitious, very confident and very funny'

You know the drill when it comes to the pantheon of Great Rock Managers. From carnival king 'Colonel' Tom Parker to the more genteel Brian Epstein, to the devilish Peter Grant, the scheming Tony Defries or the prankster Malcolm McLaren. A biography of any of them tends to be quite one-sided: it's all too easy to focus on their eccentricities, or in the case of Elton John's former manager and lover, John Reid, on his tendency to wade in with his fists in a tight spot. Indeed, Reid has earned his place in the above list several times over, having managed Elton from 1972–98, while also adroitly handling the affairs of Queen from 1975–78. How he juggled these two huge clients for that three-year period beggars belief, but it was almost certainly down to an ability to work incredibly hard, think on his feet, always aim high and to have an extremely low tolerance for bullshit.

Where did those skills come from? Instinct and talent rather than background, it seems, as Reid didn't have a leg-up into the music business, coming as he did from working-class roots. Born in Paisley, near Glasgow, on 9 September 1949, he was interested in show business from an early age – not that his career started well. A teenage attempt to manage two singing brothers, the McBrides, who attended Reid's school, went awry when some enemies of the McBrides appeared in the playground and began beating the brothers up. Attempting to intervene, Reid was assaulted too.

A more successful flirtation with the limelight came when Reid acted in an amateur dramatic company at the Glasgow Pantheon Club, appearing in musicals such as *Kiss Me, Kate*. He also sang with the house band at Glasgow's Locarno Ballroom. Later, he studied marine engineering at college, but this went nowhere and by the time he was twenty, Reid had moved down to London to try his luck there.

Once in the capital, Reid worked for Ardmore & Beechwood Limited, a music publishing division of EMI, and within a few years he had risen to the position of UK manager for the American Tamla Motown label. He did well there: it was his decision to issue Smokey Robinson & the Miracles' 'Tears of a Clown' as a British single, the American label only releasing it in the US after it was already number one in the UK.

An early friend in London was Barbara Windsor, the bubbly blonde star of the hugely popular *Carry On* film franchise, who Reid was introduced to backstage at her West End show, *Come Spy with Me*. 'He kept coming to the theatre to see me,' she later recalled. 'Even though young, he had a good head on him. There was nothing he didn't know about show business. I found this young man very exciting.' She added that Reid often talked about wanting to be a millionaire with a Rolls-Royce by the time he was twenty-one, a goal that he ultimately missed by only a couple of years.

John Reid first met Elton John in 1970 at the tenth anniversary celebrations of Motown Records in San Francisco, where Elton was making an unscheduled appearance at the new SF version of the Troubadour. Two years younger than the singer, Reid later recalled his first impression of Elton as a 'dumpy, balding little guy in a funny jump suit who used to go around cadging records'.

Elton was more impressed, writing that Reid was 'young, ambitious, very confident and very funny', and was keen to get to know him, having read Robert Hilburn's prophetic review of Elton's Troubadour show. 'He rang me up,' Reid later remembered. 'He was bubbling over with what the critics had said and dying to tell someone about it. I was the nearest Englishman – or nearest thing to an Englishman.'

The two men first slept together the following night: a particularly memorable date for Elton as it was his first such experience. By 1971, the pair were sharing a flat in the Water Gardens development on the Edgware Road, London, and the following year, Reid became his lover's manager, at Elton's own suggestion. This solved an ongoing problem as Elton's former manager, Ray Williams, had quit the role in September 1970. Since then, Dick James, his son Stephen and DJM's A&R man Steve Brown had been handling Elton's business affairs: this was a temporary solution at best, as none of them had the time to do the job properly.

When Reid was suggested for the role, Dick James was surprised but saw the logic in the idea, famously quipping to Brown: 'Who else can we rely on to get Elton out of bed in the morning than the guy he's in bed with?'

It wasn't an easy transition for Reid, who was understandably nervous about his ability to do the job. So unsure was he, in fact, that after he handed in his notice at EMI, he changed his mind when the company protested. 'They went bananas, saying, "How can you do this? We were getting you ready for great things!" So

I withdrew my notice again,' he recalled. 'Then, after a month, I thought "Oh, shit! I really should do it." I was pretty scared because I'd no management experience, no legal experience, no financial experience.'

It was agreed that Reid would become an employee of DJM on a salary of £4,000 per year – roughly equivalent to £80,000 today – which was quite a coup for the 22-year-old novice. It was understood that he would become Elton's full-time manager when DJM's contract expired in March 1973, although in the event he only stayed until August 1972 when he set up his own company, John Reid Enterprises.

Once Elton had signed on the dotted line, Reid quickly went about advising his client on every aspect of his career, bar the actual music. His first move was to suggest a change of image, from the mundane studio garb he habitually wore to a more extravagant look – a suggestion which paid off handsomely and which has sustained him throughout his career.

Elton and Reid were inseparable until around 1975, when the former's career went stratospheric: they split when he moved to Woodside the following year, having simply drifted apart. Their business relationship remained strong, difficult as that might be to believe, and if anything, Reid's command of Elton's commercial affairs went from strength to strength from this point.

Major milestones during Reid's tenure as Elton's manager include the famous lawsuit against Dick James Enterprises, the foundation and chaotic trajectory of Rocket Records and a renegotiated deal in America with MCA in 1974. When the good times rolled, they rolled hard, with Reid buying luxury property around the world as well as exotic yachts, Porsches, Lamborghinis and Jaguars, and expensive fripperies such as Fabergé clocks.

In 1975, Reid also became Queen's manager, a three-year gig that made sense at the time because Elton was taking a break from the road and Reid only had one other client, Kiki Dee.

Freddie Mercury et al. needed a manager to extricate them from a punitive contract they'd signed with the Trident company, which had left them with serious debts, and considered Peter Grant and Don Arden before settling on Reid, who had been recommended to them by EMI's chairman, Sir Joseph Lockwood.

The move paid off, with Reid freeing the four Queen members to go and make their best music while he took care of business: he also became a close confidante to Freddie Mercury, to whom he gave valuable support when the singer was struggling with his sexuality. The group enjoyed more success with *A Day at The Races* (1976) and *News of the World* (1977) but by 1978 Reid's three years were up and he signed an amicable severance agreement in the back of Freddie's new Rolls-Royce. He later described it as 'the gentlest parting of the ways of anyone I have ever worked with' – in stark contrast to later developments with Elton, to whom he returned with renewed focus after leaving Queen to manage themselves.

Chummy as that sounds, make no mistake: Reid was notorious in the music industry for his temper. As early as 1974, *Rolling Stone* had described the 5ft 6 manager as 'small and short fused', citing a source who said, 'He's diminutive, but he's a killer. He'll punch anyone.' Furthermore, Elton's biographer Philip Norman wrote, 'There [are] John Reid stories from all over the world, in tones varying from warm affection to bitter hatred, and from amusement to outright terror.'

A list of incidents had led to this reputation, usually involving Reid punching journalists. One of these was a writer called David Wheeler, who Reid assaulted in Auckland, New Zealand, in 1974: earlier that day, Reid had thrown champagne in a party organiser's face and slapped a woman called Judith Baragwanath when she tried to intervene. Reid was arrested and sentenced to a month in jail for the assault on Wheeler.

'They're isolated incidents,' Reid told *Rolling Stone* as far back as 1974. 'I don't make excuses, I'm not particularly proud of it, but any time anything like this has happened, it's been in defense of Elton or Bernie, not for personal reasons.'

In 1979, Reid was arrested again, this time in San Francisco, after hitting a hotel doorman with his silver-handled ebony cane, and yet another journalist took a Reid-shaped beating the day after Elton's marriage to Renate Blauel in 1984.

Elton and Reid had their stormy moments, too. In 1983, while filming the video for 'I'm Still Standing' in the south of France, Elton went on a night out with Duran Duran, who introduced him to vodka martinis. After downing eight of these, Elton trashed his hotel room and attacked Reid, breaking his nose.

The staff of Rocket Records often bore the brunt of Reid's temper, too. As Rocket's employee Penny Valentine told biographer Philip Norman: 'You could always tell when he was going to explode. He'd suddenly go bright red in the face. He'd got one of those tempers that, for a moment or two, are totally uncontrollable . . . I'd come in in the morning and find him sitting on the stairs with his head in his hands. "What shall I do?" he'd say. "I've fired the whole staff."'

This was noted by the press, with Nigel Dempster of the *Daily Mail* gleefully writing: 'The pathetic sight of a small group of colourfully dressed people locked out on a Mayfair pavement is the latest evidence of pop millionaire John Reid's increasing eccentricity. Passers-by in South Audley Street were treated to the vision of Rocket staff being unceremoniously bundled out on to the pavement . . . A victim of last year's screaming match, former promotions manager Arthur Sherriff tells me, "These sackings are an annual event at the very least."'

As time passed, Reid expanded his business interests, acquiring an interest in the Edinburgh Playhouse Theatre in 1976 and opening a restaurant called Friends in London's Covent Garden. He also surprised his social circle in 1978 by becoming engaged to Sarah Forbes, daughter of the director Bryan Forbes and the actor Nanette Newman, although it was soon called off. The following year, Reid was seriously under consideration as a potential Conservative MP candidate in the constituency of Orkney and Shetland, being groomed for the role by Tory backbenchers of his acquaintance, although he didn't pursue this either.

We know relatively little about Reid's personal life, but we do know that after Elton successfully tackled his addictions in 1990, Reid followed suit. He underwent rehab for alcoholism at the same clinic, the Cedars-Sinai Medical Center in Los Angeles. 'I became very depressed after a friend died of AIDS,' he told the *Daily Record* some years later. 'I was drinking lots of wine, brandy, gin – up to a bottle of spirits a day most days. If I had carried on the way I was, I would probably have killed myself.' He added: 'Elton called me regularly. He was a tower of strength.'

Reid continued to manage artists in the '90s, adding Andrew Lloyd Webber, Lionel Richie and the boyband Another Level to the roster. His most high-profile client other than Elton was the Irish dancer Michael Flatley of the hugely popular cabaret troupe Riverdance, although that relationship soured in 1994. A wrongful-termination lawsuit between them was settled with a £1 million payout from Flatley to Reid.

Elton and Reid finally parted ways as client and manager in 1998, although legal processes dragged on for a couple of years before the dust finally settled. The rift originally began when the *Daily Mirror* ran a story about how much money Elton spent on lifestyle items, information which the singer assumed had been leaked from Reid's office.

'He was incandescent with rage . . . he believed that someone from John Reid Enterprises had sold that information to the newspapers and told me in no uncertain terms to find out how it happened,' said Reid, as reported by the BBC. 'I was very angry about it too and for a couple of weeks there was a terrible tension between myself and Elton and within the office structure, because everyone was under suspicion of having somehow leaked this letter to the press.' It emerged that no deliberate leak had taken place: instead, financial documents had been taken from rubbish bins at the offices. Nevertheless, that oversight was enough for Elton to sever the relationship and Reid retired from management the following year.

In 2000, Elton sued Reid and his accountants Price Waterhouse Coopers for what he claimed was a £20 million theft in the form of unpaid touring expenses: these, he argued, should have been met out of the management's commission. Reid quickly settled out of court, paying Elton £3.4 million. But a parallel case against PWC and Reid's former managing director Andrew Haydon went to the High Court. Elton lost this case in 2001 and was obliged to meet the defendants' legal costs.

'It's very sad that the long relationship I had with Elton has ended this way,' Reid told *The Guardian* in 2001. 'I feel that the question mark that has been hanging over my integrity for the past three years has been removed and that was the most important thing to me in this case. It should never have come to trial. It was ill advised.'

As is so often the way with legal cases such as this one, the real interest for Elton fans lies in the nuggets of information that are disclosed along the way. As the *Telegraph* reported after the case closed, Reid's company earned £73.5 million from Elton's business between 1980 and 1998, with annual revenue peaking at £15 million.

We also learned that Elton was not keen to take advice about saving money for the future. As he told the court, 'I'm not a nest egg person . . . Why can't I drop dead on stage? I have no intention of retiring. I may have said in concerts that I was retiring, because I was not in a very good mood. But I'm nearly fifty-four now and I'm enjoying what I do more than ever.' When it was pointed out that many musicians end up broke, Elton retorted:

'I'm not one of them. I am earning more than I've ever done. And I always knew that.'

We last heard from John Reid seven years later, by which time he was living in Australia as a kind of celebrity expat, appearing as a judge on two seasons of *The X Factor*, having declined offers to appear on the UK version. Speaking to the Melbourne newspaper *The Age*, he said of Elton: 'We had a very strange, a very complicated relationship,' also revealing that he had written a 600-page autobiography titled *Too Close to the Candle*, although this is yet to be published.

'Elton always relied on me,' he said simply. 'We had a very solid close relationship, both business and personal. That sort of thing never went away.'

REVAMP

The past is always with us

There was a valedictory air hovering over this 2018 Elton and Bernie tribute album. Presented as Elton's personally curated project it featured a host of top pop, rock and R&B artists performing radical covers from his classic early-'70s period. Hence the startling opener 'Bennie and the Jets', featuring Elton joined by pop-punk queen Pink and rapper-producer Logic. While long-time Elton fans may have baulked at the musical upgrade – the original thumping piano chords replaced by hip-hop beats and modern minestrone production – if the point was to introduce Elton to a new twenty-first-century audience, you have to say it succeeded.

'I brought out a wish-list of people that I would love and asked them,' Elton explained, 'and to my surprise, most of them said yes.'

Ed Sheeran's hand-crafted acoustic version of 'Candle in the Wind' notched up 90 million streams. The final track by Queens of the Stone Age was another surprise: a stoner version of 'Goodbye Yellow Brick Road', chosen said QotSA frontman, Josh Homme, because of the 'psychedelic, carousel nature to it. It's really intoxicating.'

But if the idea was to bring Elton into the now, it also worked the other way. Elton was energised by his new connections, he revelled in the new, he didn't want to drift off into cosy celeb retirement. He has stayed fresh and kept his gleam like no other major artist has done, or even attempted. Proof that, as he said in 2018, 'I'm more interested in what I'm doing next rather than what I did forty years ago.'

ROCK OF THE WESTIES
A terrible photograph of a 'dusty'-looking Elton

Released just five months after *Captain Fantastic and the Brown Dirt Cowboy*, the arrival of the tenth Elton John studio album was like the unexpected arrival of a guest at a party to which they were not actually invited. A nice enough surprise, meant kindly, no doubt, but underwhelming, a bit unnecessary.

Even its title, *Rock of the Westies*, seemed a bit rote. A spoonerism on the phrase West of the Rockies, the album having been made in Colorado again. Like when the prosaically named *Caribou* followed hard on the heels of the monumental *Goodbye Yellow Brick Road*, the offhand title of the follow-up to the landmark *Captain Fantastic* seemed to mirror the good-not-great musical content.

The same for the album sleeve, horribly dull after the ornate handcrafted feel of the *Captain Fantastic* cover. His most nondescript album cover, ever: a terribly boring photograph of a decidedly 'dusty'-looking Elton, in rough dark beard, rat's tail hair and a scruffy blue cap even a creepy uncle would think twice about. Worst of all, the eyes behind the chocolate-tinted shades look dead. Dead tired. He simultaneously looked like he badly needed a bed and like he had just got out of one.

The music had fine moments. His first album without Nigel Olsson and Dee Murray, Elton seemed determined to make the most of his newfound musical 'freedom'. Roger Pope and Caleb Quaye, newly returned to prominence, bring the shimmers and shakes. Elton's voice is still able to reach for the sky despite the damage he was inflicting on it. And Bernie comes up with a fine addition to his growing list of masterful ballads, 'I Feel Like a Bullet (In the Gun of Robert Ford)'. Another real-life breakup, fresh sweet agony, amid lush orchestration, Elton demonstrating his inspiration from hymns. Building to that ravishing Davey Johnstone guitar solo, given added lustre by Caleb Quaye's melodic touch.

Extra groovy is 'Street Kids'. Get down funky rock 'n' roll, supercool riff, a close personal friend of 'Saturday Night's Alright for Fighting'. Only let down by the disappointingly hand-me-down lyrics – 'Squealers can't be trusted'; 'Beggars can't be choosers.' In the hands of Bad Company or Deep Purple, it would not matter one tiny bit, but this is Bernie Taupin – he's earned the right for us to expect more.

A collection of contradictions, the album begins dreadfully with quasi musical theatre, a veritable croc-opera entitled 'Medley: Yell

Help / Wednesday Night / Ugly'. 'Dan Dare (Pilot of the Future)' which follows spins on its own candyfloss axis. The raunchy 'Grow Some Funk of Your Own', Elton and Bernie sharing credits with Davey Johnstone – at last! But while the playing is sleek, the words again are just a little too 'generic'. Was Bernie being cute? 'Grow some funk of your own / We no like to with the gringo fight . . .' Huh? As for the 'border town . . . little cantina . . .' when along comes 'a señorita . . .', it's a struggle to care.

But that was as nothing compared to the lyrics to 'Island Girl', the jaunty first single from the album and the last Elton John solo single to go to number one in America for another twenty-two years. Along with its vanilla 'calypso' stylings, 'Island Girl' is fun and catchy – and, well, more than a little bit racist.

Elton hasn't performed 'Island Girl' live since the '80s. No explanation has ever been proffered. However, *Rolling Stone* writer Andy Greene suggested it might be due in part at least to its story of a female Jamaican prostitute in New York City and the Jamaican man who wants to take her back to Jamaica. Along with almost laughably crass lyrics such as: 'Well, she's black as coal, but she burn like a fire / And she wrap herself around you like a well-worn tire . . .'

Rock of the Westies was pretty far south of its immediate predecessors – of which there were many. The fourth Elton John album released in under two years, the quality control on *Rock of the Westies* was out of control. Non-existent, in fact. Suddenly it felt like Elton's career was outpacing his ability to keep up the quality.

Rock of the Westies would become Elton John's sixth consecutive number-one album in America. It would also be his last.

ROCKETMAN

Movies aren't about sticking to facts

'I was sixty-three when our first son, Zachary, was born, sixty-five when Elijah came along – and I did start thinking about them in forty years' time, being able to see or read my version of my life,' ruminated Elton John in *The Guardian* in May 2019.

Our man was as true as his word: his autobiographical film *Rocketman* (note the one-word spelling to avoid confusion with the song of the same name) was released worldwide in May 2019 and his wonderfully candid and insightful memoir *Me* followed five months later and became an international bestseller. Highly praised, hugely prized.

You can get almost everything you need to know about Elton John from those two productions alone – that is, as described by Elton. Both were quite different, however. The book went surprisingly deep, the movie wasn't about sticking to facts. It was Elton's fabulous lost life given the *Wizard of Oz*, Baz Luhrmann-style treatment. So – the truth but not the dull truth. A kaleidoscopic highlights package, a quality jukebox movie.

The cinema-going public certainly gave *Rocketman* a fair shot, spending almost $200 million at the box office: a decent return against Rocket Pictures' $40 million budget by any standards. Most of the critics gave it the thumbs-up and the industry rewarded it with a shelf-load of awards, including an Oscar for Best Original Song, one Golden Globe in the same category and another one for Taron Egerton, whose electrifying portrayal of Elton won him five BAFTA nominations – although *Rocketman* won none, a mild slap in the face from the old country.

Maybe the movie was a bit lightweight for the superannuated loveys awarding the BAFTAs: *Rocketman* was hardly *The Remains of the Day* or *Gandhi*, after all. Instead, it's something of a curio, landing halfway between biography and fantasy. The structure is taut, using a framing device in which Elton looks back on his life from the depths of rehab, and the screenplay lands squarely on all the right emotional touchpoints – the miserable childhood and distant parents, his blossoming in the '70s, his multiple addictions, not just to sex and drugs but to fame and money and mansions so vast he could lay lost in them for months, and the subsequent redemption through sobriety. Cue: End Credits.

Along the way, the writer Lee Hall and the director Dexter Fletcher drop in songs from the classic Elton catalogue and have fun with filmic 'magic realism': an example is the title track, which Egerton's Elton delivers from the bottom of a swimming pool. Another is a show at Hollywood's Troubadour, in which band and audience suddenly levitate from the floor, high on it all. It's mostly successful stuff, but at times it's rather like its subject: a little too self-indulgent occasionally for its own good.

One circumstantial issue may have been that *Rocketman* came out only seven months after Queen's planet-devouring biopic *Bohemian Rhapsody*, which took over $900 million against a budget one-sixteenth of that sum and scooped four Oscars. Although *Rocketman* had been in development for longer than *Bo Rhap* – partly it should be noted because Fletcher was parachuted in to finish the Queen movie when director Brian Singer was removed from the project – the inevitable feeling among the public was that Elton's film was slightly overshadowed by the bigger movie (just type '*Rocketman* versus' into Google and see which words automatically pop up next).

The two films were also slightly unequal in their lead perfor-mances, simply because Queen's Freddie Mercury was portrayed with astounding force and charm by Rami Malek, while Taron Egerton's depiction of Elton was subtler, more sensitive, less confrontational. There is also the small matter of Freddie having died young, with a heartbroken audience desperate to see him alive on screen again, while Elton remains, fortunately, in rude health.

Elton took all this on the chin, insisting in *Variety*: '*Bohemian Rhapsody* worked brilliantly . . . I'm thrilled for the guys in Queen,' although he didn't miss the opportunity to jump on accusations that the Queen film had taken liberties with Freddie's story. 'Ours tells the truth – even though it's a fantasy,' he said. 'My life can't be sugarcoated and I didn't want it to be.'

He had a point. Unlike the Queen film, in which Freddie's sexuality was almost completely absent from the screen, *Rocketman* shows the young Elton in a passionate clinch with John Reid, played by the excellent Richard Madden; he is seen in rehab and we witness a suicide attempt. The idea all along had been to tell the story in warts-and-all detail, Elton explained, adding that the film had taken so long to get off the ground because studios demanded a PG-13 certificate rather than the R rating which it finally received.

Cuts were made to the film's more provocative scenes in certain conservative countries, however. One of these was Egypt, where the head of the domestic Film Censorship Board announced: 'We do not allow any scenes that promote LGBTQ in films that are for public viewing . . . it is not for [Elton John] to allow the public to see whatever he does or whatever activities he indulges in that is not our culture.' Samoa wasn't having it either, with the relevant official declaring: 'There are acts that are not good for public viewing and against the law,' while Malaysia also made cuts and Russia took out five whole minutes.

'We reject in the strongest possible terms the decision to pander to local laws and censor *Rocketman* for the Russian market,' said Elton in a joint statement with the film-makers. 'That the local distributor has edited out certain scenes, denying the audience the opportunity to see the film as it was intended, is a sad reflection of the divided world we still live in and how it can still be so cruelly unaccepting of the love between two people.'

He was quite right in this, of course. *Rocketman* isn't simply another amusing tale of a singer who made it beyond big, did a lot of everything and burned his fuse out. It's an account, unusually told, of a unique life led in incredibly heightened circumstances.

When you read *Me* then watch *Tantrums and Tiaras* and *Rocketman*, it becomes very clear that the existence of this unconventional biopic isn't just a legacy gift for his children, as Elton intended – it benefits all of us.

ROCKET RECORDS

Fly me to the moon

Few phenomena more evoke the ridiculous levels of affluence of the early-'70s music industry than the vanity record label. The Beatles had one, of course: Apple Corps started well but failed when the rules of capitalism and the ethos of hippiedom failed to mesh. Led Zeppelin's Swan Song label and Rolling Stones Records did better, because neither label bothered to sign many outside artists. Indeed, the lesson of any successful vanity label seemed to be 'Only release records by the owners and their mates' – as was the case with Deep Purple's own Purple imprint, Frank Zappa's Bizarre Records and Jefferson Airplane's Grunt label.

On paper, Elton John understood this principle and declared that he wouldn't waste money on his Rocket Record Company, officially launched on 30 April 1973. 'We want to start a company that's for the artist, both creatively and money-wise,' he declared. 'We want to be a friendly record company. We'll pay a good advance and a decent royalty, and when we sign anybody, we'll work our bollocks off for them. It'll be like a family.'

In typical Elton-style extravagance, the new label was launched with not one but *three* parties. The first, on 25 March, was described in *Melody Maker* as 'the biggest, name-dropping rave up in recent times.' Held on a boat, the *John D*, moored on the Thames in London, guests included Rod Stewart and assorted Faces, Paul Simon, Ringo Starr, Cat Stevens and Harry Nilsson. The free booze flowed and the gathering was lent extra excitement in true '70s-style by the presence of a female stripper.

The second Rocket launch party was less name-droppy but somewhat stranger. On 3 May, a chartered train, loaded up with more than 250 Rocket Records employees, various journalists and photographers, friends and liggers, professional gate-crashers and friends of friends, left London's Paddington station bound for the sleepy picture-postcard Cotswold town of Moreton-in-the-Marsh. One carriage was given over to a full-on disco, replete with lights, loud music and strange things going on in the darkened corners. Every carriage was given over to booze and other 'party favours'.

The train was met upon arrival by a brass band, which led the cavalcade to the local village hall, specially commandeered for the occasion, where they were greeted by a medieval banquet and several gallons of vintage champagne. Two Rocket signings, Longdancer and Mike Silver, performed sets, which Elton and his band joined for the encores, which went on longer than either act's sets.

A third Rocket launch party took place shortly after in Los Angeles, on the Universal backlot usually reserved for filming westerns. The outdoor party began with a mock gunfight between two actor cowboys and starred Elton in heart-shaped glasses, his hair dyed orange and pink for the occasion, standing at the piano rip-snorting his way through 'Crocodile Rock' Jerry Lee Lewis' 'Whole Lotta Shakin' Goin' On', joined on backing vocals by Dusty Springfield and Nona Hendryx.

Rocket's branding used the smiling train image familiar from W. Awdry's *Thomas the Tank Engine* books, getting away with it because the image had never been copyrighted. As biographer Philip Norman later quipped, '*Thomas the Tank Engine* technically infringed the legal rights of Rocket Records.'

The label personnel consisted of John Reid, Gus Dudgeon, Bernie Taupin and Steve Brown, plus Elton when he was around, working out of a six-room office at London's 101 Wardour Street, in the gloriously grimy heart of Soho. But despite their talent – and budget, $5 million of which came from Rocket's US distributor MCA – chart successes were few and far between.

The insipid acoustic fare of Longdancer failed to make an impact, although the group's teenage guitarist Dave Stewart scored big a decade later as one-half of the Eurythmics, and Kiki Dee managed one significant hit with 'Amoureuse' in 1974.

The problem was obvious: Elton wasn't on the label. 'Me not being on it is what's good about it,' he had originally stated, reasonably enough. 'It would dampen everyone else. It'd be like, Elton John is on Rocket – and so is Davey Johnstone.'

He was soon obliged to revise his position. When the economics of the situation started to bite, not helped by Rocket's habit of lunching, dining, chauffeuring and flying journalists around first class, as well as the cost of their new office off Sunset Boulevard in Los Angeles, Elton became a Rocket artist.

His 1976 hit with Kiki Dee, 'Don't Go Breaking My Heart', proved that it was the right move and a period of success followed. As well as Elton's own releases, Rocket enjoyed hits with Cliff Richard, Neil Sedaka, former Zombies singer Colin Blunstone, the singer-songwriter Judie Tzuke and even scored a surprise number-six hit in 1981 with Fred Wedlock's novelty song 'The Oldest Swinger in Town'.

In November 1987, the Rocket Records directors finally called time on the label, although it was resurrected eight years later as a vehicle again for Elton's albums. It was absorbed by the Universal Music Group in the 2000s, with 2004's *Peachtree Road* its most recent Elton John release. However, the Rocket name lives on elsewhere as a management company, with the business affairs of its biggest client Ed Sheeran dwarfing any previous achievement by the brand.

ROSE, W. AXL

Every rose has its thorns

Of all the unusual artists Elton John has befriended in his career, from Rod Stewart and John Lennon to George Michael, Freddie Mercury, Britney Spears, Ozzy Osbourne, Dua Lipa and the list goes on, perhaps the most initially puzzling was the alliance Elton went out of his way to form with the notoriously volatile Guns N' Roses singer, W. Axl Rose.

At the height of their fame in the late '80s, as their debut album *Appetite for Destruction* sat at number one in America over a year after its release, on its way to selling 40 million copies, the band released *GN'R Lies*, a low-profile mini-album of material previously released only in limited-edition form. One side recorded live at an early LA club show; the other, four ostensibly acoustic songs, including the beautiful hit single, 'Patience', and the done-for-shits-and-giggles 'Used to Love Her' ('. . . but I had to kill her!').

The final track of the album however stirred up so much trouble, no one was left laughing. Least of all Axl Rose. The song was the incendiary 'One in a Million'. Specifically, the lines Axl sings about 'Immigrants and faggots' that 'come to our country' and 'spread some fucking disease'.

Even acknowledging the band's reputation for outrage, the song drew opprobrium across the board. Seen not as the dark comedy Axl would portray it as, but a vicious piece of gutter-talk in which homosexuals are depicted as disease-spreaders, the song left many of their own fans, most critics, even members of the band, deeply disturbed.

Axl had been warned the song was certain to provoke an almost unanimously negative reaction but he had insisted the track remain on the album. Given the band's position at the time as the biggest-selling act on the Geffen label, its owner and namesake David Geffen – who was gay but not yet openly – eventually demurred. Privately, however, Geffen was concerned the song might prompt criticism of him personally. The arrival in the '80s of AIDS had spawned the creation of a vocal, sometimes reactionary gay press. Geffen feared being outed in retaliation for allowing such a song to be released on a label bearing his name. He was also embarrassed when offence over the song caused the band to be unceremoniously – and very publicly – dumped from an AIDS benefit in New York, where they were to have represented the interests of the Gay Men's Health Crisis, one of the organisations involved with the show that Geffen had personal connections with.

Even his own band condemned Axl for his stubbornness in keeping the song on the album. Not least the band's lead guitarist Slash, whose mother Ola was black, and was particularly distressed by the situation. He told me, 'There's a line in that song where it says "Police and n*****s, get out of my way" that I didn't want Axl to sing. But Axl's the kind of person who will sing whatever it is he feels like singing.'

Slash did make a half-hearted attempt to defend it – 'He wasn't talking about black people so much, he was more or less talking about the sort of street thugs that you run into' – but it was clear he was uncomfortable. 'I mean, I'm part black. One of the nice things about Guns N' Roses is that we've never segregated the audience in our minds as white, black or green, you know? But Axl has a strong feeling about it and he really wanted to say it. But then, God forbid that any of us should get arrested and end up in county jail. Can you imagine?'

As for his use of 'faggot', as Axl later told *Interview* magazine, 'A lot of people have used the word "faggot" and they're not getting told they're homophobic.' He did admit, however, that 'maybe I have a problem with homophobia.' It was a theme he had explored when speaking to *Rolling Stone* in 1989, explaining how he had had 'some very bad experiences with homosexuals'. Not that he was actively anti-homosexual, he said, more that he was 'pro-heterosexual'.

With controversy over 'One in a Million' still raging, I asked Axl to talk me through the song and was taken aback to learn that the chorus came about 'because I was getting, like, really far away, like "Rocket Man" Elton John, you know, like in my head. Getting really far away from all my friends and family in Indiana.'

The mention of 'Rocket Man' prompted me to ask if he was a fan of Elton's music. He immediately began a long rant about what he called 'the genius of Elton John' and what a great fan he was of Bernie Taupin's lyrics. He said he'd like to interview Taupin about his lyrics. He had even run the idea past a few magazine editors but that, so far, there had been no takers. (Interestingly, when asked for his opinion of the young singer's lyrics, Taupin graciously replied that he was 'an admirer', particularly of the lyrics to their number-one hit and most famous song, 'Sweet Child o' Mine'.)

'Elton John is just the baddest!' Axl grinned. He said he'd learned to sing and play piano as a child in the early '70s at his stepfather's Pentecostal church but that he'd learned how to make the piano rock from listening to Elton John.

'There's nobody badder when it comes to attacking the piano and using it in a rock sense. I mean, you're gonna tell me that "Saturday Night's Alright for Fighting" or "Grow Some Funk of Your Own", or like, "Ballad of a Well-Known Gun" or "Someone Saved My Life Tonight" and things like that ain't heavy songs? There's no way! Those guys wrote seven number-one albums in the US from, like, '72 to '75. Bernie Taupin was twenty-five years old, writing off the top of his head, writing albums in two hours! And the guy's vocabulary and education . . .' He shook his head in awe. 'It was so amazing they decided to go rock 'n' roll rather than go classical or whatever. And they blended all these different styles – amazing!'

He went on: 'I play piano in a style influenced by Elton John and Billy Joel. But it's minimalistic. I know what I can and can't do, so I aim it real carefully. But it's basically influenced off Elton John's attack – and his singing. If you want to learn how to sing different styles, try singing like Elton John – anything from the blues on.'

He was on a roll now, sifting through a stack of records on the floor by the stereo, searching for *Madman Across the Water* or *Tumbleweed Connection*. 'I haven't met a group of people that after you've played everything all night and you put on an Elton John record, that don't go, "Cool . . ." and kick back. Any of the first seven or eight albums, you put one of those on and everyone just relaxes. It makes you feel good cos of the vibrations in the styles of the songs, the styles of writing. The way they take you so many different places on one album.'

He said that Elton had actually reached out to him at the height of the media storm over 'One in a Million': 'He sent these flowers and a note. It was meant towards the press and anybody else who was against Guns N' Roses. It said: "Don't let the bastards grind you down! I hate them all too . . . Sincerely, Elton John". That was just the greatest.'

According to Elton, 'Never in a million years did I think [Axl] was homophobic.' Two years later, he finally got a chance to meet Axl and work together as part of the high-profile bill at Wembley Stadium for the Freddie Mercury Tribute Concert for AIDS Awareness. Despite objections from gay rights groups, Axl led Guns N' Roses through a special commemorative concert for the Queen singer, who had died of AIDs-related causes the previous November. They performed two songs – 'Paradise City' and 'Knockin' on Heaven's Door' – before Axl, wearing a Union Jack leather jacket and T-shirt with the slogan 'Kill Your Idol' beneath a picture of Christ, teamed up with Elton for one of the highlights of the event, a stunning duet performance of 'Bohemian Rhapsody'.

'I spoke to Elton before the show,' said Axl, 'and he was kind of uneasy about meeting me, you know, I'm supposed to be the most homophobic guy on Earth.' Once he had explained his long-standing admiration for Elton – and Freddie Mercury, another piano playing rock maestro – 'he was like, "Whoa!"' He went on excitedly, 'Onstage, I was trying to be as respectful to him as I could. I was purposely vibing out, and if you look close, you can see it how much love and respect I have for Elton. There was some heavy eye contact going down. It was amazing.'

It was touch and go for a while at Wembley though. 'I do remember being determined that we'd get Elton singing with Axl,' recalled Queen drummer Roger Taylor, 'but Axl never turned up for rehearsal. It was really flying by the seat of our pants.'

Singer Joe Elliott, whose band Def Leppard were also on the bill, recalled that 'Axl was in the next room to us. Elton told us he knocked on his door and Axl's big security guy said: "Axl's sleeping." And Elton said: "Well, I'm doing a duet with him in four hours!" And the guy shrugged his shoulders and shut the door in Elton's face. So Elton comes into our dressing room and says to us: "What the fuck's wrong with that guy?" Elton had a little rant and a cup of tea and then he took off.'

No one else on stage knew quite what to expect as Elton took his seat behind a keyboard to tinkle out those first few famous notes of 'Bohemian Rhapsody'. Then, unexpectedly, he was out of his seat, mic in hand, strolling across the stage as he led the crowd in one of the loudest Wembley singalongs ever.

Then Brian May's thunderous heavy metal riff dropped, fireworks exploded and here came W. Axl Rose – bang on time, spinning across the stage like a kilted whirligig. The song reaches its crescendo before floating into its piano-driven denouement, leaving Elton and Axl to sing and gaze chummily before hugging. It's a performance that has divided many an Elton John fan since it first aired, but over thirty years on, Axl and Elton going full-Freddie together remains a singular moment for both singers.

In September that year, Elton reinforced his public affirmation of Axl when he agreed to join Guns N' Roses on piano and backing vocals for a live performance of their epic, clearly Elton-influenced hit ballad 'November Rain' at the MTV Video Music Awards, held that year at UCLA's Pauley Pavilion. The song, which would win the award that night for Best Cinematography in a Video, was very close to Axl's heart and he was desperately excited about having Elton John's tacit approval. According to GN'R drummer Matt Sorum, before recording the song, he and Axl had sat 'on the floor, we ordered some Russian caviar, we had a bottle of vodka – and we listened to "Don't Let the Sun Go Down on Me" by Elton John.'

The performance of 'November Rain' at the 1992 MTV awards was destined to be remembered for entirely different reasons, however. Nirvana, the hottest band on the planet that year, inspiring a whole new genre of rock known as grunge, had been booked to open proceedings performing 'Lithium', from their breakthrough album, *Nevermind*. But as Nirvana left the stage, singer Kurt Cobain expressed his disgust for what he saw as Axl's racism and homophobia by spitting on the keys of the piano he believed belonged to Axl.

'I saw [Axl's] piano there and I just had to take this opportunity and spit big goobers all over his keyboards,' explained Kurt. According to his guitar tech, Earnie Bailey, 'Kurt came in, laughing his ass off. He told me he'd spit across the keys of Axl's piano as he left the stage. So we're laughing about that, watching the ceremony on TV, when these two pianos come up and Kurt goes, "Oh fuck! I spat on Elton's piano by accident!" I'm not sure which was funnier, Kurt's horror at what he had done or the sight of Elton John hammering away on that piano.'

In 1994, Axl was honoured to be the one who stood on stage and personally inducted Elton John into the Rock and Roll Hall of Fame. Said the well-known gun: 'The Rock and Roll Hall of Fame honours the musicians who make the music that not only becomes the soundtrack to our lives, but actually helps us get through each day of our life. For myself as well as many others, no one has been there more for inspiration than Elton John. Also, when we talk about great rock duos – Jimmy Page and Robert Plant, John and Paul, Mick and Keith, I like to think of Elton John and Bernie Taupin.

'But also tonight, I think that Elton should be honoured for his great work and contribution in the fight against AIDS. And also his bravery in exposing all the triumphs and tragedies of his personal life. And the knowledge of these things helps ourselves get through things every day. When I first heard "Bennie and the Jets" I knew at that time that I had to be a performer. So now a man who in ways is responsible for more things than he ever planned on – Elton John.'

Russell, Leon
Rock 'n' soul brother

The late Leon Russell was a musician and songwriter with a resumé unparalleled in the context of American rock 'n' roll in the '60s and '70s. Born in Oklahoma in 1942, Russell played on albums by the Beach Boys, Jan & Dean and Dick Dale in his early years before stepping up to record with Bob Dylan, Frank Sinatra and the Rolling Stones and writing songs for Joe Cocker.

As a solo artist, he was also prolific, pulling in Eric Clapton, Ringo Starr and George Harrison for his self-titled debut album in 1970, and going on to release a couple of dozen solo and collaboration albums, both studio and live, winning two Grammy Awards along the way. This material was just the tip of the rock, souland country iceberg for Russell: he is credited on a staggering 408 albums in thirty-seven different roles, mostly on piano and keyboards but also on guitar, bass, several other instruments and often as an arranger.

If you want a quick intro to his music, listen to 'A Song for You' (1970), which you'll know from 200-plus cover versions by artists such as Ray Charles, Willie Nelson and Whitney Houston; 'This Masquerade' (1972), which has been recorded by George Benson, the Carpenters and many others. You should also give *The Union* a try: this album, recorded with Elton John in 2010, is a fascinating look inside the minds of two veteran singer-song-writers in their late prime.

Elton – who had known Russell since his first show at the Los Angeles Troubadour in 1970 – essentially signed up to the project as a favour to his friend, who he adored, musically and personally, and whose relative obscurity in the first decade of the twenty-first century he regarded as a crime. 'I want his name written in stone,' he once said. 'I want him in the Rock and Roll Hall of Fame. I want his name to be on everybody's lips again, like it used to be.'

A few high-level phone calls were made, leading to guest vocals on *The Union* by Neil Young, Bono and Brian Wilson, while Booker T. of MG's fame played Hammond organ. A crack team of session musicians was likewise recruited by producer T Bone Burnett, including Don Was on bass and Jim Keltner on drums.

Elton himself took an executive-producer credit and plunged enthusiastically into the task, engaging on a musical journey that was evidently as much about a return to his own roots as it was a showcase for Russell. The music is blues and country in essence, but loaded with gospel, brass and even funeral-march influences, with more than a nod to classic soul and Americana.

Tonally, the songs vary from optimism to world-weariness. Listen to 'Eight Hundred Dollar Shoes' in which Elton sings to Russell, 'Your songs have all the hooks, you're seven wonders rolled into one', and the single 'If It Wasn't for Bad', based on a snappy groove. 'Monkey Suit' is fun, laced with brass, and 'Hey Ahab' is a swinging, hymnal tune.

Most of the album is devoted to life's last act, though, and the two musicians are at their very best on 'Gone to Shiloh', a lament featuring Neil Young's recognisable wail, and the sombre 'There's No Tomorrow', a self-explanatory gaze into the abyss. Russell, it transpired, had undergone brain surgery just before recording the album and although he wasn't exactly ancient at the age of sixty-eight, it was self-evident that for Leon, the clock was ticking.

Elton's public approved, sending *The Union* to number three on the US chart, and the industry supported the album with a Grammy nomination for 'If It Wasn't for Bad', as well as gold and silver discs in Canada and the UK. Whether the album performed its intended purpose of restoring Russell to wider public awareness is debatable, but he was inducted into both the Rock and

Roll Hall of Fame and the Songwriters Hall of Fame in 2011, which can't have been coincidental.

Russell died in his sleep in 2016 after a life well lived, leading Elton to comment, 'My darling Leon Russell passed away last night. He was a mentor, inspiration and so kind to me. I loved him and always will.'

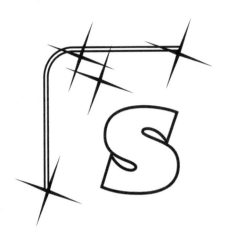

A SINGLE MAN
A single great song

When the best songwriters are going through a low period, as many do every now and then, they treat it as an opportunity to express their mood in their music. When Elton John wrote 'Song for Guy', a mostly instrumental composition that features a single, muttered line, 'Life isn't everything' towards the end, he was preoccupied with thoughts of his own mortality.

As he told *Billboard* in 1979, 'As I was writing this song one Sunday, I imagined myself floating into space and looking down at my own body. I was imagining myself dying. Morbidly obsessed with these thoughts, I wrote this song about death.'

A thoughtful song that moves from pathos to drama and back again, 'Song for Guy' would have been an affecting piece even without the sad news that accompanied it. The day after he wrote it, Elton was informed that Guy Burchett, a seventeen-year-old employed as a messenger boy at Rocket Records, had been killed in a motorbike accident. He duly named his new song after the late Burchett.

'It was like nothing I'd done before, and my American label refused to release it – I was furious,' noted Elton in his autobiography,

Me, adding that the song was a 'huge hit in Europe'. He was correct: the 'Song for Guy' single did good business in Belgium, Holland and Germany, as well as making an impact across Australasia. Even American radio embraced the song, despite the lack of a domestic release.

By anyone's standards, 'Song for Guy' is a beautiful piece of music and a songwriting masterclass. It builds towards a recognisable climax, simply by adding layers to the repeated topline melody every time it reoccurs. There's a touch of Moog and Mellotron to thicken up Elton's piano part, while the percussion – a simple drum-machine pattern – never gets in the way.

You can understand why Elton was pleased that the single did so well. It was an instrumental, in other words all his own work apart from Gary Cooper's percussion and Clive Franks' bass part. A new, untested direction for Elton, it was a success even without a chorus that radio programmers could latch onto. Most of all, he had pulled the song off without Bernie Taupin's help: the two men had parted ways in 1976, agreeing to work independently after several years as an inseparable songwriting partnership.

'Song for Guy' also represented a lifeline. *A Single Man* was Elton's first album with Gary Osborne replacing Bernie Taupin and hit singles aside, it was a disappointment. Sounding like Cliff Richard in places, David Bowie in others, even like Elton himself sometimes, it was seamlessly executed, well intended but just a little . . . dull. Forced and inauthentic. 'It Ain't Gonna Be Easy' is eight minutes you'll never get back again.

Even the vanilla hit 'Part Time Love' sounds thin and over-produced. Gus Dudgeon had been replaced by Elton and Franks. The sound, synthetic and contrived, anticipated the antiseptic pop sound that would characterise the '80s. Not much of a recommendation, in retrospect.

Ironic then that *A Single Man* also happens to contain one of Elton John's biggest and most haunting hits. 'Song for Guy' has since become a gift for TV and film soundtrack compilers. It appeared in an aviation documentary called *Diamonds in the Sky* in 1979, then in a Jane Seymour and Chevy Chase movie, *Oh Heavenly Dog*, the following year. Telly addicts in 1985 enjoyed it in the BBC comedy, *Happy Families*, which handily featured a lead character called Guy. More recently, the song has appeared in the 2017 movie *Film Stars Don't Die in Liverpool*, and in 2020 we saw Emma Corrin as the young Lady Diana Spencer whirly-gigging to it dreamily in tutu and ballet slippers in the wildly popular Netflix drama *The Crown*.

Sleeping with the Past
Elton's best-selling album of the '80s

Arriving a little later than advertised, the real Elton John comeback began in earnest in 1989 with *Sleeping with the Past*. His last album of what had been a woeful '80s, career-wise, health-wise, hat-wise, it came almost too late. Vanilla reviews and no meaningful singles led to poor initial sales everywhere. It wasn't until the second single from the album, 'Sacrifice', a flop in the UK first time around, was re-released in June 1990 as a double A-side with the album's other underperforming single, 'Healing Hands', and went straight to number one that the spotlight belatedly landed in full on *Sleeping with the Past*.

Elton's last album before voluntarily entering rehab the following year, it was also his first since the '70s that really sounded like an Elton and Bernie album. Davey Johnstone, now musical director as well as guitarist, is the only other soul-survivor, but suddenly it doesn't matter any more. Elton only played digital-keyboard in the studio but because he had the brilliantly named Guy Babylon playing all the other keyboard stuff very much 'in the style of', that didn't matter either.

From the purposely stiff white-reggae of 'Durban Deep' to the anthemic 'Healing Hands' to the joyous boogie-woogie of the title track, this was an Elton John album that no longer felt like it had a next-day sell-by-date. This was the closest to classic Elton John that Elton had come since he was releasing those classic Elton John albums. It didn't try and repeat, but it stuck closer to how those greatest hits were made, in that Elton sounds genuinely up for anything, musically engaged again, and though it doesn't always work, at least he sounds like he gives a damn.

The pearl in the oyster though was 'Sacrifice'. Contemporary production aside, 'Sacrifice' could have landed anytime between *Don't Shoot Me I'm Only the Piano Player* and *Captain Fantastic and the Brown Dirt Cowboy* and it would not have sounded out of place at all. It's just a beautiful, perfectly executed pop masterclass, impossible not to be lit up by.

Strange to relate, but when 'Sacrifice' went to number one in Britain in June 1990, it became the very first Elton John single to do so in over twenty years and upwards of eighty singles. As a result, *Sleeping with the Past* also now shot to number one, Elton's first album to do so in his home country since *Caribou* in 1974. It was his best-selling album of the '80s.

New decade, new era for Elton?

Not quite. As he later recalled: 'I was sober when I recorded *Sleeping with the Past* – just.' Except it didn't last and things would get worse before they got better. He collapsed on stage during the first week of the victory-lap world tour. The official explanation issued later claimed it was exhaustion and it probably was – but not because of anything he was doing *on stage*. 'I went off the rails,' he later admitted. Having slept with the past, Elton now needed to cut it adrift and move on.

SONGS FROM THE WEST COAST
The train is now leaving the station

In the four years that had elapsed between *The Big Picture* in 1997 and *Songs from the West Coast* in 2001, Elton John had not been idle, branching out into movie soundtracks and stage musicals. In 1999, there was the album, *Elton John and Tim Rice's Aida*: effectively a soundtrack of songs that would not feature in the main production of *Aida* until the following year.

Very pleasant it sounded, too, on the new CD player in your car. Elton performs with an array of world-class artists singing Tim Rice's words: Janet Jackson, Tina Turner, Shania Twain, Lenny Kravitz, Boyz II Men, James Taylor, some Spice Girls, various others, including the voices of *Aida* cast-members-to-be, Heather Headley and Sherie Rene Scott, on a couple of tracks. Not a big chart hit anywhere but its reach was undeniable.

Just three months later, Elton released his soundtrack album to the Hollywood comedy-drama, *The Muse*, another musical departure: a largely orchestrated score composed by him alone. Bar the solitary vocal track, the title track, 'The Make', which Bernie Taupin wrote the lyrics for. In 2000, Elton released the soundtrack album for the DreamWorks animated movie, *The Road to Eldorado*, which he and Tim Rice cowrote seven songs for, with Hans Zimmer and John Powell composing the instrumental scores.

There would be many more such projects in the future, but for now Elton brought all that newfound knowledge and experience to his next album, *Songs from the West Coast*. Indeed, the opening track, 'The Emperor's New Clothes', sounds like the crowd-pleasing opening number of a big Broadway musical. Elton's soundtrack work had seeped so far into his musical psyche, they were now one and the same. The best news of all: come-on-in-the-water's-fine tracks like 'Dark Diamond' (with Stevie Wonder on his sanctified harmonica) and the sweetly melancholic 'Original Sin', displayed neatly next to complex heavy-hitters like 'I Want Love' and 'This Train Don't Stop There Anymore'.

Elton had had so many supposed comeback albums, now the real thing had come along it came as something of a shock. This really was as good as anything he had produced in the '70s, like something that would have come from the dark depths of *Madman Across the Water* but executed with the colour and flair of *Goodbye Yellow Brick Road*.

Patrick Leonard produced the album and played keyboards, as he did when working with Elton on *The Road to Eldorado* sound-track the year before. OG Elton John Band drummer Nigel Olsson returned full-time. Rufus Wainwright sang backing vocals on the elegantly elegiac 'American Triangle', the true-life tale of Matthew Shepard, a gay college student who had been brutally murdered in Wyoming, in 1998. The album was dedicated to Shepard and Oliver Johnstone, guitarist Davey Johnstone's young son who had perished the same year. Adding to the feeling of being in the right place at the right time in the company of the right people was the not-coincidental decision to record the album using analogue tape, knowing it would make 'the voice and instruments sound warmer'.

For all that, this was now the twenty-first century and most people's big takeaway from *Songs from the West Coast* and the new improved Elton John were the videos for the singles 'I Want

Love' and 'This Train Don't Stop There Anymore'. The former, a top-ten hit in the UK, featured troubled young actor Robert Downey Jr – a Hollywood movie star that had gone so far off the rails in the past five years people feared the story could only end in death or jail. Drugs, prison, rehab, repeat, guns, drugs, prison, rehab, repeat ... As Downey Jr had earnestly explained to the judge in a recent trial, 'It's like I have a shotgun in my mouth, and I've got my finger on the trigger, and I like the taste of the gun metal.'

Yes, *that* guy. He was chosen to star in the new Elton John video, 'I Want Love'. And he was magnificent in it. As pained and vulnerable, yet somehow stronger for it, as the song itself is, Downey Jr appears alone inside an empty mansion, miming the words as though speaking to himself. A beautifully understated piece, it presented both Elton and Downey Jr in a new, far more interesting context. Directed by the English artist and photographer Sam Taylor-Wood, who also shot the cover, it was Downey Jr's first acting role since emerging from rehab (again). Eyebrows were raised in some quarters but as Taylor-Wood observed, 'The way he underplays it is fantastic.'

It was the video for 'This Train Don't Stop There Anymore' that really raised the bar, however. A brilliant Bernie lyric recalling the glam rock years of Elton's '70s superstardom, viewed from the other side of the rainbow, the arrangement a deliberate throwback to Elton's original piano-bass-drums combo with Dee and Nigel. It's a classic Elton song, in the same rarefied zone as 'Goodbye Yellow Brick Road' or 'Tiny Dancer', wincingly autobiographical and true, but it's the brilliant video that really brings home the pathos.

Directed by the American artist-photographer-film-maker David LaChapelle, with Pierre Rouger as cinematographer, it presents Elton circa-1973 played by twenty-year-old Justin Timberlake, then the biggest teen idol in America with the boyband NSYNC. The scene could be backstage at the Hollywood

Bowl, with Timberlake in overlarge pink glasses, silver boots, shiny striped suit, his hair carefully clipped to appear thinning at the front, long '70s sideburns snaking past his earlobes. It's an uncanny performance, with the backstage milieu enticingly evoked, Elton-Timberlake surrounded by lamé-clad male and female groupies, other celebs, photographers, make-up people, label sharks and other hangers-on.

Made almost two decades before the hyperreal *Rocketman* biopic, it captures in under five minutes what it took the movie two hours to achieve. The little touches were masterful. The always-on Liza Minnelli lookalike, the preening figure of John Reid, played by Paul Reubens of Pee-Wee Herman fame, sashaying Elton around while at the same time ripping up contracts and knocking the hat off a uniformed cop. The lightly bearded young dressing room assistant holding open a leather case with a dozen different bejewelled bracelets for Elton to choose from.

Most of all, there was Timberlake's utterly sublime performance as Elton '73. He is so completely convincing in the role, smiling for the cameras, air-kissing all the guests and well-wishers, then showing his real face to camera: pained, conflicted, lost, it's like stepping into a time machine.

LaChapelle extended the theme for the third and last single from the album, 'Original Sin', starring Mandy Moore and featuring Elizabeth Taylor, with the real-life Elton playing dumpy, middle-aged American dad. It's a Cinderella scenario, where the Mandy Moore character is transported by a fairy godmother from a life of drudgery to the star guest at an Elton concert – possibly the same show that Justin Timberlake's Elton presided over in the earlier video. Backstage, some familiar faces are joined by imperious-looking Sonny and Cher, Barbra Streisand and Bette Midler lookalikes.

Despite the videos receiving heavy play on VH1, the adult arm of MTV, none of the singles were hits in America, where radio was no longer dominated by FM stations playing album-oriented artists but far more targeted towards young singles' artists and hip-hop. The album, however, was a huge hit in Britain and Europe, and eventually went gold in America. The music business was changing. Although forced out of business in 2001, Napster's innovative file-sharing had led the change and the next few years would see the advent of streaming, via iTunes, Spotify and MP3s that you could store on your phone. Record stores began to close and record labels ceased being interested in last-century concepts like artist development. Even MTV began to lose its grip on public taste. Almost every major artist was left suddenly without a clue what to do.

Elton John, however, would prove the exception.

THE STARSHIP
Unfasten your seatbelts

For his 1974 tour of America, Elton John plus enlarged band and an ever-growing entourage now travelled to and from their sold-out arena shows exclusively by private jet, christened *The Starship* – a Boeing 720B, the words 'ELTON JOHN BAND TOUR '74' emblazoned down one side of its camp red, white and blue fuselage and frosted stars.

Originally designed to carry 138 passengers but converted into a forty-seater private pleasure palace, *The Starship* was owned by former singer and erstwhile American TV teen star Bobby Sherman. It had been used the year before for Led Zeppelin to tour America in and came fitted with large leather lounge seats and dinner tables, a glowing electric pseudo coal fire, a fully stocked bar and a TV lounge, a state-of-the-art hi-fi and a shelf of the latest movies on video cassette (a brand-new technology).

There was also an electric Thomas organ, which Elton studiously ignored, and, in a rear cabin, a king-sized double bed covered in shaggy white fur that would be Elton's own private boudoir in which he rarely actually slept. The bed came with its own specially fitted seatbelts so that, if he wished, the singer could take off and land in a horizontal position.

In those days there was no such thing as airport security, certainly not in the way we know it now, so, the plane would taxi to a pre-designated point at the airport, away from the terminal building used by the public alighting from commercial flights. Waiting for them would be a line of limousines.

Disembarking from the plane would be an army of tour technicians, record company bigwigs, promotion people, personal assistants, gofers, along with the freshly dubbed Elton John Band (Dee, Nigel and Davey now joined by Ray Cooper); there was also Kiki Dee, who Davey was 'having a scene with', the four-man Muscle Shoals horn section, John Reid, imperiously clutching a clipboard, their American booking agent, Howard Rose, plus *LA Times* main man Robert Hilburn and, from the Rocket Records' London office, Clive Banks and his new wife, Moira Bellas, who worked as a press officer for Warner Bros.

And last, though clearly never least, Elton himself. In a group photo taken before their maiden flight on their new floating palace, Elton stands there grinning in a white and turquoise jumpsuit and an impressively wide-brimmed Panama hat, leaning theatrically on a slender ebony cane. The cane had been used to great dramatic effect by the pimps and drug hustlers that had inhabited New York's notorious 42nd Street – known locally as 'The Deuce' – in the early '70s. It would now form a vital part of the knowingly decadent look first Elton and then David Bowie would ostentatiously adopt.

And, of course, there was Bernie Taupin, who had no role whatsoever to play on the tour except, it would seem, to have a thoroughly good time. And who could reasonably deny him? After all, it was the wonderful words he served up so elegantly to Elton that helped pay for all this. The onboard staff were very nice, too.

STEWART, ROD
Alias Sharon and Phyllis

In 1972, just as Elton John and Rod Stewart were in the first blush of their once unimaginable success, Elton bought his first rock-star mansion, Hercules. It was the era of rock stars living high in the rich English countryside, close enough to London for the action and the airport – *far enough away not to be hassled, man.* Rod Stewart and Who drummer Keith Moon lived just a few miles away, so did Donovan. They were always coming over, couldn't get rid of them. Not that Elton ever really wanted to let them leave.

Sometimes it seemed like all of London were at the house, not just Jagger or Bowie or whoever was on the scene that week, but the people around them, too. Friendships were formed. Jealousies festered. Professional alliances made. Shit happened. Out of it all though, the one real friend Elton made – and kept, regardless of whatever their latest not-so private spat was supposedly about – was Rod Stewart.

Roderick David Stewart came from a lower middle-class family in north London, the youngest and most indulged of five kids. Rod was two years older and had begun his journey long before Elton came close to having any sort of career. At the time *Empty Sky* was released, he had already starred on two hit albums in America as the singer of the legendary Jeff Beck Group, whose 1968 *Truth* album became one of the foundation stones in the history of specifically album-oriented rock.

Indeed, Rod had been around trying to make it for so long that Elton was still a schoolboy in Pinner the first time he saw him perform, when Long John Baldry's Steampacket played the local Conservative Club. Rod was just one of three singers in the line-up, including Baldry and fifteen-year-old future 'This Wheel's on Fire' star Julie Driscoll. But he was the one Reggie couldn't take his eyes off. His voice hadn't yet evolved into the warm, gravelly burr he would become famous for, but he had already earned the Baldry-coined nickname Rod the Mod for his 'funny hair' and colourful clothes.

After the show, Reggie even went backstage and asked for Rod's autograph. Something Rod teased him about years later: 'He used to come on stage with a scarf around his neck and sing "Good Morning Little Schoolgirl" . . . I thought he was great.'

Like Elton, Rod was also terminally shy, something he success-fully hid behind the peacocking rock-sparrow he transformed himself into when he joined the Faces. Rod wanted you to know he was one of the boys, a nod's-as-good-as-a-wink geezer. But he also wanted the girls to know he knew how to behave in the boudoir.

Also like Elton John, Rod Stewart was a grafter. The four studio albums he made with the Faces between 1969–73 coincided with the four solo albums he also made, including the stunning *Every Picture Tells a Story* and its immortal hit, 'Maggie May', which turned him into the biggest most fabulous rock star in America in 1971–72.

Elton John also released eight albums during that period, the last his third American number one in a row, a feat not even Rod in his prime could match. Elton's growing list of American hit singles also stood in stark contrast to Rod's meagre score of just two. Rod Stewart was still a big star everywhere, but it was Elton John who was having all the number-one hits in America.

Rod was enormous fun to be with, to hang out and have fun with. There was no question who the rock star was. But Rod was matey, loved football too, and had paid a decade's worth of dues before making it so big. Elton was the same story, concertinaed. He relished the mateyness too, just to be normal for once around someone who is definitely not a wide-eyed fan or a paid-for flunky. They connected like brothers, members of the same tribe, mercilessly taking the piss out of each other.

They just had a lot in common: 'We both love football and collecting art,' shrugged Elton. And singing and performing and 'enjoying our success'. To hell with what anyone else thinks.

The pair would bicker and moan and camp it up like an old married couple, making catty comments in the press and playing pranks on each other. They had their own drag names: Elton was Sharon, Rod was Phyllis. And they would address each other in public as 'She . . .'

When Elton played Rod a pre-release cassette recording of 'Don't Let the Sun Go Down' while driving together one day in LA in 1974, he sat impatiently behind the wheel, silently agonising over the two whole minutes it took to get to the chorus, thinking to himself: 'Fucking long single – and so slow.' Rod turned to him and said: 'Ballad, is it?'

Rod loved Reg. He got on his nerves sometimes, but he knew the feeling was mutual. Rod 'loved the fact that [Elton] was the kind of bloke who could see the comedy value in driving thirty times around the roundabout that surrounds the Marble Arch monument in the middle of London.'

They had their first public wobble in 1975 when Elton accepted the role of the Pinball Wizard in Ken Russell's spectacular film version of the Who's *Tommy*. Rod had memorably sung 'Pinball Wizard' on the 1972 classical rock version of *Tommy* recorded with the London Symphony Orchestra. It was a towering performance. As a result, a year later he had been offered the part in the movie, but Elton had advised against it, ridiculing the idea: 'Bloody hell, it'll be a cartoon series soon.'

Rod passed. But when the part was then offered to Elton, he accepted. And ran with it. Mentioning in passing, not at all regretfully, 'Rod has never forgiven for me for it.'

Not long after, Elton turned up at his own fancy-dress party in a curly blond wig, explaining he'd come as Rod Stewart. 'We try and publicise the fact that we always have a go at each other in the papers,' said Elton, 'but in fact we do that for reasons only known to us, really. We're actually very good friends.'

In 1976, at a time when Elton's personal and professional fortunes were flagging just as Rod's were on the rise again, particularly in America, where he'd just enjoyed his first number-one single since 'Maggie May' five years before, 'Tonight's the Night', Elton came up with the idea for them to co-star in a movie together, working title *Jet Lag*. As he outlined it to Rod, *Jet Lag* would be their much hipper version of the road-trip buddy movie; the hilarious yet soulful story of a pair of tax-exiled rock stars flying around the world in private jets, having madcap adventures together.

Rod thought it was a 'totally barking idea' but humoured his clearly out-of-sorts friend. The movie was never made and to Rod's relief, Elton never mentioned it again.

For the most part they just had normal every-guy fun together. When the press began 'speculating' about Elton's thinning hair and expanding pate and whether he would go for a hairpiece or not, Rod showed no sympathy. Once in the early '80s when Rod was doing a big show at Earl's Court Arena, Elton, who happened to be staying in London at a nearby hotel, looked out the window and was taken aback to find a giant blimp hovering over the venue with a picture of Rod's face on it. Elton immediately called his office and told them to hire someone to shoot it down – which they did that same day.

In 1976, after Elton watched one of those music-youth-arts shows on TV doing their best to explain what this new thing punk rock was, he instantly picked up on something one of the safety-pinned sages – Joe? Johnny? Sid? – said about 'people like Rod Stewart', who were old and useless and should stand aside for the new generation of young punks. He simply had to phone his old friend Rod and commiserate: 'My dear, how awful for you,' said Elton gleefully. 'And you still only twenty-nine, Phyllis . . .'

Rod of course derived much pleasure from this endless discourse. As he recalled in more recent times: 'Elton sent me an email saying, "I never have a headache but yesterday morning I had the biggest fucking banger I've ever had. It was because you were on the fucking radio!"'

The japes have continued as they have both grown older, though a certain crankiness can occasionally be detected. *You* know that *they* know that *we* know it's all good fun publicity but there was a little needle too in 2020 when Rod, while being interviewed on British TV, said of Elton: 'We don't talk to each other any more. Big falling-out.' The reason, it later transpired, was that when 75-year-old Rod had invited his 73-year-old playmate to his Essex home for a game of football on his own pitch, Elton had 'snubbed him'.

Rod claimed that Elton 'had the hump' because he'd been quoted as describing the Farewell Yellow Brick Road tour as 'not rock 'n' roll'. He is said to have continued: 'Last time I emailed him, I said, "I've got this football pitch, would you like the boys to come up?"' Meaning Elton's and David's children. 'You know because they both love football.' However, Rod did not receive even a cursory reply, saying he felt 'very sad' because they 'used to be good friends'.

Naturally, Elton wasn't going to let that sort of stain on his character go unchallenged but at first he said nothing – nothing publicly at least. That would come in the new chapter added to the paperback edition of *Me*, published later that year.

As an official 'source' told *The Sun*: 'Rod's continued barbed and personal criticism of [Elton's] recent successes has crossed a line beyond their usual friendly rivalry. Elton cherishes his friendship with Rod and hasn't wanted to go public so made attempts to contact Rod directly to clear the air. When his requests to speak were either knocked back or went unanswered, Elton felt compelled to set the record straight with this new chapter in his autobiography.'

He certainly did that and in hilariously spiteful fashion. Most bitingly, when he writes about how he doesn't need 'a lecture on the feral spirit of rock and roll from someone who'd spent most of the last decade crooning his way through the Great American Songbook and "Have Yourself a Merry Little Christmas".' He added with peak-Elton asperity, 'I thought he had a fucking cheek, complaining about me promoting a tour while he was sat on a TV show promoting his own tour.'

Checkmate, old chap. In fairness, Rod immediately backed down, blaming TV producers for 'plying me with alcohol' before he made his comments on the chat show. He added: 'They make sure you get drunk before you go on. Four big shots of neat vodka and with me being a butch man, I knocked them all back.'

He went on ruefully: 'She [Elton] doesn't like me at the moment. I was bang out of order. Correct, but bang out of order. I said that 300 dates in three years sounded a bit money-grabbing to me. Look, I know where's he's coming from. He's just got two kids very, very late in life, but I'm planning my tours around my kids. I think he'll miss it. I can't wait for the next show.'

Or the next insult/joke, you decide. Or, as Boy George tweeted, 'Rod Stewart and Elton have fallen out? The world is less glam!'

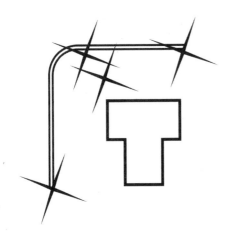

Tantrums & Tiaras
'I'm on fucking holiday!'

A marvellously indiscreet 1997 documentary directed by David Furnish and produced by Rocket Pictures, Elton's sporadically active film, *Tantrums & Tiaras*, offers an excellent view into the more than slightly mad world of its subject, or at least its subject as he was back in 1995.

So where was Elton at in the mid-'90s? Energised by his recent sobriety, for sure, but also prickling with sensitivity for the same reason and prone to fits of pique. Forty-eight years old and looking surprisingly fit, he's trailed by the boyish-looking Furnish – who throws a sequence of leading questions at him – on a promo tour of France and Spain, at home in Windsor and Atlanta, on holiday in France and then behind the scenes on his 108-date 1995–96 world tour. Mum Sheila Dwight pops up to deliver some curt comments, as do Elton's assistant, hairdresser and therapist.

You might expect Furnish to portray his partner's eccentricities affectionately, and indeed he does, but at the same time both director and subject are to be commended for their willingness to let all hang out on camera – the good, the bad and the sometimes toe-curlingly embarrassing, all are featured in *Tantrums & Tiaras*. Most famously, for the highly amusing scene in which he stormed off a tennis court at a hotel in Antibes in the south of France after a fan called out, 'Yoo-hoo!' to him. 'I'm on fucking holiday!' he screamed back. 'I'm never coming to the south of France again!' he announced, before ordering his private jet to take him elsewhere.

For this reason, the best way to watch *Tantrums & Tiaras* is with the expanded Director's Cut version released in 2009: Elton's audio commentary, in which he laughs at his own bad behaviour, adds a huge amount of context. As he told *GQ*, 'I think *Tantrums* is hilarious, it's one of the funniest things I've ever seen. The bits I really love are the bits when I'm behaving appallingly . . . they're the bits you want to see; you don't want to see me be nice to everybody.'

Still, Elton must wince whenever – if ever – he re-watches the scenes in which his stage nerves become overwhelming before the 1996 Oscars, or when he yells at a hapless assistant on a video shoot or berates florists for their supposedly 'disastrous' flower-arranging. His catty remarks about his peers may be brilliant – before yet another interview, he snipes, 'How does Mrs Jagger do it? He'll talk to a wildebeest' – but at the same time, he comes across as incredibly contradictory. Desperate for alone time, he can't manage without his team of helpers; people annoy him intensely, but he's addicted to their validation.

That's a recommendation, by the way: few rock-star docs are this honest and compelling.

TAUPIN, BERNIE

You can't plant me in your penthouse

Few creative partnerships are structured quite like that of Elton John and Bernie Taupin. Talented musicians pair up with skilled lyricists all the time, of course, but there has rarely been a duo that has been as successful, or that has maintained that success for as long, as Elton and Bernie. Only Elton's idols, Lennon and McCartney have exceeded their worldwide sales. But their professional relationship lasted a mere ten years, where Elton and Bernie first began working together over half a century ago and with a couple of temporary gaps, have been together ever since. According to Bernie, 'Elton and I were inseparable from the time we met.'

Furthermore, rarely has such a creative partnership flourished between such different personalities. Elton was the insecure child who turned himself into an extrovert peacock and blew millions on drugs and luxuries, while Bernie was the quietly spoken Yorkshire lad from a background of relative privilege who never learned to love the limelight. Opposites attract, we know that – but as Elton has said himself, the fact that Bernie's lyrics express Elton's own emotions so accurately defies all analysis. How the dickens have they pulled it off for all these years?

'I don't know why. I can't explain it and I don't want to explain it,' declared Elton in his memoir, which is his prerogative, of course. However, we may be able to do a little better than that.

Consider the following. Bernard John Taupin was born on 22 May 1950 in rural Lincolnshire, where he grew up in a farmstead called Flatters House. When he was nine years old his parents, Robert and Daphne Taupin, moved the family to the north Lincolnshire village of Owmby-by-Spital, where Robert ran a battery-chicken farm. Bernie, as he was known to family and friends, had an older brother, Tony, and a younger one, Kit.

The Taupin family weren't wealthy, the privilege referred to earlier a cultural resource rather than a financial one. Robert Taupin was of French heritage, having been educated in Dijon, while Daphne had lived in Switzerland, where she studied French literature. Her father, John Cort, was a Cambridge-educated classics teacher who taught Bernie to appreciate reading and poetry.

The academic side of this was evident in older brother Tony, a grammar-school kid who went on to university. Bernie, however, did not follow in his footsteps, leaving school at fifteen. He could write well enough, so he applied for a job as a trainee in the print room of the *Lincolnshire Standard*, the local newspaper. This didn't last long, however.

Bernie says he thought the job would be more along the lines of 'ace reporter, but I ended up in the machine room [and] that drove me crazy.' He recalled a 'northern factory-type' environment, 'very dark and gloomy and little men walking around asking for their sixpence a week to join the union.'

He was fired, he said, 'for trying to find another job during working hours.' He spent the next couple of years either unemployed 'just doing nothing really' or taking manual jobs on local farms. He laughingly recalled: 'I was playing a lot of snooker and drinking a lot of beer and staying out all night.'

Aged seventeen, Bernie answered an advert in the *New Musical Express* that connected him with Reg Dwight, a budding musician three years his senior. The Liberty Records label, newly independent after leaving the EMI group, were looking for songwriters, and although neither man passed their audition, the label's A&R man Ray Williams handed Reggie an envelope containing Bernie's lyrics. He read them on the tube on the way home to Pinner and was impressed, contacting Bernie shortly afterwards.

A film, *Two Rooms*, was made in 1991 and followed the songwriting process that the soon-renamed Elton and Bernie quickly developed. It came out twenty-four years after the two had first met, but nothing had really changed about their method in the interim; today, thirty-two years later, the process is still the same.

What we're told is that Bernie writes the lyrics, occasionally inspired by something that Elton has suggested, but more usually not; he then sends them to Elton, who builds music around them with no further input from Bernie. The two men will occasionally meet in the studio as the songs take shape, but most of the time, Bernie has no idea what a finished song will sound like.

At least, that's the received wisdom about their process. In practice, their songwriting roles overlap to a certain extent. For example, Elton comes up with the occasional lyric himself, 'Life isn't everything' from 'Song for Guy' being a notable, if simple, example. More importantly, he is not beyond cutting words from Bernie's lyrics if they don't fit his perception of the song.

As Elton said in the liner notes of the *To Be Continued . . .* box set in 1990, 'I used to do some things to his lyrics which were really heinous crimes . . . [I'd] just cross out things and say, "Oh, sorry, Bernie." That's why the last verse of "Daniel" was never there, which explained the whole song. I said, "Too long, sorry." Somebody else would have gone nuts. But that's part of our relationship – we give and take.'

In the same interview Elton revealed that Bernie's early lyrics weren't constructed in a formal manner, a fact which is more significant than it first appears. 'In the beginning, [Bernie] wrote in the narrative; he didn't write songs. The early lyrics weren't in verse and chorus form at all . . . he just wrote what he liked. Things like 'Madman Across The Water', 'Indian Sunset', 'Talking Old Soldiers' were written in the narrative form. I used to be able to get 12 words in one line, because he had written 12 words in one line.'

In other words, Bernie wrote lyrics unconstrained by rhythm or rhyme, and to a lesser extent by meter. He addressed this early naiveté once in *Rolling Stone*, explaining: 'At that time I was really faking it. The whole idea of how to construct a song was foreign to me. The idea of verse/chorus/bridge was big-pants terminology to me. Back then, I was throwing it down on the page. It was brain-to-pencil sort of freeform.'

That freedom wasn't shared by Elton, however, whose job was to create a chord sequence for a given song, arrange its structure, find a suitably appealing topline melody, and add harmony. In these tasks, all of which require much talent and even more effort, he would be aided hugely by the option to chop a word here and there: if this were disallowed by Bernie's ego, he would effectively be forced to build a house around the corners of its furniture, so to speak.

None of this would be particularly interesting in the case of lesser songwriters. However, the simple fact is that both men are phenomenally gifted at what they do. Bernie, an early devotee of the poetic lyrics of Bob Dylan and Joni Mitchell, has the knack of taking the listener into emotionally resonant territory that feels very much of the here and now. His words can certainly be fantastical, especially in the earlier songs he wrote for Elton, but that doesn't mean they feel elevated or irrelevant.

Eleven hugely successful studio albums representing an enormously productive decade of writing together, made it even more mystifying when Elton and Bernie decided to stop working together in 1977. To this day, we don't really know why they did it. Elton has always dodged the question, simply saying that they didn't want to get stuck in a rut. Bernie has rarely said anything at all on the subject, so we can only speculate here as to why it happened. Was Bernie hungry for solo success? Did the two men fall out? Was there a business problem? The answers are apparently not; possibly; not that we know of.

The most likely answer is that, at after working so closely for over a decade, the two men – both still young, Bernie just twenty-seven. Elton now thirty – they both felt the need for some space from each other, as well as just being curious about what else they might achieve without the other.

The separation didn't last long; Bernie's nominal replacement, Gary Osborne, was gifted but his work with Elton was not nearly as prolific in producing never-to-be-forgotten hits. In addition, while it has often been pointed out that Bernie is able to write lyrics that perfectly suit Elton's personality and delivery, he was less able to do this with other artists. He'd already given it a shot with the singer-songwriter David Ackles in 1972, but the album for which he wrote lyrics, *American Gothic*, was more written about than listened to, a worthy effort soon forgotten. Even a 1971 album of his own, titled *Taupin*, was destined to remain a career footnote, consisting of jammed, sitar-based music over which he recited autobiographical poetry.

However, Bernie did better with the Alice Cooper concept album *From the Inside*, released in 1978 during the break from Elton. Musically, the songs are of a type with the veteran shock-rocker Cooper's '70s sound, in other words mildly beefed-up hard rock – delivered in this case by a band that included Elton's guitarist Davey Johnstone and bassist Dee Murray. Lyrically, however, it's evocative and vivid, with Bernie's lyrics based on Cooper's 1977 incarceration in a New York sanitarium due to his alcohol abuse. Far from the contemporary model of a rehab facility, however, Cooper found himself in an actual insane asylum, sharing padded cell space with patients suffering from severe mental illness.

The subject allowed Taupin to indulge his love of Americana. 'Was it Texas or was it Canada? / Drinking whiskey in the morning light' he writes on the title track. As well as some classic Taupin poetic metaphors: 'We just played with the wheels of a passenger train / That cracked on the tracks one night' – from 'Inmates (We're All Crazy)'. Not for the first time in his career, Bernie also turned his thoughts to the subject of sex ('I'm suddenly twice my size / My pants are all wet inside', from 'Nurse Rozetta'). Although in that instance we perhaps could have done without the details.

Speaking in 2014, Bernie's main memory of working with Alice, he confessed, was the amount of cocaine the two began to consume together. 'At the time,' Bernie confessed, 'I had a drug problem. It was the old thing of, 'I'll be right back' then go to the bathroom where I'd be doing coke. And Alice, he's not a stupid guy, he's catching wind of something here.'

Having conquered his alcoholism, Cooper felt 'well, I quit drinking, I can probably allow myself to do something like this. And I started like everybody else having just a little hit of this and a little hit of that . . . '

But the little hits Bernie was sharing with Alice quickly turned into a full-blown addiction to freebasing the coke. In case you've only just been born or perhaps were born a little too long ago, freebasing is a more efficient method of self-administering alkaloids – such as cocaine – by smoking it through a homemade plastic pipe. In '70s LA, snorting coke was considered classy, like offering your guests vintage champagne. But freebasing, which was only just becoming a thing and mainly confined still to the mean streets of East LA, was considered tacky, uncool. For Bernie it looked positively dangerous.

'I remember freebasing with him, which I'd not done before,' Bernie recalled. 'It's easy to get caught up in something new.' Eventually though he had to tell Alice: 'I said, "A bit of coke's okay, dude, but when you start smoking that shit, it's like smoking your home."'

But Alice wasn't listening, and the next few years vanished up his nose and into his lungs. 'It broke my heart,' said Bernie, forced to walk away. 'It was one of the hardest things I ever did. But I remember leaving that pool house and going, "I just can't stay here because I'm gonna go down, too . . . "'

The great romantic writer of lines about horny-backed toads and howling old owls in the wood also turned his mind to more carnal themes of love. Apart from the excellent quality cocaine, what else was there to do in LA in the '70s than enjoy sex with some of the most goodlooking people on the planet.

There was the – unintentionally no doubt but highly problematic – 'Jamaica Jerk-Off' from *Goodbye Yellow Brick Road*. Elton chirruping in a faux 'islands' accent over a vague reggae lilt: 'Let the ladies and gentlemen be as rude as they like / On the beaches, oh in the jungle where the people feel alright . . . '

From the same album, 'All the Girls Love Alice', a beautifully crafted pop epic, that now fair reeks of a certain lasciviousness, familiar to every major tour band in America in those early empire-building days. The dark flipside to 'Tiny Dancer'.

'It is a pretty blue record,' Bernie conceded when the *LA Times* brought the subject up some years later. 'I was a young kid, a horny 23-year-old, among a lot of other horny twenty-somethings. I read a tremendous amount all through my life, and I'm not sure how I would have drawn some of those songs out of Tolkien or C. S. Lewis. I was basically writing about my fantasies at the time.'

In 1971, he'd married Maxine Feibelman, a beautiful, dynamic American girl who he'd met in Los Angeles the previous year. They remained together for five years, during which time Bernie moved permanently to LA, officially granted US citizenship in 1990. Maxine was the inspiration for several of Bernie's songs during this period, whether he admitted it in public or not. Bernie's love for Maxine was expressed most famously in 'Tiny Dancer' from *Madman Across The Water* and 'Mellow' from the following year's *Honky Chateau*.

Inspiration was also drawn from other areas of Bernie's relationship with Maxine. For example, the phrase she used whenever Elton was in a filthy mood again became 'The Bitch Is Back'. When their marriage broke down and she began an affair in 1976 with Elton's then-bassist Kenny Passarelli, Bernie wrote poignantly in the *Blue Moves* track, 'Between Seventeen and Twenty': 'I wonder who's sleeping in your bed tonight . . . Could it be a close friend I knew so well who seems to be so close to you instead?'

During his break with Elton, Bernie investigated new creative territory, to build more of a name for himself than merely 'Elton John's lyric writer'. He acted and sang in a 1978 episode of the US TV teen drama *The Hardy Boys/Nancy Drew*, 'The Hardy Boys & Nancy Drew Meet Dracula', singing backup to Shaun Cassidy.

He not coincidentally resumed his solo recording career with a new solo album the same year, his second: *He Who Rides the Tiger*. Bernie cowrote all the songs with former Buckinghams guitarist Dennis Tufano and finally took the plunge as a vocalist, singing lead. Despite the presence of Elton on some backing vocals plus various members of his band – including, interestingly, Kenny Passarelli – the album sold poorly. That was the last time Bernie Taupin tried anything as crazy as singing his own songs. Bernie retreated from the public eye for the next five years.

With the benefit of hindsight, it would be only a matter of time before Elton and Bernie renewed their creative partnership. A 1978 single-only release, tellingly titled, 'Ego' had been a moment of enjoyable drama to keep the fans happy.

A leftover from *Blues Moves*, "Ego' was just something I had lying around,' shrugged Elton without any trace of irony, 'I wanted to release it for a long time.' When it failed to make the charts anywhere, he was disappointed, said Elton. 'I really had hoped it would do well because I really liked it. I wrote the song jointly with Bernie Taupin, and we never thought of it as an autobiography until it came out. It's about the silliness of rock 'n' roll stars, and the video film was supposed to show just how stupid rock 'n' roll can be. It's the grotesque side of rock 'n' roll. And it's turned out to be one of the most sincere songs we've ever written.'

American-born film and TV director Michael Lindsay-Hogg, famous for dozens of promotional clips for both the Beatles and the Stones, was brought in to make a video for Elton's new single, 'Ego'. Although it was not a hit, barely making the top forty in

Britain or America, 'Ego' became the first Elton single to be given the full-on video treatment.

It may look tame now but in 1978 the 'Ego' video was considered upscale and featured 'theatrical' scenes starring a young British actor named John Emberton, who plays Elton as a small boy acting out a scene from *Romeo & Juliet*, while his real-life sister Penny plays a suitably impressed member of the audience. Designed to launch a new look, more 'new wave' sounding Elton John, the video for 'Ego' saw him ditch the glasses in favour of contact lenses and debut a chiselled chin with a hint of five o'clock shadow, his sleek suit and tie set off with a snazzy fedora hat, his face twisted into his version of a punk sneer. He does not look comfortable at all.

The video, set in a mansion, was meant to satirise the life of a pompous out of touch rock star, and cost £40,000 to make, ten times as much as Queen's game-changing video for 'Bohemian Rhapsody' in 1975. If only it had sold even half as well, it might truly have ushered in a new era for Elton. Alas, it just wasn't very good. Nevertheless, in its ambition to marry music and image, 'Ego' was very much a harbinger for the coming age.

Indeed, in terms of Elton's and Bernie's professional relationship, it was the beginning of their Great Reconciliation. Within another two years the pair were collaborating on a handful of songs for each new Elton album. When Elton and Bernie finally resumed working together on a full-time basis, *The Fox*, *21 at 33* and *Jump Up!* had been and gone, and it was 1983. Bernie's lyrics had become more focused and direct over the years, and the payoff was noticeable. Elton's biggest '80s hits – among them some of his biggest hits whatever decade, 'I'm Still Standing' (1983), 'I Guess That's Why They Call It the Blues' (also '83), 'Sad Songs' ('84) and 'Nikita' ('85) – were taut, punchy and focused on a clear emotion, whether that meant defiance, misery or plain old love-love-love. There was little room for existential pondering or homages to Americana in Bernie and Elton's Middle Years.

Even more focused on quick thrills rather than cerebral musing, Bernie's songs 'We Built This City' (1985) and 'These Dreams' ('86) – released by Starship and Heart, respectively – were perfect, unashamed pop disguised as soft rock. 'Marconi plays the mamba' was a memorable phrase from the former, although Bernie spoiled it somewhat when he gleefully admitted that it meant nothing whatsoever.

In 1987, Bernie released another solo album, *Tribe*. Like its predecessors, it failed to make an impact, despite the appearance in two videos of the pulchritudinous actress Rene Russo. Not coincidentally, she was the sister of Bernie's second wife Toni Russo, to whom he was married from 1979 to 1991, and who provided the inspiration behind Bernie's lyrics to 'I Guess That's Why They Call It the Blues'.

Although Bernie and Elton enjoyed slightly diminishing commercial returns in the '90s, despite the latter's post-rehab rebirth, the former occupied himself with some interesting projects, as well as spending 1993 to '98 married to his third wife, Stephanie Haymes Roven, the daughter of old-time American TV faces Dick Haymes and Fran Jeffries. A collaboration with the French-American musician, producer and soundtrack composer Josquin Des Pres was fruitful, with many of their collaborations becoming modest hits for other artists around the globe.

A new band called the Farm Dogs was more interesting for several reasons. Formed in 1996 and ploughing a broadly similar furrow to fashionable alt-country bands of the time such as Wilco, the Farm Dogs featured Bernie on guitar and vocals alongside guitarists Jim Cregan and Robin Le Mesurier, both veterans of Rod Stewart's solo band. Critics noted, not unfairly, that Bernie's performance was adequate rather than scintillating, and the group's debut album *Last Stand in Open Country* while warmly received failed to stamp its authority on country radio.

A club tour didn't do much business, and a second album, 1998's *Immigrant Sons*, seemed to mark the end of the Farm Dogs. Still, there was life in the songs, one of which, 'Bird of Prey', appeared to make a vitriolic reference to a former spouse. Bernie singing of 'a wedding ring just hid the whore' and referred to a woman keen to steal his money. Asked if its subject was his first wife Maxine, Bernie said: 'You think I'm going to admit to that. I'm surprised you even know the name. You judge for yourself. I will tell you as much as this. It's definitely from experience.'

Five years later, anyone who had dismissed the Farm Dogs as a vanity project was forced to eat their words when none other than Willie Nelson covered three of the group's songs on his album *The Great Divide*. One of these, 'Last Stand in Open Country', was a duet with the rap-metal artist Kid Rock; the others were 'This Face' and 'Mendocino County Line'. The latter was another duet, between Nelson and the singer-songwriter Lee Ann Womack – and it won the 2003 Grammy for Best Vocal Collaboration in Country Music. Bet *that* made Elton sit up . . .

After that high point, it was time for the Farm Dogs to go back into their kennel, but that didn't mean that Bernie's American obsession had slackened off. If anything, he dug deeper into a real-life version of the Wild West, moving to a ranch in Santa Barbara, where he competed in cattle-herding contests. Bernie, now in his early seventies, still lives there with his current wife, Heather Kidd, who he married in 2004 and with whom he has two daughters, Charley Indiana and Georgey Devon.

Every now and then Bernie will do an ad hoc writer-for-hire job, as he did in 2004 when he cowrote Courtney Love's song 'Uncool', and most memorably, in 2005, a song called 'What I Really Want for Christmas' with none other than Beach Boys' resident genius Brian Wilson.

These don't get in the way of his ongoing collaborations with Elton, with whom there's the occasional failure such as 2006's

Lestat: The Musical, based on the Anne Rice gothic vampire novels. But most of their work together is both critically and commercially successful. An example is the album *The Captain & the Kid,* also released in '06, which made number six in the UK and the top twenty in the US.

These were good times for Bernie, who received a massive pat on the back from the establishment in the form of a Golden Globe Award for the song 'A Love That Will Never Grow Old' from the film *Brokeback Mountain.* Elton, too, was keen to stress Bernie's importance to him, including his lyricist in the cover art of *The Captain & the Kid* album, and telling the audience during the filming of the *Elton 60: Live at Madison Square Garden* DVD the following year that there would not be an Elton without a Bernie.

Although neither man really needs to create new music, separately or together, they keep doing it because they love it and, as Bernie once said, 'What else should we do?' Some of it is definitely worth your time, such as *The Union,* a collaboration album that Elton and his idol Leon Russell released in 2010. Other songs are best regarded as a bit of fun, like the tunes they wrote for the 2011 movie *Gnomeo and Juliet* and the related *Sherlock Gnomes* seven years later.

Along the way they've kept a weather eye on the day job, collaborating on Elton's *The Diving Board* and *Wonderful Crazy Night* albums in 2013 and 2016, and raking in critical plaudits with the *Rocketman* movie three years further on. An Oscar for Best Original Song for the film's closing song '(I'm Gonna) Love Me Again' was richly deserved.

A nostalgic release in 2021 of *Regimental Sgt Zippo,* an album of the youthful Elton's quasi-psychedelic songs recorded fifty-three years earlier, bears scrutiny for Bernie's vivid, slightly schoolboy lyrics. You can imagine the young Taupin scribbling 'There's a picture in the nursery of a well-known soldier man / And he wants to be like Father when he grows up if he can . . . '

Bernie had spent the past ten years exhibiting and selling his original artwork. Brushing aside his name and the modest cachet it afforded for wealthy or would-be art collectors, the work itself, large, mixed-media canvases, were more Americana fan collage than deep David Hockney dive. You applaud the endeavour.

The picture we're left gazing at on the wall, is of someone not unlike Elton John. A man of intriguing, sometimes dark contradictions. Yet in more fundamental ways the two men are the opposite of each other. Bernie was a prodigiously gifted poet from humble farming stock, a star who both craved and shunned the spotlight, an America-bedazzled young Brit who literally became what he beheld.

Awarded a CBE in the 2022 New Year Honours list, Bernie is no less a star than Elton, but he takes up far less space – which answers the earlier question about why the two work so well together. As their personalities dictate, one recedes from exposure while the other revels in it. They are yin and yang, sun and moon, town and country. Words and music.

THE THOM BELL SESSIONS
Elton in a Philly-soul funk of his own

The creative hub that had sustained Elton John for so long finally came apart at the seams as the '70s staggered to a bleary close. Bernie Taupin's wife, Maxine Feibelman, the LA woman he'd written 'Tiny Dancer' for, had left him for Elton's new bassist, Kenny Passarelli, of all people. Bernie drifted into morning drinking and night-time coking – until a doctor warned him about the perilous state of his liver. On the advice of smarter kinder friends, he checked into a high-class rehab facility in Acapulco. He needed to dry out. He needed to control his drug use. He needed to rethink his life.

Rocket Records, meanwhile, still relied completely on Elton's record sales – the very thing he had vowed would not happen. However, MCA still released all his work in America and if Rocket was to survive, it badly needed new acts that generated their own hits for the label. Producer Gus Dudgeon found his suggestions for acts they might sign and develop for Rocket were too often overlooked.

Then suddenly, without any conspicuous bust-ups or obvious 'musical differences', something apparently permanent had shifted. The *Blue Moves* album had marked the end of a tightly knit era of Elton's creative life. Punk rock was running riot through older musical sensibilities. Elton, always impatient, grew itchy for new and different experiences. He was also coked out of his gourd for much of the time and a born-again thrill seeker. He was sick of the lot of them, he would do whatever the fuck he wanted.

The split with Bernie was also a natural reaction to a decade of intense artistic intimacy. They both needed the break. Taupin became involved in a writing project with shock rock king Alice Cooper. Elton in turn would work with lyricist Gary Osbourne, who he'd met through their work for Kiki Dee. Before that partnership began to flower, however, Elton took the chance to fly to Seattle to record 'a few songs' with Thom Bell, a storied and highly talented writer and producer of the Philadelphia soul sound that Elton had given an approving nod to on 'Philadelphia Freedom'. Bell was noted for his hits with the Stylistics, the Delfonics, the Three Degrees and the Spinners, an all-American, all-black, all-proud sound that David Bowie had created a fantastic simulacrum of on *Young Americans* two years before and been rewarded with his first American number-one single, 'Fame'.

There was a lot about trying something different like that, that appealed to Elton John in 1977. He had turned thirty in March and suddenly felt for the first time in his life . . . not *old* but definitely *older*. He had done it all. Now he was open to suggestions.

Bell had recently relocated to Seattle, so recording took place not at Bell's cherished Sigma Sound in Philadelphia, but in a top Seattle studio handpicked by the producer. However, the overdubs would be done back at Sigma, something which pleased Elton, who otherwise appeared to have little or no say in proceedings.

As well as producing the resulting three tracks, all cowrites shared between Bell's nephew, LeRoy Bell, and his singing partner, Casey James, Thom cowrote a shiny potential pop diamond that he unfortunately blanketed in eight minutes of soul-opera testifying. Not even the Spinners adding rolling waves of harmonies and heartaches could save it from simply going on and on too damn long.

Zero hit single potential. Great if you like that sort of thing, but, honestly, a bit boring.

It was called 'Are You Ready for Love'.

They recorded six tracks in total but according to Philip Norman, Elton decided that the sessions were 'overproduced' and the orchestration 'too sweet'. The project was shelved, given a PR burial, as Elton performed a volte-face with the next thing he recorded, a leftover track from *Blue Moves* called 'Ego', written with Bernie and released as a one-off single early in 1978 that was musically about as far removed from Philly soul as you could get.

Two years later, three of the tracks – 'Three Way Love Affair', 'Mama Can't Buy You Love' and 'Are You Ready for Love' – were issued as the EP, *The Thom Bell Sessions '77*. Like a magician sawing his lovely assistant in half, 'Are You Ready for Love' was folded across both sides of a single formatted as Parts 1 and 2 and released in May 1979. It was especially disappointing when it failed to have any impact as, timeline-wise, it was perceived as the follow-up to 'Song for Guy', his biggest single since 'Don't Go Breaking My Heart'. America ignored it. In Britain it didn't even make the top forty.

But of course, the story didn't end there . . .

TikTok

The clock is always ticking

When Elton John embarked on his Farewell Yellow Brick Road world tour in 2018, the name TikTok had not yet entered the lexicon. Five years later, as the tour entered its final leg, everyone had heard of TikTok. Not everyone still knew what it was exactly, or what it was for, or even how it was supposed to work, but they had heard of it the way everyone has heard of Twitter. If you were under the age of twenty, however, you not only knew all about TikTok, not only used and viewed TikTok, you *were* TikTok.

Owned by the Chinese company, ByteDance, and first test-launched in 2018, TikTok hosts user-submitted videos, ranging in duration from three seconds to ten minutes. The most popular home videos are all music-related. Sometimes professionally produced videos for established or unknown wannabe musicians and singers, the same as on YouTube and all the other social media sites. But the vast majority of TikTok videos are made by people just taking existing songs and having fun with them. Being creative. Taking old gold and alchemising it into freshly minted currency. And viewed on computers, iPads and tablets but mainly enjoyed on phones . . . billions of phones.

Corporations, sports franchises, movie and TV companies all rushed to get involved. By October 2020, TikTok had surpassed 2 billion mobile downloads worldwide. Morning Consult, the global business intelligence company, officially listed TikTok as the third-fastest growing brand of 2020, after Zoom and Peacock. In 2021, Cloudfare, the world's largest cybersecurity company, ranked TikTok the most popular website of 2021, surpassing even google.com. The same year, TikTok reported that it had earned $4 billion in advertising revenue.

In October 2022, TikTok was reported to be planning an expansion into the e-commerce market in the US, following the launch of TikTok Shop in the UK. The company posted job listings for staff for a series of order fulfilment centres in the US and was reportedly starting the new live shopping business before the end of the year. According to data from app analytics group Sensor Tower, in March 2023, advertising on TikTok in the US grew by 11 per cent just that month, with companies including Pepsi, Amazon and Apple among the top spenders. According to estimates from research group Insider Intelligence, TikTok is projected to generate $14.15 billion in revenue in 2023, up from $9.89 billion in 2022.

The impact this has had on the music business has been seismic. Beyond that even of MTV in the '80s, when video really did kill radio stars, the immense reach of TikTok has transformed the way music – both new and old – is now consumed. An early tipping point came in October 2020, when a young American named Nathan Apodaca posted a clip of himself on TikTok, sipping cranberry juice and lip-synching to 'Dreams' – a number-one single in 1977 for Fleetwood Mac – as he skateboarded down the street after his vehicle broke down on the way to work, and the video went viral.

'We love this!' the band tweeted when they saw the post. When drummer Mick Fleetwood and singer Stevie Nicks then posted their own versions of the video, with Nicks singing along to herself while lacing up roller skates, 'Dreams' went to number one in the *Billboard* streaming chart. TikTok capitalised on the trend by making a TV commercial from the original video and its knockoffs, which ran during Major League Baseball playoffs. The phrase 'pop will eat itself' has never seemed more apt – or prophetic. The popularity of that one clip prompted 8.47 million streams of 'Dreams' in just a week in the US, beating the previous high of 3.83 million. The song also returned to the UK charts, while the classic album from which it heralded, *Rumours*, returned to both the US and UK charts, forty-three years after its original release.

Suddenly the music industry was all over TikTok. Every 'heritage' act in the business was suddenly finding their recording careers resurrected because of TikTok. And one of the most popular artists in this new field of expression was Elton John. At last count – and the numbers continue to rise every day – classic Elton hits account for millions of TikTok videos, with the most popular, like his 2021 Dua Lipa collab, 'Cold Heart', accounting for almost half a million different videos alone.

There is no discernible pattern, just whichever Elton songs fit any one individual's needs at the time. Hence 'Sacrifice' has been used in TikTok videos almost 200,000 times, 'Bennie and the Jets' and 'I'm Still Standing' account for around another 200,000 videos. But not as many as 'Hold Me Closer', Elton's 2022 collab with Britney Spears.

TikTok now features its own Top Elton John Songs page, as well as its own niche song charts updated every twenty-four hours. Spotify now features its own TikTok songs page and TikTok trending page, as does Apple Music. Amazon sells all the bits of kit you need to make your own TikTok videos, from tripod stands and boom mikes to a Bluetooth scrolling ring and wireless fingertip gadget shutter. Meanwhile, TikTok-themed books, clothes, games, apps, now dominate the online market.

The big driver though is still music. And Elton is still one of the biggest TikTok song-drivers of all. So that now it no longer matters whether Elton's music is played on radio or TV, or how old he is, or what he looks like or what *his* new video looks like. Elton John's music – his name, his appeal, his freshly laundered reputation and name-recognition among the children of the 21st-century online revolution – now sits comfortably alongside that of Taylor Swift and Harry Styles, Dua Lippa and Lizzo, Post Malone and Megan Thee Stallion, Doja Cat and the Weeknd.

Needless to say, Elton John now has his own TikTok page with almost a million subscribers. Welcome to the future.

'TINY DANCER'

Meet my cool new American girlfriend

Written about Bernie Taupin's cool new American girlfriend, its music created in not much longer than the time it takes to play, barely a hit first-time out and now one of the best-known songs in Elton John's vast catalogue, the long and strange history of 'Tiny Dancer' is one of the great romantic stories in rock and pop.

The song was almost thirty years old when Cameron Crowe used it for a few ecstatic moments in *Almost Famous*, his elegiac, semi-biopic of his time as one of *Rolling Stone* magazine's youngest writers. The fictional band Stillwater are cast in the image of '70s goliaths like Led Zeppelin and the Eagles, both of whom the young Crowe covered extensively for *Rolling Stone*.

The scene where they are enduring a tense after-show bus ride is so beautifully realised by the director, especially the moment where the mood is instantly transformed by 'Tiny Dancer' coming on the radio twinkling and shedding fairydust, and the passengers, one by one, begin singing along. If it hadn't before, 'Tiny Dancer' now took its place in the canon of the very greatest of '70s love songs.

Bernie met Maxine Feibelman in LA in 1970, when she arrived at the band's hotel with a hairdryer for the group's drummer, Nigel Olsson. It was the week of the Troubadour dam burst and the pair made an instant connection. Feibelman would inspire lots of Bernie's lyrics over the course of their subsequent relationship, marriage and breakup six years later. The first of those was 'Tiny Dancer' and there exists a film, shot just days after the song was written during the *Madman Across the Water* sessions, which explains the instant alchemy of its creation. In it, Bernie and Maxine watch Elton at the piano as he grabs a sheaf of Bernie's lyrics.

'There's one here I done the other day, "Tiny Dancer" – and it's about Bernie's girlfriend . . . ' an impossibly young and cool-looking Elton says.

'He tends to write very fast as he doesn't have the patience to spend days or hours on anything . . . that's Reg,' remarks an apple-cheeked Bernie.

Elton, looking through the lyrics to 'Tiny Dancer', goes on: 'As soon as you get to the word "ballerina", you know it's got to be slow.'

He begins to play and sing, Bernie and Maxine looking on. It is magical to see.

When 'Tiny Dancer' was recorded, it came in at more than six minutes long, meaning it had to be edited if it was to be a single, and everybody agreed it had to be the single. Yet it barely scraped the top forty in America, was never released in the UK and for a while seemed as though it would be a part of the yesteryear catalogue cherished only by the most ardent fans, yet it was ultimately too good to hide.

Elton kept the song in his set and although he and Bernie were writing and creating at a phenomenal pace, 'Tiny Dancer' held its own, rising all the way to the timeless classic status Crowe's brilliantly evocative film triumphantly confirmed.

THE TROUBADOUR

It happened one hot night in Hollywood . . .

In 1970, the Troubadour, sited at 9081 Santa Monica Boulevard, West Hollywood, was a magnet for the new post-hippy, double-denimed singer-songwriter crowd typified by Linda Ronstadt and her band, two of who will go on to form the Eagles, Jackson Browne, Tom Waits, Joni Mitchell, David Crosby and Stephen Stills. All rubbing shoulders with the new LA demi-monde that included writer Eve Babitz, famously photographed playing chess naked with the French artist Marcel Duchamp; comedian-cum-banjo player Steve Martin, who opens for rock groups, doing loopy magic tricks and pretending to mess up on the banjo.

The Troubadour is where you might find Harry Dean Stanton looking gloomy and nursing a beer. Where rising stars like Kris Kristofferson hung out with Hollywood hipster Jack Nicholson. Where Janis Joplin showed up just days before she died. Even the waitresses are different. There's Big Tit Sue, Bigger Tit Sue and Black Sylvia. Towering above it all, sometimes appearing naked on the stage, 43-year-old Doug Weston, the club's charismatic owner, standing 6 foot 6 inches. 'The 'tallest queer I ever knew,' according to Ted Markland, who played Reno in the hit early-'70s TV western *The High Chaparral*.

The Troub's bar was the place where the regulars plunged into 'over-boogie', as they called it. Monday night was Hoot Night, just a dollar to get in, the joint turned into a showcase for unsigned talent. If you got to sing three numbers, you were winning.

Into this melting pot, in August 1970, tiptoes Elton John. Neither he nor the people who showed up that night had any idea of what was about to happen. The cognoscenti drooled in groovy anticipation of the kind of low-lit, self-absorbed posture suggested by 'Your Song'. But that was decidedly not what Elton John had in mind. 'The photo on the cover of the *Elton John* album led people to believe I'd be quite folksy and Randy Newman-esque,' he recalled. 'When I walked out on stage wearing flying boots with dungarees, everyone was genuinely taken aback.'

Beginning on Tuesday 25 August, Elton John played eight shows over six consecutive nights at the Troubadour: shows that helped turn him from a strangely named unknown into rock's biggest star since the Beatles. Not that anyone could have predicted that happening.

In a 1970 *Record Mirror* readers' poll, Elton came just fifth in the Most Promising Newcomer category, trailing behind Juicy Lucy and Pickettywitch. He had already released seven singles and two albums and so far, zero hits. 'I'd been performing as a solo artist for about a year in England by that point,' he recalled. 'I felt I still needed to properly break the UK first and I wanted to keep my focus there.'

He had performed some shows in Europe, but they had not gone so well. Booed off stage in France, 'I certainly didn't think we were ready to try breaking America.' In fact, every American label had passed on signing him, except for one: the LA-based UNI Records, short for Universal City Records, a modest imprint of MCA Records, but whose only name artist was Neil Diamond. When UNI head Russ Regan offered a signing advance of just $0.00, Dick James was forced into a 'stick or twist situation'. Dick decided to twist and put a final $10,000 into getting Elton and crew over to America.

'It was Dick James who really pushed for me to go to the Troubadour,' said Elton. 'He thought it would kick-start things – and he was right!'

The original offer from Doug Weston for the Troubadour stint was just $150 per show. Not enough to even cover expenses, James told Elton and Bernie, 'If this doesn't work, you can all come back and I'll get you jobs in a shoe store on Oxford Street.'

Thus, a worried Elton touched down at LAX airport in August 1970 full of trepidation. His first time in America, in addition to his two-man band of bassist Dee Murray and drummer Nigel Olsson, he was also accompanied by Bernie Taupin, his then manager Ray Williams, DJM producer Steve Brown, album sleeve artist David Larkham and just one roadie, Bob Stacey: 'We were very much a gang,' said Bernie.

The gang could scarcely believe their eyes when they got through airport customs control to find that UNI had splashed out on a red open-top British double-decker bus, written on the side: ELTON JOHN HAS ARRIVED. Some bystanders were said to have concluded that 'Elton John' must be some kind of new toilet.

The night before the first Troubadour show, Elton was in a state of almost nervous collapse. 'I'm not doing this gig,' he announced at one point, 'I'm going home!' Ray Williams was aghast: 'I said, "You can't do that, you'll ruin your career."' A loud shouting match ensued, which only calmed down after Elton had thrown Williams into the hotel swimming pool. 'Elton was so nervous,' remembered Williams. 'Finally, he said, "All right, I'll do the shows." His tantrums, which he's now famous for, had already started.'

His nerves remained coiled tight, right up until the first show. When Williams informed Elton that through the extraordinary efforts of Russ Regan and UNI publicist Norm Winter, they had filled the Troubadour guestlist with everyone from superstar producer Quincy Jones and his fiancée, actress Peggy Lipton, to fellow musos Linda Ronstadt, Mike Love, Van Dyke Parks, Don Henley, Randy Newman, David Crosby and as many other regular Troub scenesters as they could round up. None was more important or influential, however, than thirty-year-old Robert Hilburn from the *Los Angeles Times*. Hilburn had begun his career as a news reporter on the suburban Los Angeles newspaper, the *Valley Times TODAY*. His interest in writing about popular music began in the mid-'60s when, like millions of others, he became in thralled to the more intellectualised pop of Bob Dylan and the Beatles.

In 1966, he began submitting pieces to the *LA Times* on such figures as Johnny Cash and Janis Joplin. Then in 1970, he was offered the chance to become the newspaper's first official pop music writer. Over the next few years Hilburn would garner a hard-won reputation for taking no prisoners in his reviews. Reviewing Elton John's first show at the Troubadour, however, was of a different, higher order and spectacularly prophetic.

'Rejoice!' Hilburn announced in his review. 'Rock music has a new star.'

'I'd never heard of Elton until I started getting calls from UNI Records,' he said. 'Russ Regan or Norm Winter called me every day for six or seven days: "This guy's got the same publisher as the Beatles." I didn't care who the publisher was.' As it happened, Hilburn made it a point to always be at the Troubadour on Tuesday nights: 'It was the most important club in the country.'

Hilburn recalled how shy Elton appeared on stage at first: 'He played almost with his head down, like he was hiding. They were pretty songs, but he wasn't selling them in any way. For the first ten minutes, I thought, "This is gonna be a disaster."'

But then Elton surprised everybody, even Dee and Nigel, by kicking over the piano bench and turning into a cross between Little Richard and Jerry Lee Lewis, standing there with his head thrown back singing, or hoisting up his platform-booted feet to pound the keyboard. When he started doing handstands on the piano, the club went wild.

'It was the end of the '60s,' Hilburn recalled. 'An era had ended. We'd been through all of that fire and rain. Elton was calmer, a little less frantic. He had those great songs that reminded me of the Band and then there were Bernie's lyrics: "I hope you don't mind that I put down in words." I loved that line.'

Speaking in the *LA Times* years later, 'The atmosphere during those nights at the Troubadour was electric,' said Elton. 'Something inside me just took over. I knew this was my big moment and I really went for it. The energy I put into my performance caught everyone off guard. Even before the reviews came in, we knew that something special had happened.'

'It was like a ball of fire hit the Troubadour,' said Linda Ronstadt. 'When he got to "Take Me to the Pilot", the place levitated. They were a trio, but they sounded so tight, like a garage band.'

Once Hilburn's *LA Times* review hit the newsstands the following day, every one of the seven remaining shows sold out immediately. Suddenly the LA trip turned into one long glorious celebration. Leon Russell, a genuine Elton hero, who had also been there that first night, came backstage and offered to take Elton out as the support act on his next run of US shows. He also gave him a friendly tip on how to keep his voice in good shape: 'He told me about gargling with cider vinegar and honey – and I still do it to this day.'

UNI arranged limousines to take Elton and his entourage for a day out at Disneyland. That night, Nigel, Dee and Bernie were sitting in the tiny Troubadour dressing room when Elton came in with Mickey Mouse ears on his head, announcing, 'I'm going on stage like this tonight.' 'It was horror and laughter at the same time,' laughed Nigel Olsson. 'I think that was the start of his crazy stage wear.

Three months later, Elton returned to California, but not for more shows at the 300-capacity Troubadour, rather to headline the 3,000-capacity Santa Monica Civic Auditorium. Three weeks later, he was back again, this time to headline the 9,000-capacity Anaheim Convention Center. Less than a year after that, Elton performed for seven straight nights at yet another iconic LA venue, the 4,000-cap Greek Theatre. Next stop the 18,000 LA Forum, followed by his crowning Californian achievement: two sold-out nights in 1975 at the 56,000-capacity Dodger Stadium.

But nobody ever forgot about those Troubadour shows. *Rolling Stone* included them in a list of the '50 Greatest Concerts of the Rock Era'. And in 1975, to mark their fifth anniversary, Elton returned to the Troubadour to perform three short sets, along with his much bigger band, plus Bernie, Kiki Dee, John Reid and enough friends, employees and hangers-on to fill the club entirely.

As Robert Hilburn says now, 'The love affair with LA has never stopped, on both sides.' Something that Elton still gives Hilburn credit for. 'I've gotten occasional Christmas cards from Elton,' he relates. 'There's a bond from that night that has continued. In almost every interview he does, he mentions my review. That's very gracious.'

Tumbleweed Connection
California dreaming

Written and recorded months before Elton John and Bernie Taupin arrived for the first time in Los Angeles but released in the wake of the unexpected triumph of the August 1970 Troubadour shows, at the culmination of Elton's first lengthy American tour, twenty-six shows that took him coast-to-coast, *Tumbleweed Connection* was the perfect album to reinforce his status as America's newest singer-songwriter superstar. It was as if Elton and Bernie had fully anticipated their new career trajectory, coming up with fresh and startling material that sounded for all intents and purposes like it was written and recorded in America by American singers and musicians, rather than at Trident Studios during a cold rainy March in London.

As Bernie later explained to the British music historian John Tobler: 'It was totally influenced by The Band's album *Music from Big Pink* and Robbie Robertson's songs. I've always loved Americana and I loved American westerns. I've always said that "El Paso" [an American number one in 1960 written and sung by country singer Marty Robbins] was the song that made me want to write songs, it was the perfect meshing of melody and storyline, and I thought that here was something that married rhythms and the written word completely.'

Certainly, you can immediately hear the difference in the opening track, 'Ballad of a Well-Known Gun', with its slinky lead guitar from Caleb Quaye, burbling percussion from Roger Pope and the tenderised backing vocals, featuring Dusty Springfield, Madeleine Bell and Lesley Duncan. Said Elton, 'Lyrically and melodically, that's probably one of our most perfect albums. I don't think there's any song on there that doesn't melodically fit the lyric.'

It's there again for all to hear on tracks like 'Country Comfort' – garnished with some authentic pedal steel guitar from Gordon Huntley of Matthews Southern Comfort, who enjoyed one of the biggest hits of 1970 with their version of Joni Mitchell's 'Woodstock'. And it's there on the funky, country-cool 'Son of Your Father', the come-get-some 'Amoreena' – the first track both Dee Murray and Nigel Olsson appeared on together on an Elton album – and again on the gospel-country of the rollicking 'Burn Down the Mission'.

But while Elton strove to distance himself from the harpsichords and flickering shadows of much of his previous *Elton John* album, he still ensured his finely poised pop sensibility was fully expressed on almost too fragile tracks like the sublime 'Come Down in Time' and, most especially, 'Love Song', a staggeringly beautiful song written by Lesley Duncan, one of the most cruelly underrated pop chanteuses of the era.

There was another fateful Elton track originally recorded during the *Tumbleweed Connection* sessions, entitled 'Madman Across the Water' and featuring a fiery then unknown guitarist named Mick Ronson, soon to become uber-famous as David Bowie's right-hand man. But while the song would become the masterful title track of the next Elton John album, it was ultimately left off the finished *Tumbleweed* collection.

Interesting footnote, for an album featuring at least two stone-cold hits, 'Come Down in Time' and 'Love Song', there were actually no singles released from *Tumbleweed Connection*. At the time the album was released in Britain, in October 1970, 'Your Song' was belatedly on its way to becoming a multi-million seller in both Britain and America (although 'Country Comfort' was released in Australia and New Zealand). When the album was finally released in America, in January 1971, the title track to a soundtrack album for the movie *Friends* was about to be released as Elton's next single.

In an era of artists releasing at least two albums a year and up to six singles in the same period, it was thought simply that the moment had passed. At the time it hardly seemed to matter as Elton and Bernie were already hard at work on their next collection of soul-stirring classics.

TOO LOW FOR ZERO

Elton conquers the blues and stands tall again

Released in 1983, Elton John's seventeenth studio album was
seen as something of a comeback for him. The first Elton album
to feature all John/Taupin material since *Blue Moves* in 1976, it
also marked the return full-time to the fold of guitarist Dave Johnstone, bassist Dee Murray, drummer Nigel Olsson, percussionist
Ray Cooper, along with guest appearances from singer Kiki Dee
and harpist Skaila Kanga, last heard on *Tumbleweed Connection*
more than a decade previously.

The result was a more focused if still somewhat incoherent
collection of songs. As the writer Don Shewey put it, reviewing
the album in *Rolling Stone*: 'Although *Too Low for Zero* is a big step
up from losers like *Blue Moves* and *A Single Man*, it doesn't hang
together, either.'

It did however boast two of Elton's biggest hit singles of the
'80s, in 'I Guess That's Why They Call It the Blues' and 'I'm
Still Standing'. The former was written by Elton and Bernie in
conjunction with Davey Johnstone and had an irresistible roiling
swagger and gospel-tinged vocals. It also featured Stevie Wonder
on his beautiful harmonica. The best Elton singalong since 'Philadelphia Freedom', it immediately found a home in both the UK
and US top five.

For once there was a cool video to go with it, too. Directed
by Russell Mulcahy, the talented Australian film-maker who had
made his name in Britain directing hit videos for Culture Club
and Duran Duran, among many others, the 'I Guess That's Why
They Call It the Blues' video told the story of two '50s-era young
lovers who are separated when the man is called up for National
Service in the army. Following his misadventures there, the lovers

are reunited by the end of the song and everyone goes home happy.

Mulcahy also directed the video for 'I'm Still Standing', which made the top five in Britain and sold more than a million copies in America. The song, which would not have sounded out of place on *Goodbye Yellow Brick Road*, has gone on to become one of the most memorable hits of Elton's career. Not least because of the Mulcahy video, which the recently launched MTV kept on 24/7 rotation.

Shot over a hectic 48-hour period on the Côte d'Azur in France, the first day's filming had to be shot again after Mulcahy fell into the sea while holding the camera. This was also the infamous occasion when Elton went on a bender with Duran Duran, who happened to be staying in the same hotel.

In his book, *Wild Boy: My Life in Duran Duran*, guitarist Andy Taylor wrote: 'There were lots of celebrities around in Cannes and one day we discovered that Elton John was in town, filming the video for his song "I'm Still Standing". This was before Elton became teetotal, so he was still a steaming party animal. We went up to see him at his hotel and spent the afternoon getting blasted on martinis. We decided it would be a laugh to get him drunk and we were slinging the drinks down him. "Ooh, you are lovely boys," he screeched, loving every minute of it. We got him so drunk that eventually he went upstairs and threw a wobbler in his suite. It caused all sorts of chaos, but it was a great party.'

In 2019, the original 16mm film negatives were rescanned and the computer graphics recreated to create a new version of the video. It is this version that serves as the ending to *Rocketman*, with Taron Egerton rotoscoped in. It may not rate as one of his very best albums, but people still sing along to 'I Guess That's Why They Call It the Blues' when it comes on the radio and no one can deny the boisterous 'I'm Still Standing' – or the exuberant video that went with it.

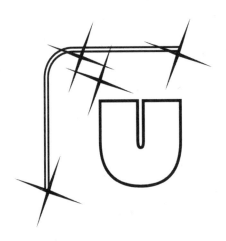

Uni Records

Signed for exactly no dollars, no cents

Universal City Records, founded in 1966, commonly referred to in the business as 'Uni' and rendered with a slick UNi logo, was the work of two American executives, its founder Ned Tanen of Uni's owner MCA Inc, and its president Russ Regan, who is the man who signed Elton John to the label in 1969 – even though he wasn't particularly enamoured with his music. Dick James, who'd had no luck at all in trying to get any other US label interested, offered Elton to Uni, through Regan, for the principal sum of exactly no dollars, no cents. All he asked in return was that the label distribute the *Elton John* album in America.

The accomplished English songwriter Don Black, then hot with the theme tune to the drama *To Sir, With Love* (1967), rated Elton's work, saw the potential – like a lot of serious musicians – and when Regan asked him for his opinion on the young song-writer, Black heartily recommended the new talent to him. Regan eventually agreed to sign Elton if Uni could also have DJM's band Argosy. Dick James, who was in no position to argue, agreed to the deal and was paid a $10,000 advance for Argosy and nothing for Elton, an ironic outcome since the former vanished without trace and the latter is still doing business fifty-four years later.

That said, Uni's initial release of Elton's 'Lady Samantha' and 'Border Song' singles made little impact in the US: it was only when *Elton John* arrived on Regan's desk that the wheels really started to turn. 'I couldn't believe my good fortune,' he told Philip Norman. 'I called the whole staff of Uni into my office, about thirty people.' Regan ordered all calls to be put on hold while he played them the album, all thirty-nine minutes from start to finish – 'Everybody fell in love with it.'

Regan's PR supremo Norm Winter embarked on a publicity campaign to promote the album, sending it to every radio DJ he knew and smothering LA record stores with posters. The week at the Troubadour blew everything up and before Elton landed in America in late 1970 to begin his first lengthy US tour, Uni released 'Your Song' – which quickly rose to number eight in the US chart.

In 1971, Uni merged with the indie and soul labels Kapp and Revue, as well as the US arm of Decca, to become the new MCA Records – transferring their artists over to the new, much larger company. The first official MCA release in November 1972 was Elton's single 'Crocodile Rock', Elton's first US number one and a million-selling hit. History was made and Elton remained signed to MCA in North America until 1980, when his manager John Reid negotiated an even better deal for him with the newly formed Geffen Records label, who had just signed John Lennon.

Uni itself was revived in 1988 as a niche label, with a roster that included Eric B & Rakim and Steve Earle, and in 1991, MCA used the name for its sales network, Uni Distribution Corp. Geffen controls the Uni catalogue today after acquiring MCA in 2003, bringing Elton's classic '70s releases under one roof.

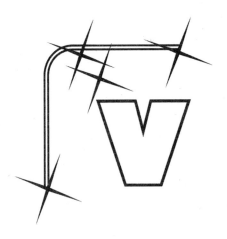

VERSACE, GIANNI

Song for a gay

It might be easy to dismiss the friendship between Elton John and the late fashion designer Gianni Versace as predictable and light-weight, given their mutual penchant for camp outrageousness, but you would be mistaken. While of course they shared many of the same extravagant tastes – outlandish attire, lusty appetites for both sex and drugs, absolute excess in every department, and of course great artistic talent directed into impossibly glamorous and successful careers – theirs was more of a brotherhood than a mere friendship, tragically cut short in the cruellest way possible.

The two men met in the late '80s, when Versace was still a small clothing store in Milan rather than the mega-brand it soon became. Elton loved the clothes, already well known for their flashy prints and ultra-bright colours, but he loved the man who designed them even more. The two were remarkably similar, he later noted: both gay, only a year apart in age and with restless minds that rarely switched off. Versace's favourite song was 'Song for Guy', which he praised as incredibly brave; Elton was somewhat bemused by this until he realised that his chum had misunderstood the title as 'Song for a Gay'!

The other personality trait that the two men shared was their ability to spend money: Versace would, recalled Elton, go out to buy a watch and come back with twenty of them. He once implored Elton to buy a tablecloth that was hand-stitched by nuns over a period of thirty years and cost a million dollars. Even Elton thought this was over the top, but a disappointed Versace completely failed to understand this. Still, the pair remained close until 15 July 1997, when Versace was shot dead at his home by an American serial killer named Andrew Cunanan, who took his own life a couple of weeks later. BLOWN AWAY IN HIS VERSACE FLIP-FLOPS, as the tasteless headline in the *Daily Mirror* crudely put it. Elton was beyond devastated, comparing the murder to the death in similar circumstances of John Lennon.

Just as he would have to do for Princess Diana only six weeks later, Elton performed at Versace's funeral, which took place at the Milan Duomo on 22 July 1997. He sang a duet with Sting, delivering a rendition of the 23rd Psalm with difficulty because he was overwhelmed with grief. The event was almost derailed by a couple of the Duomo's clergy, who asked pointed questions of Elton and Sting because neither man was a Catholic.

In the years following the murder, Elton remained close to the Versace family, at one point staging an intervention for Gianni's tragic sister Donatella, who had developed a serious cocaine addiction. He also took note of the circumstances of his friend's demise and adopted a policy of hiring professional security, something he had never previously considered – not even after the shocking assassination of Lennon. Sadly, such precautions are now part and parcel of twenty-first-century celebrity life.

VICTORIA AND ALBERT MUSEUM

A good home for the 3ft powdered wig and the 15ft feather train

Opening the day before Elton John's final British show at Glastonbury on 25 June 2023 was a new exhibition at London's Victoria and Albert Museum entitled *DIVA*. The V&A, as it is customarily known, is the world's largest and most prestigious museum of applied arts, decorative arts and design, home to a permanent collection of over 2.27 million objects.

What made the *DIVA* exhibition so special for Elton fans was that among the more than 250 objects drawn from the V&A's collection and loans from across the world, including clothing and over-the-top costumes worn by those who have been given the title of diva, would be the Louis XIV costume he wore to mark his fiftieth birthday in 1997, a never-before-displayed outfit comprising a 3ft powdered wig and a 15ft feather train.

Elton was not alone among the male celebrities included in the show which the V&A announced was dedicated to the 'fluid' concept of 'the diva'. Among the iconic dresses and attire of women including Maria Callas, Marilyn Monroe, Mae West and Tina Turner are the work and images of other famous male divas, Prince and drag queen RuPaul.

Kate Bailey, curator of the show, said: 'The *DIVA* exhibition narrative explores how the term has been embraced, redefined and reclaimed. Diva is a fluid and open concept that is channelled and harnessed by performers on and off stage to inspire creativity and expression through their art, costumes and music.' She added: 'Today the word diva holds a myriad of meanings. At the heart of this exhibition is a story of iconic performers who with creativity, courage and ambition have challenged the status quo and used their voice and their art to redefine and reclaim the diva.'

Displays would inform visitors about the exceptional talent of such individuals and how they used this and their individual style to transcend various social norms and expectations. Whether they would also feature a section devoted to the famous 'tempers' and 'tantrums' of certain male divas remained to be seen at the time of writing.

VOICE PROBLEMS

Open up and say ah . . .

Generally, a fit and strong fellow, Elton John was largely injury- and disease-free for the first four decades of his life, meaning that when his voice first started giving him problems in 1985, he didn't pay much attention to it. A lot of singers have throat issues, especially those that have spent fifteen years headlining stadiums and selling millions of records, and those that have not looked after their voices as well as they should.

In the early days of longform touring in the early '70s, Elton always relied on a Leon Russell-recommended blend of honey, cider vinegar and hot water to pull him through. As the years sped by and the party just never stopped, Russell's elixir simply didn't cut it any more. Elton was shocked on tour in Australia when his voice oscillated unpredictably between normal- and zero-performance. Sometimes he could only croak and wheeze, sometimes he couldn't even speak between the songs. A show in Perth was cancelled and he finally sought professional help after a concert in Sydney when he coughed up a lot of repulsive-looking gunk.

An ear, nose and throat specialist, Dr John Tonkin, had a look at Elton's larynx and diagnosed cysts on his vocal cords, which sounded manageable until he revealed that in fact those cysts could either be benign or cancerous. Concerned by Elton's habit of smoking spliffs and doing lines of coke, Tonkin duly scheduled surgery.

Elton was terrified, both by the existential threat and by the practical implications of being unable to sing if, in the event of a cancer diagnosis, his larynx had to be removed. He was advised to cancel his remaining Australian dates but was unwilling to do so as a live album was scheduled for recording. Somehow, he recorded the material and finished the tour before going under the knife on 6 January 1987.

To everyone's relief, the operation, in which the cysts were cauterised by laser, revealed the cysts to be benign, but the surgery did have an unexpected side effect: it lowered Elton's vocal range. He was happy with his new voice, fortunately, even though he was no longer able to reproduce the falsetto that had enriched songs such as 'Tiny Dancer' and 'Someone Saved My Life Tonight'. They are still great songs when he sings them now, made more poignant perhaps sung by the older man.

WATFORD FC

Don't bend down when Elton's around

Football was a strictly working-class game in England before the 1990 World Cup in Italy, after which the chattering classes started professing great interest in it. But for the working-class kid Reg Dwight, the sport was a lifelong source of fascination and comfort. Like his friend Rod Stewart, a staunch Celtic FC fan, the soon-to-be Elton John kept the same team close to his heart into adulthood, although – unlike Rod – his beloved club was something of a joke.

'I've always supported Watford football club since a child,' he told Michael Parkinson in 1986. 'Even though my cousin, Roy Dwight, played for Fulham – and scored the first goal in the 1959 [FA] Cup final.'

Watford's lowly Third Division status, crumbling home stadium and precarious finances made them an unappetising prospect for most football fans in the mid-'70s. The club first benefited from Elton's beneficence when he played a fundraiser there in 1974, prompted by Julie Webb, a journalist from *NME*. She was also a Watford supporter and suggested Elton put on a concert in aid of the club.

So it was that on the afternoon of 5 May 1974, clad in a black-and-gold striped jacket and matching trousers (the team's playing colours), Elton bounded onto the specially erected stage at Watford's home stadium, Vicarage Road, to a crowd of over 31,000 – five times the number of people who usually showed up for the team's league matches. Joined on stage for a song by an all-in-white Rod Stewart, the show was such a success that Elton then bought shares in the club and became its vice-chairman, before buying it outright and moving up to chairman two years later. He appointed a hotshot manager, the 32-year-old Graham Taylor, and the two agreed a plan of action.

'This was at a time when I was wearing 8-inch high-heeled shoes – and had pink hair.' He said that 'although they must have laughed their heads of as soon as I walked out the door,' it was the people that he met who worked there that really encouraged him to get involved. Because they treated him as a normal person, which nobody had done in the music business since he first became a star.

'For example, the washing lady, Molly, who was a lovely lady. She used to say to me, "I don't like your new record. Why don't you make something like 'Daniel' again?"'

With Elton's considerable spending power at his disposal, Graham Taylor completely revamped the club and its team, renovating the ground and buying talented young players such as the teenage John Barnes, a future Liverpool and England superstar. With Taylor's strategy of playing two hefty centre-forwards flanked by fast wingers on the flanks, Watford began to win their games and were promoted in their first season under the new regime. By 1981, they had risen from the Fourth to the First Division, qualifying for European competition for the first time in their history by finishing the 1982/83 season with only Liverpool ahead of them.

The pinnacle of the Elton-owned Watford came in 1984, when they played the FA Cup Final at Wembley Stadium in front of over 100,000 fans. Elton shed tears of joy in front of the TV cameras when he realised how far his team had come: even their 2–0 defeat by Everton didn't diminish his pride. He knew he'd taken the club as far as he could, though, and when Taylor moved on in 1986, Elton went with him. Both men returned for a brief spell in the '90s, but Elton quit for good in 2002. He remained on close terms with Taylor until the former manager's death in 2017.

Elton later claimed that Watford FC saved his life, primarily because he couldn't be an overindulged rock star when he was at the club: as its owner, he was required to always behave professionally: 'There were no holds barred but they were very, very protective of me and very, very loving.'

Elton recalled turning up one Boxing Day at Vicarage Road, where Watford were playing Luton Town: 'At the time I was drinking very heavily, and I wasn't particularly very happy. He knew I was in a state and Graham Taylor said, "I want to see you for lunch." I thought, "I know what he's gonna say, he's gonna give me a lecture." So, I went to his house for lunch and he said, "Here you are" and he put a bottle of brandy on the table. He said, "Have that. That's what you want, isn't it?"' It was a lesson he never forgot: 'I needed someone to lecture me, I never could get one over on him.'

Surrounded by yes-men and lackeys as he normally was, it was refreshing for Elton to have his feet placed firmly on the ground once again and even to be embarrassed – as he was when thousands of away supporters took to singing whenever he was there, 'Don't bend down when Elton's around, or you'll get a penis up your arse!' Far from being offended, Elton cheerfully accepted the humour in his treatment: being able to handle it without throwing a tantrum was, he acknowledged, important for his and Watford's survival.

'What the fuck do you know about football?' laughed Rod Stewart when Elton originally told him of his grand plan to buy the club and bring it to glory. 'If you knew anything, you wouldn't support this lot!' But it was Elton who had the last laugh. He may have saved Watford FC, but they saved him in return.

WEALTH

What do you do with your money, honey?

It's impossible to gauge anyone's wealth with any degree of accuracy once their assets exceed £10 million or thereabouts – not because that's a large sum in today's era of psychotically inflamed capitalism, but because most of what they own is fluid in value. These people didn't get rich because they earned a salary, like the rest of us. Their wealth lies in stocks and equity, and not only are those assets subject to opaque taxation rules, but their value also rises and falls with the economy in which they are sequestered.

In estimating the wealth of Elton John, a reliable starting point might be the annual *Sunday Times* Rich List, and specifically its richest UK-resident musicians' category. The list obviously limits its estimates to publicly available information, so it can't tell you exactly how much a particular multi-millionaire pop star has in his various bank accounts. However, in the post-subprime world you'd be insane to trust a bank with a life-changingly large sum of money. We can therefore assume that most of Elton's fortune is tied up in limited companies, whose annual accounts you can readily consult at the Companies House website.

In 2000, the Rich List placed Elton fifth on their musicians list with assets of £160 million. According to the same paper five years later, he was worth £185 million, a figure that remained the same for the next five years, possibly because of the 2007–09 recession. A footnote from 2005: in that year, Elton made the top of the list of wealthy charity-givers, donating an estimated 12 per cent of his £185 million to good causes.

A decade later he'd added another £100 million to his fortune and every year from 2016 to 2020, his assets appreciated by another £20 million or so. In 2021, Elton was the fourth-richest musician on the *Sunday Times* list with £375 million and held that position in 2022 at £395 million. The pandemic had clearly made little impact on his assets, suggesting that by now most of his income might come from investments and appreciation rather than touring. For reference, the top-three places on the musicians' list usually swap between Sir Andrew Lloyd Webber, Sir Paul McCartney and U2, the latter entry being a touch unfair as there's four of them.

Can we go further back? Not easily, given the opacity of book-keeping before 2000, back when the keeping was done in writing in actual books. We do know from court records in the DJM Records case that Elton's declared gross income in 1994 was around £40 million. Half of that was from touring, we learn, but we have no indication of his total assets at that point. However, his amusing confession in court that he blew £2 million a month for eighteen months in 1996–97 indicates that he had, as they say down Pinner way, plenty put away for a rainy day. In exchange, Elton has given everything that's his to give – his talent, his energy, his time, his life. He has earned every penny.

WILLIAMS, RAY

It's a shame about Ray

Born in 1947 in the London suburb of Middlesex, Ray Williams is a successful music producer for film and TV, with some big credits – from even bigger productions – under his belt: these include music supervision roles on Bernardo Bertolucci's nine-time Oscar-winning *The Last Emperor* (1988) and Lars von Trier's Oscar-nominated *Breaking the Waves* (1996). Long before he entered the film world, however, Williams was the man who connected Elton John with Bernie Taupin, subsequently becoming Elton's first manager before John Reid came along. It's been many years since he was involved in Elton's business in any significant way, but his pivotal role in the yet-to-be-famous singer's career cannot be overstated.

Williams had his first taste of showbiz at the age of sixteen, hanging out on the set of the TV show *Ready Steady Go!*, where his local band, Cliff Bennett & the Rebel Rousers, were playing the first of their two top-ten hits, 'One Way Love'. A well-dressed Mod, Williams caught the eye of presenter twenty-year-old Cathy McGowan, who asked him to help with auditioning extras to dance on each week's show; this made Ray instantly popular with the hordes of kids who lined up at Rediffusion TV's studio in Kingsway, London, every Friday night. He became one of those with-it young faces that appeared in televised interviews when overseas camera crews arrived in London to cover the capital's swinging vibe and had appeared in *The Mod's Monthly* magazine.

Through *Ready Steady Go!* Williams met the Beatles' manager Brian Epstein and the group's PR man, Brian Sommerville, who gave him a job as an assistant in his Tin Pan Alley office. After doing PR for the Kinks, Sonny & Cher and Tommy Roe, Williams set up the short-lived Mayfair Public Relations, in Berkeley Square. By the time he was eighteen, Ray had famously added Buffalo Springfield, the Hollies and Cream to his roster.

In 1967, Williams was given the grandly titled job of European head of artist and repertoire by the American Liberty Records label, which was setting up a British operation. With no acts yet signed to the label, Ray drafted an advert for the *New Musical*

Express, where it ran on 17 June that year. 'Liberty wants talent,' ran the copy. 'Artistes, composers, singers, musicians to form a new group. Call or write Ray Williams for appointment or mail audition tape or disc to 11 Albemarle Street, London W1. Tel. Mayfair 7362'.

The ad received thousands of responses, one of which came from a young wannabe named Reggie Dwight, then playing in a group called Bluesology. Williams later described Reggie as 'a bit fat, a bit forlorn' at their first meeting, where he asked him to demonstrate his talents.

'I always remember a sentence that he used: "I feel lost." He just didn't know what to do,' Williams recalled in the *Daily Mail* half a century later. 'He was frustrated very much by the fact he was only a backing singer and a piano player. I had a piano in my office and asked him to go and play. He had a great voice and he was a great piano player, but he couldn't write, he had no ability to write lyrics.'

Williams liked Reggie's singing and playing enough to arrange for him to record a demo at Regent Sound studio in Denmark Street – London's version of Tin Pan Alley – where music publishers would send their promising songwriters to record basic versions of potential hits. But when he recommended that his bosses at Liberty sign the bespectacled young hopeful, they weren't keen. On Reggie's next visit to the office, Ray handed him an envelope containing Bernie Taupin's response to the *NME* ad, reasoning that the lyricist and musician might be able to work together; he also arranged for the two youngsters to meet.

This was the moment that kickstarted Elton John's career, of course, but at the time Williams thought nothing of it: he had bigger things on his mind, namely budding connections with pop-surrealists the Bonzo Dog Doo-Dah Band and Jeff Lynne, then of the Idle Race, later the Move then the Electric Light Orchestra (ELO). After Williams left Liberty in order to become Lynne's full-time manager he didn't hear from Reggie or Bernie again until 1970, by which time the former had signed his deal with Dick James Music.

'I lived near Chelsea at the time and Elton and Bernie came by. It was just a nice surprise to see them,' Williams recalled. 'We went to the pub, the Duke of Wellington, and Elton said, "I want you to manage me." I gave up everything I was doing at that time to manage him.'

A deal was struck with James in May 1970, in which Williams would co-manage the now-renamed Elton John and receive half the management commission, and the new manager promptly began booking engagements for the singer and his hastily assembled two-piece backing band. Everything changed however after Elton's soon-to-be legendary August residency at the Troubadour in LA. Although the trip was a tremendous success, it led indirectly to the end of Elton and Ray's working relationship. With a couple of free days before the Troubadour show, Williams organised a day trip to Palm Springs, the resort outside LA: Elton refused to accompany them and was duly left to his own devices for the day.

'Elton was the only one that didn't want to go and we thought, "Fine, stay." In retrospect it was probably completely the wrong thing to do,' Williams later revealed. Speaking years later, he described Elton's frame of mind that evening: 'He was very, very weird. I realised that being left alone all day had put him in some kind of bad mental state. He was sulking – and petrified.'

The next day, Elton was in an even worse mood. At breakfast, he told Williams: 'I'm not doing this gig, I'm going back to London.' According to Ray, 'He was shit scared, he was nervous. I said, "Yes you are" . . . He had a huge tantrum and it all kicked off. What I hadn't realised at that point is he'd rung Dick James and Dick took advantage of it and started to sow seeds of doubt.'

Back in London, Elton asked Williams to stand down as his manager, although not, it should be noted, in an unfriendly manner. Williams agreed that his client needed someone to manage him in a more hands-on way: 'Another thing was that, with his success, he was starting to get away with murder,' Ray told Philip Norman. 'He was very quick, very witty, very funny, and people just let him do anything he liked. I'd been standing up to him and that hadn't been going down well.' It was during the same period that Elton was finally coming to terms with his true sexual identity and the conventionally straight Williams, 'found that another pressure on our relationship.'

Still, Williams was confident that he and Elton would remain friends, particularly as the singer agreed to honour the deal they had signed: this awarded Williams a commission for Elton's first five albums, as well as a percentage of the revenue from live dates. Dick James had other plans, however, and called Williams in for a meeting, where he told him in no uncertain terms that the deal was off: Williams could either sue him or accept a payoff of £500. In a tight spot, and with a young family to support, Williams chose the latter option, negotiating it up to £1,100 (worth around £22,000 in 2023).

Unhappy with James's behaviour, Williams tried to contact Elton, who was touring the US at the time. 'Of course, there was a smokescreen of getting through to him,' Ray told the *Mail*. 'I think Dick did the dirty and Elton just avoided the issue because he had other stuff on, and that's been the same thing all his life, he's been able to avoid quite a lot of stuff. And it's dealt with by other people.'

That was it for Elton John and Ray Williams until 1982, when Dick James was sued for unpaid royalties and copyright terms: Williams was asked to assist with contacting witnesses, which he agreed to do. The pair didn't meet again, however, until 1991, when they had dinner together in Paris, and Elton apologised for the way Williams had been treated.

Twenty years later still, Williams wrote to Elton, annoyed about an interview the star had given to *Rolling Stone*, in which he had been referred to as 'a guy' who connected the singer with Bernie Taupin. A reply came from Elton's lawyer and manager Frank Presland, which Williams described as 'a very rude condescending letter. It basically said, "Really Ray, you had very little to do with Elton, it was a serendipitous moment, a happy thing, and we're very sorry you've had no success in your career". It was such an arrogant letter.'

It was also inaccurate: Williams went on to form a partnership with the Kinks' manager Robert Wace, launching the career of Stealers Wheel and that band's singer Gerry Rafferty, before entering the film world. Any remaining rancour on his part appears to be directed at the late Dick James rather that at Elton and indeed the singer himself wrote in his memoirs: 'Ray Williams was a lovely man, I owed him a great deal and he was incredibly loyal.'

Finally, Philip Norman summed the whole story up aptly when he wrote, 'If there were any justice in the world, the making of this one connection [between Elton and Taupin] would have given Ray Williams riches for life. But we can be assured, there is no justice in the world.'

WILSON, BRIAN

'He was not well at the time'

As with every aspiring pop star in the '60s, the young Elton John was completely in thrall to the extraordinary music of the Beach

Boys, and in particular, the troubled songwriting genius behind their greatest hits, Brian Wilson. As Elton explained: 'I love the Beatles, but I don't actually think they influenced me as song-writers.' The Beach Boys, he said, 'were a much bigger influence.'

When Elton discovered that Mike Love of the Beach Boys had been among the many famous names in the audience for his first show at the Troubadour in LA in 1970, he was glad no one had told him beforehand, as it would have made him too nervous. When later during that same crazy week Danny Hutton of Three Dog Night (who had recorded versions of 'Lady Samantha' and 'Your Song' on their earlier albums) offered to take Elton and Bernie Taupin to meet his good pal Brian Wilson at his Hollywood mansion, the wide-eyed young Englishmen could not believe their luck.

It was known at the time that Wilson had retreated from the world, under a thick haze of psychedelic drugs and plantations worth of pot, so nobody knew what to expect. Accordingly, the meeting began on a completely surreal note when the Beach Boys' legend responded to being introduced to Elton and Bernie by bursting into song: 'I hope you don't mind, I hope you don't mind . . .' Brian Wilson was singing 'Your Song' to them.

Things continued to get weirder after Brian invited them into his home. 'He was not well at the time,' explained Elton in the understatement of the year. 'We had dinner and the dining room was filled with sand. He went up to introduce us to his kids, woke them up. "This is Elton John. I hope you don't mind . . . I hope you don't mind . . ."'

Never having taken drugs at this tender early stage of their careers, Elton and Bernie freaked out. But not as much as when, after dinner, Wilson sat Elton and Bernie down and began playing them some demos he'd been working on alone in his state-of-the-art home studio. He also wanted to play them the master tape of 'Good Vibrations' but couldn't find 'the right one'.

They stayed up playing music and talking non-stop until seven in the morning. Elton recalled the drive back to the hotel with Bernie, thinking about how he'd never done anything like that before. It was exhilarating! He felt like he could keep going for another few hours, that's how good he felt. 'Years later,' he recalled, 'Danny told me that they put cocaine in my food. I'd no idea the first time I did cocaine.'

WOODROW, LINDA

'I felt so sorry for her'

'You almost had your hooks in me, didn't you, dear?' sings Elton John in 'Someone Saved My Life Tonight', the only single from 1975's *Captain Fantastic and the Brown Dirt Cowboy*, before a friend, unnamed in the song, intervened in the nick of time.

Harsh words, in retrospect? Probably, and when their target – Elton's early fiancée Linda Woodrow – heard them, she was understandably irked. 'In a way, I was disappointed,' she told the *Record* in 2010. 'It was Bernie Taupin that actually wrote the words. Bernie has probably said more negative things than Reg has. I mean, unbelievable things that were said. In some of the songs, I was very hurt.'

There's a lot of information in that little quote. First, Linda talks of being 'disappointed' and 'hurt' by those sardonic lyrics, which shows a great deal of restraint: some of us might be furious to hear a famous former partner publicly belittling us in that way. Second, and in a way brilliantly, she still calls Elton 'Reg' after all these years: it's a very '70s, very middle-England name, suggesting that to her, he never became the star, worshipped by millions, that we all know. That he would always be the same weak lost boy she had known before Reg was famous, before he became the singer known as Elton John.

Indeed, the Reg that Linda knew does cut a pathetic figure in the accounts that we have of this early period in his life. When the unlikely couple met at a Bluesology gig in Sheffield in 1968, Elton was twenty-one and Linda twenty-four; he was 5ft 7 and she was 4 inches taller; he was a struggling musician and she was the heiress to a fortune.

The two did have something in common – show business. Linda's father Alexander Woodrow had been in the limelight in a variety of roles, as a drummer in the Cameron Highlanders, as a standup comic in Variety, as a wrestling promoter and even as a stage magician. In 1968, he was running a Soho bar called the New Cottage, hence his nickname, Cottage Al. His family owned a company called Epicure, which made pickles and preserves: the firm had been successful enough to fund a private education for Linda at an academy in Reigate and then at a finishing school in Eastbourne.

A trust-fund girl, well educated in the verities, Linda towered over poor Reg both literally and in social terms, yet however improbably, the two hit it off almost at once and a relationship began. That night in Sheffield, she was in the company of a short-statured fellow called the Mighty Atom, who worked as a disc jockey at the city's Locarno Ballroom.

Elton later told *Rolling Stone*: 'She was going out with a midget in Sheffield who drove around in a Mini with special pedals on. He used to beat her up! I felt so sorry for her, and she followed me up the next week to South Shields.' Linda contradicted this, stating that she was not involved with the Mighty Atom and that the two were merely companions.

She and Reggie began to go on dates, with Linda coming down to Pinner to stay with Sheila and Fred Farebrother. After

Elton quit Bluesology and signed with Dick James Music, the two moved into a basement flat in Furlong Road, Islington. Bernie Taupin moved in too, although this inevitably caused tensions as time passed: as Bernie later revealed to biographer Philip Norman, he and Elton played tricks on Linda behind her back. They once spilled soap powder into part of a treacle sponge pudding, allocating that part to her – conveniently forgetting that she was supporting them financially while they tried largely in vain to make money out of their songs.

Sex was a problem from day one. Linda recalled that the first time they slept together, Elton – still a virgin at twenty-one – had booked them into an old Victorian hotel for the occasion. The earth failed to move for either of them, she told Norman: 'When we rolled into bed, he was clumsy and, frankly, didn't have a clue. He was a gentle person by nature and he was that way in bed. I was so keen on him that I didn't really mind.'

Other than physically, the relationship progressed conventionally for the times. Elton attended her friend Janet's wedding; he and Linda drove to her brother Neil's twenty-first birthday party; they visited her parents' home in Lincolnshire – although the stay was nearly ruined when Elton wrote off his Hillman Imp in a motorway pile-up. The couple walked away unhurt, apart from a minor arm injury for Linda.

They did make for an odd couple, most agreed. 'Cottage Al' Woodrow snickered in amusement when Linda told him that her boyfriend was going to be a star. Caleb Quaye, then working for DJM as a young studio engineer, laughingly recalled Elton 'trotting along beside Linda in his fur coat, with one of her little dogs on its leash. He looked so ridiculous with her towering over him.'

Elton and Bernie both claimed that Linda had hit her boyfriend on more than one occasion, although she denied this. Even so, the couple got engaged on Elton's birthday in March 1968, using a ring that Linda had bought for herself, as the groom-to-be was as usual skint. She had told Elton she was pregnant and not knowing how else to respond, he had mumbled, 'Well, I suppose we should get married then.' A date was duly set for the third week of June.

'We do not intend to get married yet, or at any rate not until my career takes shape,' he wrote disingenuously in a letter to Sheila. 'She is a very understanding girl and realises that at the moment my work comes first.'

Elton was miserable about his situation, aghast at the prospect of becoming a young married father and depressed about his lack of progress as a songwriter. But he wasn't going to admit that to his mother, of all people. One day, Linda and Bernie were taking a nap at the Furlong Road flat when they were woken by a noise. It was Elton, who had turned the gas oven on and stuck his head inside atop a pillow he had placed in there, illogically opening the kitchen windows first.

As suicide attempts go, it was at best half-hearted, a clear cry for help, and once Bernie had pulled him out of the oven, life went on. 'I'd backed myself into a wall by saying I was gonna get married,' Elton later recalled. 'You know inside you're making the wrong move. You deal with it by being preposterous.' So preposterous that the very next day Elton and Linda ordered a wedding cake and furniture for a new flat in Mill Hill, where they planned to set up their marital home.

Still, it was obvious that blissful nuptials for Elton and Linda were never likely to materialise and the last straw came when he, Bernie and Long John Baldry, who Elton had asked to be best man at the wedding, went out drinking at the Bag O'Nails club in Soho. Ostensibly a stag 'do' held a couple of weeks before the wedding, Baldry, who was six years older than Elton and openly gay, had seen it all before. With homosexuality still illegal in most of Britain in the late '60s, Baldry had seen too many male gay friends getting married simply because straight society demanded it. He was not about to allow his young friend Reggie Dwight to be plunged into the same abyss: 'You don't really love her,' Baldry kept repeating. 'Don't be a damned fool . . .'

Elton had burst into tears, finally seeing sense at last and, intoxicated though he was, informed Linda when he got home that the engagement was off. After sleeping on Bernie's bedroom floor that night, he spent the next morning trying to console his former fiancée, who had locked herself in the bathroom and was threatening to kill herself by injecting an air bubble into a vein. 'I remember the two of us outside, saying, "She can't, can she? She hasn't got a syringe",' recalled Taupin.

Fred Farebrother was duly summoned and transported a much relieved Elton, Bernie and their belongings in his van to his and Sheila's flat in Northwood Hills. That was the end of the saga of Linda Woodrow, who never saw Elton again. However, over the years her name has occasionally popped up in print.

In 1984, as Elton was preparing to marry Renate Blauel, the British Sunday newspaper *The People* tracked Linda down for an interview. Now a married mother of four, she was living near Cambridge. Linda told them: 'I'm not a bitter woman. I really hope he makes a success of marriage,' before adding: 'If Renate is expecting romance, though, she's picked the wrong guy. He was lousy in bed.' She had also heard, although the source is not known, that Elton had blamed her for 'putting him off heterosexuality' and had paid a solicitor £1,500 to launch a libel case: 'Nothing ever came of it,' she said.

In 2019, she was asked to appear on the ITV show *Good Morning Britain* to comment on the *Rocketman* movie, in which her story was omitted. 'I never actually believed he would become such a superstar as he is,' she admitted. 'I don't know what I would say to him, but I'd like to see him . . . There's no resentment and there's certainly no bitterness. It would be a joyous meeting if we did meet, I'm sure.'

The ending to this star-crossed lovers' tale is heart-warming, or at least leg-warming. In 2020, Linda was a triple divorcee, living in Dallas, Texas, and working at a doctor's surgery, but she was having problems with one of her knees. However, she couldn't afford the necessary operation.

'My knee is awful to walk on and I've been having shots . . . I thought of Reg and whether he could help. It was a long shot,' she told the British tabloid paper the *Daily Mirror*, still referring to Elton by that contextually ridiculous name. 'In the late '60s, Reg and Bernie weren't earning any money, so I was hoping, from one friend to another, whether they could help me through this financial blip,' she said.

When informed about Linda's problem, Elton funded the required surgery. 'He didn't hesitate for a second to help out,' said a source. 'He remembers how good she was fifty years ago, when he and Bernie needed the support, and is really pleased to be able to help her in her hour of need.'

'I am so touched by Reg. After all these years, it's so kind,' Linda told the papers. 'I am thrilled to bits that he is offering to help.'

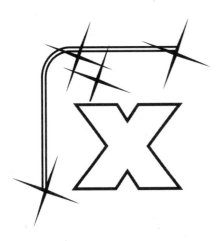

X, GRAHAM

Marks the spot

The UK's tabloid newspapers don't enjoy a particularly respectable profile these days, but, compared to how they behaved in the '80s and '90s, their modern incarnations are positively toothless. At the height of the global AIDS epidemic – which, remember, was regularly described as a 'gay plague' by red-top editorials and columnists – it was common practice for the *News of the World*, its ostensibly higher-brow equivalent the *Daily Mail* and, most of all, *The Sun*, to portray homosexuality as the sin to end all sins. As such, Elton John, a supremely rich, closeted gay man who didn't hesitate to speak his mind, was considered an obvious target for the muckrakers of the tabloid press back then. He didn't help matters by living a life of ostentatious debauchery, of course, but then that applied to almost every major rock star of the period. None of which justified the deliberate smear campaign which *The Sun* launched against him in 1987 and which dragged on for the entire year. No one came out of it looking good, as we'll see.

It all began when a nineteen-year-old male prostitute identified as Graham X, but whose real name was later revealed to be Stephen Hardy, appeared in *The Sun* with a series of lurid stories about Elton. He claimed to have attended parties at the Finchampstead, Berkshire, home of Rod Stewart's manager, Billy Gaff – a prominent member of what became known as the Velvet Mafia: the group of gay men who managed some of the biggest stars of the music business, including Brian Epstein (the Beatles), Kit Lambert (the Who), Robert Stigwood (the Bee Gees), Simon Napier-Bell (Marc Bolan) and many others – where he claimed to have witnessed Elton engaging in gay orgies and taking copious amounts of drugs. 'Elton In Vice Boys Scandal' ran the headline, with Hardy claiming to have procured other rent boys as partners for Elton and Gaff, each youth supposedly paid £100 'plus all the cocaine they could stand'.

As always with these ridiculous stories, the paper threw capitalised verbs at its rabid readers. Elton apparently 'LOVED his boys to be tattooed skinheads or punks with spiky hair, SNORTED cocaine throughout the orgies, which lasted up to four days, and BEGGED the teenagers to indulge in his bondage fantasies'. *The Sun* also made a point of contrasting these tawdry tales with solemn mentions of Elton's new wife, Renate Blauel, and couched the whole sordid fable as a moral lesson, with Hardy whimpering: 'I am ashamed of what I did . . . I am speaking out to show how widespread this sort of thing is and to warn other gullible young kids to steer clear of people like these.' The fat fee the newspaper reportedly paid for his stories probably didn't hurt either.

This could have gone on forever, but *The Sun* put its proverbial foot in it when it wrote that Hardy 'took two youngsters to Gaff's home on 30 April last year. It was the last time he saw Elton.' It emerged that Elton had been in New York on that date in 1986, a fact that several eyewitnesses were able to corroborate – and a writ was duly issued by Elton's solicitors, Frere Cholmeley.

The Sun doubled down with the headline: 'The story they're all suing over!' and ran a story titled 'Elton's Kinky Kicks'.

The parade of surreal nonsense continued, with *The Sun*'s rival tabloid, the *Daily Mirror*, coming to Elton's defence and pointing out the detail about him being in New York at the time of the alleged party the previous year. A statement also came from Billy Gaff, who explained in fact that Elton had never been to his house and furthermore, he too was out of the country on the supposed orgy dates. The *Daily Mirror* even produced a copy of an invoice from the limousine firm that took Elton to John F. Kennedy Airport in New York on the date in question.

The Sun's reply was simply a headline that ran 'You're a Liar, Elton!' By now, Elton's lawyers had issued a second and third writ, with the star himself making light of the situation while on tour in Australia: hosting an awards ceremony, he quipped that he'd always thought 'bondage' was a beach in Sydney. More seriously, he sent a strong message to the *Daily Mirror*: 'I'm going to nail the paper that wrote all those lies. I'm doing it to clear my name, not for the money. But £50 million would not be enough to compensate for all the harm they have done me.'

The battle continued to rage, with *The Sun* recruiting another former male prostitute called John Boyce to lure young men into saying they had slept with Elton. Boyce later confessed: 'It was all pure crap.' The paper's next move was to publish some partially nude pictures of Elton under the headline: 'Elton Porn Photo Shame', although these were not particularly graphic.

Elton's team had issued no fewer than twelve writs by this point and the strain was starting to show. As he later recalled in the 1991 biography, *Elton*: 'I hardly went out, because I couldn't stop crying. One minute I'd be fine, the next – "waaaa". I'd get up, have breakfast, then go back to bed. Eat ice lollies and watch TV all day.'

He was also eating 'six times what I should have' and drinking heavily. 'I started drinking vodka martinis. You're supposed to sip them . . . but I used to just woosh them back. I would need three or four before I went out in the evening. Then I'd go on to red wine.'

Fortunately, the public were tiring of *The Sun*'s relentless prurient attacks on Elton and its sales figures decreased on days when he occupied the headlines. The final straw came when the paper alleged that the guard dogs at Elton's home had had their 'voice boxes sliced through' to keep them quiet, a story that was quickly and easily disproven.

In late 1987, Stephen Hardy told the *Daily Mirror* that his stories about Elton John were fake, admitting: 'It's all a pack of lies. I made it all up. I only did it for the money and *The Sun* was easy to con. I've never even met Elton John . . . I've never been to one of his concerts or bought one of his records.' Ironically, if irrelevantly, he added: 'I hate his music.'

By the end of the year, a court date had been set, but before that could take place, settlement talks were already underway. *The Sun* ran the headline 'Sorry Elton' and wrote: '*The Sun* last night agreed to pay megastar Elton John £1 million libel damages. The settlement followed allegations published in *The Sun* last year about his private life. A delighted Elton said last night: "This is the best Christmas present I could wish for. Life is too short to bear grudges and I don't bear *The Sun* any malice."'

Some years later, the paper's then-editor, Kelvin MacKenzie, wrote in the *Evening Standard*, '*The Sun* was forced to pay out a record £1 million libel damages to Elton John for wholly untrue rent boy allegations. So much for checking a story. I never did it again.'

Not to Elton John anyway.

X-ES

'Dozens of men could theoretically have sold a sex and drugs exposé on me'

When Britain's most notorious daily tabloid, *The Sun*, began its poisonous smear campaign against Elton John in 1987, using the supposed testimony of a man called 'Graham X' to make unpleasant – and untrue, as later proven in court – allegations about his private life, Elton pondered the irony of the fact that he had never met the chap – even though, as he later wrote, 'There were dozens of men, all around the world, who could theoretically have sold a sex and drugs exposé on me: ex-boyfriends, disgruntled one-night stands.'

Of course, in his wondrous position as drop-dead rich, single, ugly-duckling-whose-immense-talent-transformed-him-into-a-swan, Elton would be expected to sow his seed, so to speak, far and wide. Along the way, however, he also spent time in longer relationships, of varying degrees of commitment and sanity. We know that he was engaged to Linda Woodrow for a few months in 1968; we know that he was in a serious long-term relationship with John Reid right at the height of his fame from 1970 to 1975-ish; and we also know that he has been with David Furnish – first co-habiting, then in a civil partnership, and finally a marriage – since 1995. But in his memoir, *Me*, Elton refers to a sequence of men, some named, others anonymous, to whom he was romantically connected between those more significant partnerships.

The first of these wasn't identified: we know only that the object of Elton's desire suddenly decided one day in 1978 that he wasn't gay after all, although as Elton elegantly observed, 'He didn't seem very straight when he was in bed with me.' Adding insult to injury, the same flame then hooked up with one of the stewardesses from *The Starship*, Elton's private plane, rather than join him at Woodside for a cosy Christmas. Fortunately, Elton's then lyricist and temporary Bernie Taupin replacement Gary Osborne and his wife Jenny took pity on the bereft singer and gave up their own plans to spend the holidays with him.

A few years later, an Australian named Gary was reportedly on the scene. All seemed tickety-boo until Elton shocked even himself by announcing his intention to marry Renate Blauel. That left Gary in a tough spot. He was the boyfriend of the world's most closeted gay rock star. *Who was now getting married?* Elton never did treat Gary all that well. He had persuaded him to leave his hometown of Melbourne and come live with him at Woodside in England, only to be sent packing by Elton's assistant Bob Halley whenever the errant singer got bored. After a while Elton would start to miss Gary and the process would begin again.

Some of these liaisons were risky, in more ways than one. Elton reflected in his memoir that he had not been 'hugely discriminating in my choice of partners.' Certainly not in the '70s or '80s. Worse, once the spectre of AIDS made itself known, two of Elton's exes were infected: Tim Lowe and Vance Buck.

A relationship with Hugh Williams, from Atlanta, Georgia, was important because it led to Elton at last finding the courage to address his reliance on drink and drugs and a sudden willingness to enter rehab for his many addictions. Williams, a drug-user himself, had put himself into a treatment facility and cleaned up just as Elton was approaching his personal nadir, although the singer took some persuading.

It was only when Elton tired of spending his days – in his own words – 'sat around, wanking, in a dressing gown covered in my own puke' that he agreed to a session in rehab of his own. The treatment was a success, but it ended the relationship with Williams, as life-transforming experiences so often do.

In 1992, when Elton launched his AIDS Foundation, he did so with a new boyfriend named John, who ran the charity for its first two years from his kitchen in Atlanta. That's all we know about John despite the Foundation's high profile, probably because he prefers his details to remain private, a universal right. Even when Elton was devastated by the suicide of a former lover in 2010 – who reportedly killed himself because he couldn't reconcile his sexuality with his religious beliefs – he didn't name him, and quite rightly so.

Elton's love life may have been gothically tragic, but the curtain finally fell on that part of his life the day he met debonair, empathic and handsome David Furnish.

'YOUR SONG'

I hope you don't mind . . .

In 1975, in an interview with *Rolling Stone*, John Lennon was asked what he thought of Elton John's music. He immediately brought up the subject of Elton's first hit, 'Your Song'. 'I remember thinking, "Great, that's the first new thing that's happened since we [the Beatles] happened." It was a step forward,' he declared in his typically forthright way. 'There was something about his vocal that was an improvement on all of the English vocals until then. I was pleased with it.'

With this comment, Lennon identified an important part of the success of 'Your Song', one of Elton's most enduring releases and a significant entry in the songbook of great '70s ballads. He was right about the vocal: Elton hadn't adopted a fully American accent in the song, but he wasn't singing in a provincial English voice either. He'd landed on a transatlantic hybrid which, coupled with the song's James Taylor-like guitar arpeggios and Leon Russell-indebted piano, gave it a feel that worked in both British and American markets.

It worked, all right. Everything about 'Your Song' was and remains perfect. Bernie Taupin's lyrics about a young songwriter struggling to get his emotions out sat perfectly when delivered by the 23-year-old Elton. Paul Buckmaster's beautifully arranged strings gave the song depth and warmth, and with four layers of melodies from voice, piano, guitar and strings, the innocent listener could not help but be seduced.

A romantic myth later circulated that Taupin had written the evocative line 'I sat on the roof and kicked off the moss' while actually sitting on the roof of Dick James's office at 20 Denmark Street, London, where Elton worked as an office boy. However, the lyricist soon quashed the idea, explaining that the song had been written in the rather more prosaic environs of Sheila Dwight's kitchen in Northwood Hills.

'Your Song' made number eight on the *Billboard* Hot 100 and number seven on the UK Singles Chart in January 1971, and was Elton's first big international hit, pushing the self-titled parent album to gold and platinum status worldwide. It's an amusing irony that, not for the last time in his career, the hit was originally relegated to a B-side, in the US at least. It wasn't even on the first single from the *Elton John* album: 'Border Song' had come out beforehand but failed to chart in the UK. 'Your Song' eventually appeared in America as the B-side to 'Take Me to the Pilot', but radio DJs preferred it to the A-side and arbitrarily decided to play 'Your Song' instead.

To understand the song's importance, consider its context. Elton's three-year career to date had produced seven singles and an album, 1969's *Empty Sky*, none of which had enjoyed more than nominal success. How long could he have continued if 'Your Song' hadn't come along and elevated him and Taupin to the Lennon -approved status of songwriters of their generation? 'Your Song' established Elton John as a commercial name to be reckoned with and carried him through the rest of 1971 – until he was essentially home and dry from November that year, when *Madman Across the Water* was released and his imperial period kicked off in fine style.

The critics liked 'Your Song', with John Mendelsohn of *Rolling Stone* labelling it a 'pretty, McCartney-esque ballad', the highest praise any song could receive in the early '70s. However, the description isn't particularly helpful as 'Your Song' doesn't sound remotely like a Beatles' composition, being more influenced by American songwriting greats of the day such as Carole King.

On that note, the first version of the song was actually released by the American band, Three Dog Night, for whom Elton had opened in concert: they had recorded 'Your Song' for their 1970 album *It Ain't Easy* (which also contained their first number-one single, 'Mama Told Me Not to Come'). Although it's difficult to prove from this distance, the story goes that the group had elected not to release 'Your Song' as a single simply because they liked Elton and wanted him to have the first crack at it – although experience tells us that the music industry is rarely that generous and stories such as this one rather too convenient. Either way, check out their version: the chord sequences are slightly different and the vocals much less convincing than Elton's, so the right decision was made, however it was reached.

Elton has played 'Your Song' at almost every concert he's ever played, which means between 3,500 and 4,000 times, depending on which source you consult. Several live versions exist and indeed many other musicians have taken it upon themselves to record versions of it. The first of these came as early as 1972, when the soul singer Billy Paul recorded an excellent, mildly funked-up version as the B-side of his huge international hit single 'Me and Mrs. Jones' – an ancillary bonus being that Bernie Taupin, then newly married, was grateful for the vast extra income that Paul's cover generated.

There were dozens of later covers of 'Your Song', from the surprisingly sincere 1992 version by Rod Stewart to the camp-verging-on-silly Ewan McGregor version in Baz Luhrmann's 2001 film *Moulin Rouge!*. Ellie Goulding performed 'Your Song' at the reception party of Prince William and Catherine Middleton's wedding at Buckingham Palace on 29 April 2011, to which the couple shared their first dance. It was also originally going to be the song Elton sung at the funeral of Princess Diana. Then, in 2018, Elton was depicted performing a specially adapted version in the annual Christmas TV ad for British department store chain John Lewis titled 'The Boy and the Piano', with Elton John looking back on his life in reverse, finally receiving a piano for Christmas as a child.

Elton has sung it at every show he's ever done since it was released. Sometimes it's deeply personal, sometimes it's a universal feeling of hope it engenders: the Concert for New York City in October 2001, in the wake of 9/11; duetting with opera singer Alessandro Safina at Sport Relief in 2002; and as the opening song for the Concert for Diana in July 2007. Ultimately, 'Your Song' is always '*Our* Song'. A beautiful ballad, its charm is it could be any of us singing it. Or merely listening, enthralled.

ZIPPO, REGIMENTAL SGT

But is it any good?

Although officially Elton John's thirty-first – and last – studio album, *Regimental Sgt Zippo* is actually the first album Elton ever recorded. Conceived over several fly-by-night sessions at DJM's demo studio between November 1967 and May 1968, during the first days of Elton working with Bernie Taupin, it remained unreleased until Record Store Day in June 2021, when an original mono-only version was issued on 12-inch vinyl, limited to just 7,000 copies. A stereo vinyl version of the album would be released a year later, along with a CD of both stereo and mono versions.

All very well, one might say, but is the record actually any good? Well, the polite answer would be to point to the decision not to release it at the time, sending Elton and Bernie back to the drawing board. Tracks like the singalong-a-Swinging-London 'The Angel Tree' or the misguidedly titled 'Tartan Coloured Lady', on which use of harpsichord and strings brings to mind a Jake Thackray-style dirge. Just the titles tell the story: 'A Dandelion Dies in the Wind', 'When I was Tealby Abbey' and of course 'Regimental Sgt Zippo'.

'What were these songs even about?' asked music publisher Dick James. They weren't even catchy. In fact, the more he thought about it, the more he decided, correctly, that it simply wouldn't do as a first album from Elton John. On the eve of the record being pressed, he shelved the project and ordered Elton back into the studio with the instruction to keep it simple this time – and try writing a hit. He came back with 'I've Been Loving You', a lush big-production number that Dusty Springfield or Tom Jones or maybe Engelbert Humperdinck could have turned into pop history. Except they didn't.

As a historical document, however, *Regimental Sgt Zippo* is interesting, less for its queasy pop psychedelia, but for the fact the sessions brought together Elton and Bernie for the first time in a studio. Invaluable experience, it also introduced Elton to future musical stalwarts Caleb Quaye, who acted as producer on the sessions and cowrote 'Sitting Doing Nothing', and drummer Roger Pope, who played alongside Quaye in the rock band Hookfoot. Another obscure detail, a year later Plastic Penny, then featuring future Elton drummer Nigel Olsson, released their own version of 'Turn to Me'. It was not a hit and the band split soon after, leaving Olsson free to join Elton.

Musically, however, there is nothing here you will rush to play again. As Bernie later admitted, the album's self-consciously 'trippy' sound was more than 'a tip of the hat to *Sgt Pepper*.' The legendary Beatles' album, released at the height of 1967's senses-altering Summer of Love, became the flagbearer of the new LSD-enlightened pop consciousness that now seeped into all the best art. The title *Regimental Sgt Zippo* so clearly 'influenced' by the title *Sgt Pepper* it could be parody. Except it's not.

'It certainly proved that we were hanging on the coattails of things that were currently popular,' admitted Bernie. 'Things like 'A Whiter Shade of Pale' were in vogue at that particular point in time. I think, in a way, I was literally trying to be part of a gang.'

Bernie succeeded – just not with the gang he thought it was.

Lucky Elton, lucky us.

ACKNOWLEDGEMENTS

The author wishes to thank the following people, without whom this book would not be nearly as good:

Pete Selby
Melissa Bond
Matthew Hamilton
Joel McIver
Jon Hotten
Linda Wall
Mark Blake
Alan Jones